Open theism offers a God who, like us, does not know the future. Its sponsors see this humanizing of God as logical and devotional gain. Bruce Ware sees it as a way of misreading Scripture and impoverishing the life of faith, and he makes a compelling case for his view. I heartily commend this thorough and insightful book.

— J. I. PACKER
Professor of Theology, Regent College

Open theism, which denies that God can foreknow free human choices, dishonors God, distorts Scripture, damages faith, and would, if left unchecked, destroy churches and lives. Its errors are not peripheral but central. Therefore, I thank God for Bruce Ware's loving, informed, penetrating, devastating critique of this profoundly injurious teaching. I pray that God would use this book to sharpen the discernment of leaders and prepare the people of God to recognize toxic teaching when they taste it. O how precious is the truth of God's all-knowing, all-wise, all-powerful care over our fragile lives. For your name's sake, O Lord, and for the good of the suffering church who rest in your all-knowing providence, prosper the message of this beautiful book and shorten the ruinous life of open theism.

— JOHN PIPER
Senior Pastor, Bethlehem Baptist Church, Minneapolis

Evangelical theology faces a crisis of unprecedented magnitude. The denial and redefinition of God's perfections will lead evangelical theology into disintegration and doctrinal catastrophe. The very identity and reality of the God of the Bible is at stake. The real question comes down to this—does God really know all things, past, present, and future? Or, is God often surprised like all the rest of us? The Bible reveals that God is all-knowing and all-powerful. Bruce Ware sets out the issues carefully in *God's Lesser Glory*. This book is a much needed antidote to contemporary confusion, and it is a powerful testimony to the truth of God set forth in Scripture. I can only hope that Christians will read it and rejoice in the knowledge of the true and living God.

— R. ALBERT MOHLER, JR.
President, The Southern Baptist Theological Seminary

At once businesslike and practical, Bruce Ware's restatement of classical Christianity in the face of contemporary challenges to it within evangelicalism is bold and bracing. Driven by the pastoral and practical importance of God's greatness, Ware's approach keeps his defense from bogging down in pedantic rhetoric. This book clearly demonstrates that the historic Christian view, against centuries of antecedents to "open theism," has been favored for so long for one reason: It is so evidently biblical.

— MICHAEL HORTON
Associate Professor of Historical Theology
Westminster Theological Seminary in California

Not even God knows whether you will decide to buy this book or read it, at least according to "open theism." But Bruce Ware shows that this position, which is seeping into evangelical churches, is contrary to Scripture, internally contradictory, and destructive to our Christian lives. This is a clear, fair, well-reasoned, and Bible-centered critique of a doctrinal error so far-reaching that it ultimately portrays a different God than the God of the Bible.

— WAYNE GRUDEM
Chairman, Department of Biblical and Systematic Theology
Trinity Evangelical Divinity School

The movement known as open theism claims to be a more biblical and more practical alternative to the traditional view. Bruce Ware systematically refutes both of those claims, showing that the traditional view better handles the biblical evidence and the issues of Christian living while better preserving the glory of God. His examination of the biblical material is especially strong.

— MILLARD J. ERICKSON
Distinguished Professor of Theology
George W. Truett Theological Seminary, Baylor University

Bruce Ware offers a compelling scriptural defense of an informed classical theism—that God's knowledge of the future is exhaustive, his providential governance is complete, and his eternal purposes will triumph—while fully preserving our authentic humanness. This book exalts the God who is truly God in undiminished greatness for the confidence, hope, and victory of his people.

— BRUCE DEMAREST
Professor of Theology and Spiritual Formation, Denver Seminary

While I (basically a traditional Arminian) do not agree with all of Ware's answers, I applaud his keen discernment of the questions and issues raised by openness theology. He clearly sets forth the key differences between this view and traditional views of God, both Arminian and Calvinist; and he perceptively identifies its major weaknesses. I benefited especially from Ware's treatment of the biblical teaching on God's foreknowledge.

— JACK W. COTTRELL
Professor of Theology, Cincinnati Bible Seminary

Bruce Ware's book is not the last word on this crucially important subject. Rather, it is the first book-length serious response to open theism—a movement that is beginning to inflict serious damage on confessing evangelicalism. Presenting itself as a legitimate variant within evangelicalism, "open" theism in reality so redefines the God of the Bible and of theology that we wind up with a quite different God. Ware's work demonstrates that this is so, and launches a courteous but firm attack against the incursion.

— D. A. CARSON
Research Professor of New Testament, Trinity Evangelical Divinity School

God's Lesser Glory is a carefully reasoned and well-argued critique of open theism. Employing both philosophical rigor and outstanding biblical exegesis, Ware convincingly shows why the great minds in church history have with near unanimity affirmed that the God of classical theism is the God of Abraham, Isaac, Jacob, and Jesus of Nazareth. Every pastor, philosopher of religion, and theologian should have this book in his or her library.

— FRANCIS J. BECKWITH
Associate Professor of Philosophy, Culture, and Law
Trinity International University, California Campus

In their controversy with classical Christian theism, open theists have tried to seize the evangelical high ground by claiming that their view of God is truer to the Scriptures. *God's Lesser Glory* rebuts this claim. Bruce Ware goes to the heart of the hermeneutical issue, cogently arguing the biblical case for classical Christian theism and showing why open theists should themselves be uneasy with some of their biblical interpretations.

— MARK R. TALBOT
Associate Professor of Philosophy, Wheaton College
Vice Chairman, Alliance of Confessing Evangelicals

GOD'S LESSER GLORY

The Diminished God of Open Theism

BRUCE A. WARE

CROSSWAY BOOKS

A PUBLISHING MINISTRY OF
GOOD NEWS PUBLISHERS
WHEATON, ILLINOIS

First printing, 2000

Printed in the United States of America

Library of Congress Cataloging-in-Publication Data
Ware, Bruce A., 1953-
   God's lesser glory : the diminished God of open theism / Bruce A. Ware.
    p.   cm.
   Includes bibliographical references and index.
   ISBN 13: 978-1-58134-229-1 (alk. paper)
   ISBN 10: 1-58134-229-2
   1. Providence and government of God. 2. God. I. Title.
BT135.W37   2000
231'.5—dc21   00-010765

VP		17	16	15	14	13	12	11	10	09	08	07
19	18	17	16	15	14	13	12	11	10	9	8	7

"But if God has shown us bad times ahead,
it's enough for me to know that He knows about them.
That's why He sometimes shows us things, you know—to tell
us that this too is in His hands."

Betsie's words of confidence in God, spoken to Corrie as Holland
was being dragged into war with Germany.
The Hiding Place

To my precious wife, Jodi.
Your encouragement, support, wisdom,
and love bring me such strength and joy.
What a gift you are from such a gracious God.

Contents

Preface

Readers will find this book unkind to open theism. I hope that in no respect and in no place is it unkind to open theists. It is the views of this movement and its advocates that I oppose, not the individuals who advocate them. Some people do not make this distinction, and when they do not, the church is harmed. If, for the sake of warm and affirming personal relations with brothers and sisters in Christ, we tolerate views that are contrary to Scripture and detrimental to the health of the church, we show great disregard and lack of love for the broader membership of the church and we become, by our passivity, negligence, and/or lack of courage, complicit in the advocacy of these errant teachings.

In the introduction to his book *God of the Possible*, Greg Boyd includes a section titled, "Our Attitude in Discussing Controversial Issues."[1] I wish to affirm with him his call to conduct our private and public disagreements in love for one another. Personally, I know and have deep respect for several of the central players in the open theism movement. I have cherished memories of theological banter and pleasant laughter with Greg Boyd, when we taught together at Bethel College and Seminary. I have deeply appreciated over several years warm and mutually respectful conversations with John Sanders and Clark Pinnock, and I pray and wish for God's richest blessing upon their lives. Of course, there are others whom I do not know, but for whom I wish only the best.

I differ with Boyd, however, in his assessment of the significance of this issue. Boyd writes that "the debate about the nature of the future is an important issue. . . . But compared to our common faith in the person of Jesus Christ and the importance of our loving unity in him, this issue and most other theological issues are peripheral."[2] I believe and intend to demonstrate that this debate with open theism is central, not peripheral. It has everything to do with the God whom we trust, follow, honor, and obey. It has everything to do with whether he is worthy of

---

[1] Gregory A. Boyd, *God of the Possible: A Biblical Introduction to the Open View of God* (Grand Rapids, Mich.: Baker, 2000), 19-20.
[2] Ibid., 20.

our uncontested reliance, our unqualified devotion, and our unreserved worship. It affects the whole picture of who God is and what life in his presence is all about. And actually, I believe that a fair reading of the openness literature will reveal that, in fact, openness proponents believe the same thing. The difference is, we have very different views of what the God of the Bible is like and of what life in relation to him is to be. What is at stake here, then, is central and must be engaged.

As I conclude the writing of this book, I wish to give particular thanks to many who have helped and encouraged me in its writing. Western Seminary in Portland, Oregon, invited me to deliver the Fall 1999 Bueermann-Champion Lectures. I used this occasion to develop three lectures which have formed the basis for this book, and am grateful to have had this opportunity. Colleagues and friends at The Southern Baptist Theological Seminary, where it is my privilege to teach, have graciously read portions of these materials and have given helpful feedback. Danny Akin, Craig Blaising, Rob Lister, Al Mohler, Steve Wellum, and others have been a constant source of encouragement, insight, and assistance. Tom Schreiner, in particular, has demonstrated his dear friendship to me once again through his willingness to read and comment on drafts of various chapters, and by his constant and cheerful encouragement. I also am appreciative of Paul Engle, who offered wise counsel in writing techniques. My secretary, LuWinn Lister, helped me greatly in getting these chapters into shape. She no doubt will remember for life the handwritten copies of materials I gave her after flights on which I scribbled out nearly illegible sections. What service and what kindness. Lane Dennis and Marvin Padgett at Crossway Books have been so encouraging and supportive, and Bill Deckard has served with skill and competence as editor. I am grateful to Crossway for their willingness and desire to publish this book.

My deepest and most heartfelt thanks goes to my family. My parents, Bill and Ruth Ware, and my mother-in-law, Esther McClain, have prayed for me hour on hour in this process. The magnitude of their contribution will only be known in heaven. My precious daughters, Bethany and Rachel, have watched their dad write with never a complaint and always an encouraging and interested word. I love them dearly. Above all on earth, my precious wife, Jodi, is the joy of my life, and once again in this project she has shown her unfailing love and devotion to me. I could never repay her loving care, nor would she want repayment, but I can say how much I love her.

May God be pleased. May he receive all the glory. In the end, this is all that matters. Where I am here wrong, may God be merciful, may I humbly stand corrected, and may any harm done to the church be rectified. But where the argumentation of this book is right, where it reflects God's own Word and truth, may God be pleased to bring bold and gracious reform. With Jesus, I affirm that only in knowing the truth can we truly be set free. O God, sanctify us in the truth. Your Word is truth.

Foreword

Divine providence as a *reality* is ever steady, stable, steadfast, sure, and strong. Would that this were true for divine providence the *doctrine*. Divine providence as a doctrine is in great turmoil. Theological earthquakes shake its foundation. This is no time for the weak-kneed and spineless to travel its volatile terrain. The forces are strong that would topple the classical doctrine of providence, and so must be the resolve of those wishing to reinforce it.

As goes the doctrine of divine providence, so go vast portions of our entire doctrine of God and with it our conception of God's glory. But again, do not fear. The glory of God as a *reality* is vast, boundless, infinite, splendor-filled, and wondrous. As such, the glory that is God's alone is absolutely unshaken and undiminished by human proposals that would seek to make finite what is infinite, bounded what is boundless, and humanlike what is, eternally and uniquely, God's own.[1] Yet, our *conception* of the glory of God will be shaped largely by our understandings of his nature, his perfections, his sovereignty, his wisdom, his knowledge, his moral holiness and goodness, and through all of this, his providence. Furthermore, our conception of his providence will necessarily impinge upon everyday Christian life and experience in a multitude of ways.[2] So, while the turmoil over how best to formulate the doctrine of divine providence affects not a whit the actual greatness and glory of God (he is who he eternally is regardless of what anyone says of him!), this turmoil has an enormous impact on Christian thought and life. To get it wrong here is to create a thousand related problems, both theological and practical. Our humble plea must be, "By your grace, O God, show us your glory!"

---

[1] Consider the memorable statement by C. S. Lewis (*The Problem of Pain* [New York: Macmillan, 1962], 53): "A man can no more diminish God's glory by refusing to worship Him than a lunatic can put out the sun by scribbling the word 'darkness' on the walls of his cell."

[2] As A. W. Tozer (*The Knowledge of the Holy* [New York: Harper and Row, 1961], 6) so aptly comments, "The low view of God entertained almost universally among Christians is the cause of a hundred lesser evils everywhere among us"; and, "A right conception of God is basic not only to systematic theology but to practical Christian living as well. It is to worship what the foundation is to the temple; where it is inadequate or out of plumb the whole structure must sooner or later collapse. I believe there is scarcely an error in doctrine or a failure in applying Christian ethics that cannot be traced finally to imperfect and ignoble thoughts about God" (10).

This book proposes to summarize and critique a leading contemporary reconstruction of the doctrine of divine providence. Open theism offers a bold reconceptualization of the nature of God and his relation to the created order. At the heart of the openness proposal is a new model of divine providence. Because those making this proposal are self-professed evangelicals, and because they claim to make this proposal, in part, in faithfulness to Scripture, their view deserves careful investigation. May God grant to his people wisdom and courage to study, know, and embrace the teaching of his holy Word to the end that we may think, live, and worship to the praise of his matchless, glorious name.

Introduction

Why You Should Be Concerned

A Future Unknown to Us and . . . to God?

Life contains daily reminders of our limited human knowledge. How often, and for how many different reasons, do we think to ourselves, "If only I had known . . ."? Have you ever sat frustrated behind the wheel of your car in an unexpected traffic jam because you didn't know that a stalled car up ahead was blocking the lane? No doubt you thought, "If only I had known, I would have turned off and taken a different route." Or have you agonized over an unforeseen accident that happened to one of your children? You naturally think, for example, "Had I known she was about to slip, I would have held her hand." Yet we realize that even the wisest and most perceptive drivers and parents endure traffic jams and injuries in part because they simply cannot know what the future holds.

But think for a minute. What if this inability to see into the future is true not only for human beings but for God as well! What if God in fact faces the same limitations as we do in not being able to know what will happen in the next moment, or day, or year, or century? How would this affect your trust in God, your confidence in facing the future, your motivation to pray and leave everything in his hands?

One of my dad's favorite "vacation songs" has a line that says, "Many things about tomorrow, I don't seem to understand, but I know Who holds tomorrow, and I know He holds my hand." What a beautiful, reassuring, faith-building, hope-inspiring truth! How many Christians have been strengthened to know and believe and rely on the fact that God knows absolutely everything about their future, even if they know nothing of it? But now, consider: What if it simply is not true that God "holds tomorrow"? What if, in fact, he does not know what tomorrow will bring? What if it turns out that God may be just as alarmed and taken aback by what happens as we are? What, in fact, if God even looks back with regret at many of his own decisions and thinks, "If only I had known"? Can such a God really be trusted? Can we really have confidence in his direction and will for our lives? Is this God really in control of the unfolding events and progression of human history? Can we be confident that his purposes, both individual and cosmic, will be accomplished? Can we be absolutely sure that God in fact will win in the end? Is such a God worthy of our worship, our praise, our adoration, our uncompromising devotion, and our unqualified obedience? And even more basic, is such a God the God of the Bible?

Many readers may be surprised to learn that this very view (namely, that God does not know much of the future and has to learn what happens as that future unfolds) is being advocated by a growing number of biblical scholars, theologians, and philosophers who identify themselves as evangelicals, some of whom teach at highly respected evangelical colleges and seminaries. These scholars call the position they advocate "open theism"[1] because they like to make central the notion that, for God as well as for us, much of the future is "open" and hence not foreknown or foreordained.

The reasons open theists give for denying God's comprehensive foreknowledge (i.e., comprehensive knowledge of the future) are biblical, philosophical, and practical.[2] Biblically, openness proponents seek to defend their position as being in accordance with the full range and texture of biblical teaching. According to this view, while Scripture does

---

[1] I choose here to use the label "open theism." This movement is also variously called, "open-view theism," "openness theism," "presentism," and often "freewill theism." This last term, however, is ambiguous. It is not always clear exactly to what school of theology "freewill theism" refers. Although it may refer to all variations of a broad Arminian theology in which libertarian human freedom is affirmed, in actual usage those who self-consciously align themselves with the movement of "freewill theism" comprise a sub-division of Arminianism in which the doctrine of divine foreknowledge (i.e., particularly knowledge of future free human choices) is denied so as not to preclude (as they see it) the genuineness of future contingencies and future free human choices. Hence, the future is "open" and hence, the appropriateness of the more precise term "open theism" for this movement. For an interesting analysis of the term "freewill theism," see David Basinger's *The Case for Freewill Theism: A Philosophical Assessment* (Downers Grove, Ill.: InterVarsity, 1996), 32-37. See also Basinger's comment (135, f.n. 5) that he believes that he is "the first person to have used the phrase 'freewill theism'" as a label for the theological movement that denies that God can grant humans freedom and also control unilaterally the decisions they make. This may be so, but it is also the case that many today use the terms "open theism" and "freewill theism" as virtual synonyms.

[2] See chapters 2 and 3 below for a much fuller discussion of the openness proposal.

sometimes teach God's knowledge of select future actions or events, a strong pattern of biblical teaching would suggest that generally God does not know what will happen in the future. Passages that speak of God changing his mind or regretting his past actions are not treated fairly in the classical tradition, it is claimed. If these passages are taken in a straightforward manner and allowed to say what they mean, they demonstrate that the future is open, for indeed God learns what this future holds as it occurs.

Philosophically, open theists argue that true human freedom is possible only if the future is open. If God *knows* all that will occur in the future, then we are not free to do differently than what God knows, and hence we are not truly free. Furthermore, since God can know only what is real, he cannot by definition know the future—because it has not as yet happened and so is not real.

Practically, open theists argue, if God knows in advance all our thoughts, feelings, and actions, then our real relationship with him is called into question. How can our ideas, prayers, or decisions make a difference to God if he knows all of those things from eternity?

What Difference Does It Make?

While much more will be said in due course on the openness proposal, enough has been said to raise an important question: What is at stake in this proposal, and why does it matter whether or not we adopt an openness view? Although the critique of open theism presented in subsequent chapters will be much more specific, let me suggest here that our *overall conception of God* and our *broad understanding of living the Christian life* are both deeply affected by the openness view.

First, consider *God*. If open theism is correct, we must acknowledge that the openness God, when compared to orthodoxy's view of God, is quite deficient in his understanding. It follows that his wisdom and providential control are greatly affected. God not only learns what happens moment by moment (as do we), but he also realizes moment by moment which of his beliefs about the future have been *wrong*. Yes, the God of open theism is *mistaken* about much. Furthermore, since he is so mistaken in many cases, we must conclude that God would often be filled with *regret* over his own past decisions. Just how often this is the case, we do not fully know. But it stands to reason that, since God cannot know any future free decision, choice, or action, many times he is faced with some turn in events that takes him by surprise and reveals to him that his thoughts about the future and his past decisions were, disappointingly, erroneous and misguided. What, then, do we make of the wisdom of God? Since wisdom is the application of knowledge to devise good and right ends, this deficiency in God's knowledge cannot but negatively impact his wisdom. As we considered earlier, how often do we think, "If only I had known . . ." The shocking reality is that the God of open theism faces just this same frustration in relation to his wisdom, planning, and predictive ability.

And what do we make of God's providential oversight of the unfolding of human history? Deficient knowledge and wisdom surely mean that neither we nor God can be certain about just what will happen in the end. Will God succeed in fulfilling his goals? Will history move in the direction he hopes it will? Are God's predictions and promises sure? The only answer open theists can give to these questions is that they are hopeful that God will somehow pull it off. God is resourceful, we are assured! But providential guidance is risky business for God, according to this view, and the future is unknown and uncertain. In short, the God of open theism suffers greatly from this lack of knowledge and it affects his plans, wise counsel, predictive ability, and providential control of history.

Consider also some implications of the open view of God for *living the Christian life*. While open theists claim that their view enhances the reality and genuineness of relationship with God, the truth is that the gains they propose are not real, while the losses incurred are tragically great. In a word, what is lost in open theism is the Christian's confidence in God. Think about it. When we are told that God: can only guess what much of the future will bring; is relatively reliable only when predicting things close at hand; cannot be trusted to give accurate guidance on matters that are far into the future; constantly sees many of his beliefs about the future proved wrong by what in fact transpires; reevaluates the rightness or wrongness of his own past conduct based on what he learns moment by moment; even regrets at times that his own decisions or his counsel to those who have trusted him have actually resulted in harm instead of the good he intended—given this portrayal of God (and more—read on!), what happens to the believer's sense of confidence before God? Can God be trusted to give accurate guidance or to lead us in a direction truly best in light of future developments? Can hope in God to fulfill his promises be founded without mental reservation or qualification? Can a believer know that God will triumph in the future just as he has promised he will? All this and more is greatly harmed and ultimately undermined by the open theism proposal.

While claiming to offer meaningfulness to Christian living, open theism strips the believer of the one thing needed most for a meaningful and vibrant life of faith: absolute confidence in God's character, wisdom, word, promise, and the sure fulfillment of his will. The strengthening and reassuring truth of Romans 8:28 ("God causes all things to work together for good . . .")[3] is tragically ripped out of our Christian confession as it becomes an expression merely of God's resolve to try his hardest and to do the best he can.

Lest one think that this revisionist model of God and the Christian life is affecting just a few theologians and Bible scholars in the backwaters of academia, it is important to note the impact of this issue on some major evangelical institutions and denominations. The Baptist General Conference (BGC) has been divided over the question of whether open theism's denial of comprehensive divine foreknowledge is an acceptable view within their churches and their denominational college and seminary (Bethel College and Seminary, St. Paul, Minnesota). Largely due to the advocacy of open theism through the writing[4] and teaching of Gregory Boyd (professor of theology at Bethel College and senior pastor of the BGC Woodland Hills Church in St. Paul), a major controversy has arisen. Several BGC pastors who oppose Boyd's view on this issue proposed a resolution at the 1999 annual meetings of the Baptist General Conference affirming God's knowledge of all future actions and events. After debate on this issue, the confer-

---

[3] Unless otherwise noted, Scripture quotations are taken from the New American Standard Bible version, updated 1995.

[4] To my knowledge, Boyd's first published support for the openness perspective came in his *Letters from a Skeptic: A Son Wrestles with His Father's Questions about Christianity* (Colorado Springs, Colo.: Chariot Victor, 1994), 30, where he wrote: "If we have been given freedom, we create the reality of our decisions by making them. And until we make them, they don't exist. Thus, in my view at least, there simply isn't anything to know until we make it there to know. So God can't foreknow the good or bad decisions of the people he creates until he creates these people, and they, in turn, create their decisions."

ence delegates declined to adopt the resolution, thus affirming *de facto* that Boyd's view is acceptable within the BGC,[5] even if most BGC churches and church members would disagree with Boyd's view.[6] Then in the 2000 annual meetings of the BGC, a somewhat confusing pair of statements was adopted. First, an overwhelming majority approved the following statement:

> Be it resolved that we, the delegates of the Baptist General Conference (*who are also the delegates of Bethel College and Seminary*) affirm that God's knowledge of all past, present and

[5] Following the BGC annual conference decision refusing to adopt the proposed resolution on exhaustive divine foreknowledge, Boyd published a letter on the "open theism" website in which he concluded by saying, "To Openness readers of this letter who are planning on going into ministry or teaching, let me just say, be of good courage. We will suffer some losses, but we are also making great advances. At the very least, you can know that there's one safe haven out there for you: my own denominational home, the BGC" (Sept. 15, 1999; http://www.opentheism.org/resolution.htm).

[6] In their coauthored letter dated September 30, 1999, George Brushaber, president of Bethel College and Seminary, and Robert Ricker, president of the Baptist General Conference, attempted to disabuse their constituencies of the notion that the BGC is adopting open theism. But as I attempted to point out in a letter to Brushaber, October 15, 1999, earlier statements in support of Boyd and his position (dating back to the spring of 1999, preceding the summer annual meetings of the BGC) may have misled readers to think that Boyd's views here were in agreement with the BGC generally. A portion of my October 15, 1999, letter to Brushaber reads:

President Brushaber, I call to your attention the inconsistency between statements in your March 19, 1999 and September 30, 1999 letters. In your March 19 letter to the denomination, you (with others) wrote:

We find a perplexing challenge before us. On the one hand, we readily affirm our unqualified belief in God's omniscience as well as His complete sovereign control over history. So does Dr. Greg Boyd, the person whose writings have prompted this proposed resolution.

Just recently, in your September 30 letter with Dr. Robert Ricker, you wrote:

We want to be clear where the BGC and Bethel's leadership stand on the issue. Many of us have heard Greg Boyd's explanation several times, and do not agree with him. . . . Neither of us, nor any member of the BGC Executive Ministry Team (President and all Vice Presidents), nor any member of the Bethel President's Leadership Team espouses Boyd's position.

Based on your recent testimony (September 30 letter), you deny Dr. Boyd's position on divine foreknowledge. Therefore, you do not hold Boyd's view of "God's omniscience as well as His complete sovereign control over history." But, to say as you did back in March that you and Boyd both affirm your "unqualified belief" in God's omniscience as well as His complete sovereign control over history is just plain false. What was your intention in saying that you did agree with him? . . . If your defense on these questions appeals to the fact that you and Boyd both affirm the term "omniscience" of God, this is about as hollow as when I heard that John Hick affirmed the "deity" of Christ just as much as he affirmed the deity of all of us! In other words, the terms by themselves are shells; the definitions are what matter. Your definition of omniscience and Boyd's definition are radically different.

The reply I received from Brushaber appears to be a form letter which did not address the specific issue I had raised.

future events is exhaustive; and, we also believe that the "openness" view of God's foreknowledge is contrary to our fellowship's historic understanding of God's omniscience.[7]

Later the same day, the following statement also passed by a 423 to 363 (54 to 46 percent) vote:

> Be it resolved that the statement on the doctrine of God in the 1951 Affirmation of Faith is sufficiently stated; and, in regard to the subject of open theism, as delegates of the Baptist General Conference (*who are also the delegates of Bethel College and Seminary*) we affirm the Position paper unanimously approved by the Board of Trustees of Bethel College and Seminary on June 24, 2000.[8]

The relevant section of the "Position paper" spoken of, says,

> We affirm the unanimous vote of the Committee for Theological Clarification and Assessment occurring on May 13, 1998, that Dr. Boyd's views did not warrant his termination as a member of the Bethel College faculty and by inference that his views fall within the accepted bounds of the evangelical spectrum.[9]

So, the BGC adopted one statement which says that the openness denial of exhaustive divine foreknowledge "is contrary to our fellowship's historic understanding of God's omniscience" and on the same day adopted another statement saying that Dr. Boyd's denial of exhaustive divine foreknowledge falls "within the accepted bounds of the evangelical spectrum." I dare say that the last word on this matter has not been said in this denomination.

In notable contrast to the ambiguity reflected in the BGC, at the 1999 annual meetings of the Southern Baptist Convention a resolution was proposed and unanimously endorsed affirming that God does know all

---

[7] Passed June 28, 2000, BGC annual meetings, St. Paul, Minnesota (emphasis in original). For the complete statement, see: http://www.bgc.bethel.edu/4know/resolu1.htm.

[8] Passed June 28, 2000, BGC annual meetings, St. Paul, Minnesota (emphasis in original). For the complete statement, see: http://www.bgc.bethel.edu/4know/resolu2.htm.

[9] Included in the statement passed, June 28, 2000, BGC annual meetings, St. Paul, Minnesota. See website in previous footnote for full text.

future contingencies, including all future free choices and actions.[10] And at their summer 2000 annual meetings, the messengers (delegates) of the SBC voted overwhelmingly in favor of a revised version of *The Baptist Faith and Message*. A number of key changes were introduced to the previous (1963) edition, one of which is the addition of a clear affirmation of God's exhaustive foreknowledge. In part, the 2000 revision reads: "God is infinite in holiness and all other perfections. God is all powerful and all knowing; and His perfect knowledge extends to all things, past, present, and future, including the future decisions of His free creatures."[11] Clearly the SBC leadership and messengers see this issue as central enough to warrant a forthright declaration that defines the boundaries of this major denomination's core beliefs.

The issue has affected other major evangelical institutions. InterVarsity Press has determined that open theism should be known

---

[10] The full statement of the resolution affirming God's comprehensive foreknowledge can be found at http://www.sbcannualmeeting.org/sbc99/res2.htm. It reads as follows:

WHEREAS, The one true and living God has revealed Himself to us in the Holy Scriptures that we might have knowledge of Him; and

WHEREAS, The biblical doctrine of God is the first and central axiom of Christian theology; and

WHEREAS, The Bible reveals that God is the Maker, Preserver, and Ruler of all things and that He is infinite in His perfections; and

WHEREAS, Among these perfections revealed in the Bible are God's omnipotence, omniscience, and immutability, by which we affirm and confess His infinite power, knowledge, and changelessness; and

WHEREAS, These essential and biblical affirmations are now under attack by those who would revise the church's historic doctrine of God, and would deny or diminish God's omnipotence, omniscience, and immutability; teaching that God's power is limited, His knowledge is incomplete, and His character and nature can change; and

WHEREAS, Such compromises of the biblical doctrine of God imperil the church and threaten its witness.

Therefore be it RESOLVED, that we, the messengers to the Southern Baptist Convention, meeting in Atlanta, Georgia, on June 15-16, 1999, affirm the biblical teaching concerning the omnipotence, omniscience, and immutability of God and call upon all Christians to confess the living God of the Bible, whose attributes and powers are without limitation, and whose eternal purposes are realized in the saving work of Christ, the Son; and

Be it further RESOLVED, that we affirm God as the Almighty, the Lord God who reigns omnipotent, and who rules the universe by the power of His Word; and

Be it further RESOLVED, that we confess and proclaim that the omniscience of God extends to all creation and throughout all time, to all things actual and potential, even to the thoughts and actions of His conscious creatures, past, present, and future; and

Be it further RESOLVED, that we acknowledge the immutability of God in whom there "is no variableness, neither shadow of turning" (James 1:17).

Be it finally RESOLVED, that we stand united in the faith precious to the church throughout the ages, and bear witness to the limitless majesty and glory of the King eternal, immortal, invisible, the only wise God.

[11] Passed June 14, 2000, SBC Convention meetings, Orlando, Florida. For the complete text of this revision of *The Baptist Faith and Message*, see: http://www.sbc.net/default.asp.

more broadly and its case published. Most of the current volumes advocating open theism have been published by InterVarsity Press.[12] Recently Baker Books decided to join InterVarsity in allowing its readers exposure to the case for open theism. Baker's publication of Boyd's *God of the Possible* caused some grave concern as it delighted others.[13] Add to this the February 7, 2000, editorial in *Christianity Today* titled "God vs. God: Two Competing Theologies Vie for the Future of Evangelicalism," in which open theism was extolled[14] as a viable albeit imperfect evangelical model of God and his relations to the world. *Christianity Today* has published several other articles relating to open theism in recent years.[15] These data indicate that open theism is anything but a backwater movement, and its impact is increasingly being felt in some of evangelicalism's most significant denominations and institutions.

All of this elicits deep, prayerful, and earnest concern. To the extent that the openness model of God penetrates our churches, we can anticipate a greatly lessened confidence in God and a much greater temptation to trust in our own insights and abilities. We can anticipate weakened prayer lives and more confidence in our own accomplish-

---

[12] Observe in the footnotes to follow the several InterVarsity titles supporting open theism.

[13] I spoke in my office with a representative from Baker Books, who acknowledged that they had received quite an outpouring of concern over their publication of Boyd's *God of the Possible*. In Baker's defense, he cited the decision discussed above in the BGC to allow openness teachings, numerous papers read pro and con regarding open theism at several annual meetings of the Evangelical Theological Society, and recent articles in *Christianity Today* debating the open view as evidence that open theism is *de facto* part of the current evangelical discussion.

[14] I used this exact term in a letter to the editor of *Christianity Today* regarding the "God vs. God" editorial. My letter, published April 24, 2000, 18, reads:

What shall we say of the new proposal that God does not know the future free actions of human beings? According to *Christianity Today*, these open theists "appeal boldly to Scripture and seem to take the biblical high ground." This is both instructive and distressing, since Isaiah's assessment of any supposed god or gods who cannot tell what will take place in the future is: "Behold, all of them are false; their works are worthless, their molten images are wind and emptiness." Instead of extolling open theism as a viable albeit imperfect option for evangelicalism, as this editorial does, we ought to bemoan the very notion of such an unworthy and unbiblical deity. Really, this debate with open theism is not "God vs. God," but "god vs. God."

To this published letter, the editors of *Christianity Today* appended a notation directly following it which reads, "The editorial does not extol open theism, as the writer suggests, but introduces tools for dialogue between opposing camps." I stand by my use of the term "extol." The editorial begins by describing the classical view, associated by the editorial's writer with the ever-pejorative philosophical theism (!), as *boring*, whereas later, as I noted in my letter, the open view is said to be taking "the biblical high ground"! I will let the reader of this "God vs. God" editorial judge whether open theism is here "extolled."

[15] Articles by Timothy George, Douglas Kelly, Alister McGrath, Thomas Oden, Roger Olson, and Clark Pinnock weighed the merits and problems of open theism in recent issues of *Christianity Today* (January 9, 1995; and February 9, 1998).

ments. God will be viewed increasingly as a pathetic sort of figure, possessing good motives but terribly faulty in his attempts to steer the direction of our lives and of human history. We will see more emphasis on the importance of human will and work, and less confidence that God's will or work will prevail. Worship will be muted and, in the end, smothered because this God of faulty vision, action, and purpose will be seen, in time, as unworthy of unqualified honor, glory, and blessing. Fear of the future will grow as people begin to realize that God may be just as taken aback by the unexpected as we are. In short, then, both *the undiminished glory of God* and *the unqualified good of Christians* are at stake in this new and deeply flawed vision of God and the Christian life known as open theism. For the sake of God's greater glory, we must take seriously the argumentation offered by open theists—lest the church be led, with them, to affirm this God of lesser glory.

THE ORGANIZATION AND CONTRIBUTION OF THE SECTIONS TO FOLLOW

This book contains three main sections. In Part One, a summary of the central elements of and support for open theism will be presented. Fairness and accuracy will be sought in this description, though its brevity will require that some aspects of the openness model be neglected.

Part Two will offer a critique of the biblical, theological, and philosophical arguments supporting open theism's view of God and his providence. I will endeavor to demonstrate that, in the end, open theism suffers from serious and fatal problems. Contrary to the openness proposal, I will show that the God of the Bible does in fact possess comprehensive knowledge of the future and so is omniscient in the classical sense. Furthermore, God is not the risk-taker that open theism espouses. To the contrary, Scripture indicates over and again that God rules over heaven and earth and thus is fully in control of all that occurs. Careful attention will be given to biblical passages, and several sobering doctrinal implications of open theism will be developed.

Part Three will focus on practical issues that arise from an openness understanding. How prayer, divine guidance, and Christian hope are understood and lived out differ greatly between the open view and the more traditional views of God. How suffering and pain are interpreted and dealt with by open theists differs altogether from the long-standing

Christian view that God reigns over all of life, including its tragedies as well as its triumphs. Practical differences of major proportion are evident. It is incumbent on us that we think and live out the truth of God's Word on these and other related practical questions.

The stakes are indeed great in this debate over the nature and work of God. The view of God and of the Christian life that we adopt and then pass on to our children is in the balance. Will we—and our children—know the true God, the God revealed in Scripture, the God who proclaims, "I am God, and there is no other; I am God, and there is no one like Me, declaring the end from the beginning. . . . Saying 'My purpose will be established, and I will accomplish all My good pleasure'" (Isa. 46:9b-10)? Will we and our children be able to offer unreserved worship to God alone? Will we and they have wholehearted confidence that God's will and leading are perfect? Doctrinal and practical issues need to be faced here, and it will become apparent that the stakes in this debate over the nature and work of God are indeed great. Not least at stake here is our understanding of God's glory. *Soli Deo gloria* requires our careful, prayerful, biblical, and fair treatment of these issues so central to the faith we place in our infinitely glorious God.

PART ONE

What Does Open Theism Propose?

*EXAMINING GOD'S
LESSER GLORY*

2

The Perceived Inadequacy of the Classical Arminian View of God

THE RISE OF OPEN THEISM

Open theism has been emerging for the past twenty years as a prominent alternative to the classical Arminian model of divine providence.[1] With the publication in 1994 of *The Openness of God: A Biblical Challenge to the Traditional Understanding of God*, coauthored by Clark Pinnock, Richard Rice, John Sanders, William Hasker, and David Basinger, the openness proposal moved from backstage to find its place under the spotlight. Pinnock offers a succinct summary of the key notions, doctrinal commitments, and values of open theism:

> In this book we are advancing . . . the open view of God. Our understanding of the Scriptures leads us to depict God, the sovereign Creator, as voluntarily bringing into existence a world with significantly free personal agents in it, agents who can respond positively to God or reject his plans for them. In line with the decision to make this kind of world, God rules in such a way as to uphold the created structures and, because he gives liberty to his creatures, is happy to accept the future as open, not closed, and a relationship with the world that is dynamic, not static. We believe that the Bible presents an open view of God as living and active, involved in history, relating to us and changing in relation to us. We see the universe as a context in which there are real

---

[1] Although less noticed, the contemporary open theism movement dates earlier to the publication of Richard Rice, *The Openness of God* (Minneapolis: Bethany, 1980); reprinted as *God's Foreknowledge and Man's Free Will* (Minneapolis: Bethany, 1985).

choices, alternatives and surprises. God's openness means that
God is open to the changing realities of history, that God cares
about us and lets what we do impact him. Our lives make a difference to God—they are truly significant. God is delighted when
we trust him and saddened when we rebel against him. God made
us significant creatures and treats us as such.[2]

Proponents of open theism are, in one sense, committed Arminians.
That is, they affirm such cardinal Arminian doctrines as 1) the universal and impartial love of God for all humanity and his true desire that
all be saved; 2) God's creation of humans with what they often call "genuine" or "significant" freedom of will (i.e., libertarian freedom); and
3) the necessity of such genuine freedom for true worship of God, love
for God, and human moral accountability. While embracing wholly
these Arminian commitments, open theists are also disturbed with other
aspects of the Arminian theological tradition. Particularly they object to
the notion that the divine omniscience includes comprehensive knowledge of the future. Omniscience (i.e., in its most general sense, the doctrine that God knows all that can be known or is knowable) must be
defined, they say, as God's comprehensive knowledge of the past and
present only. All of the future that is undetermined by God (which
includes *all* future free choices and actions), since it has not happened
and hence is not real, cannot be an object of knowledge. This future,
they say, is logically unknowable,[3] and as such not even God can rightly
be said to know what cannot in principle be known.[4]

---

[2] Clark Pinnock, in Clark Pinnock, Richard Rice, John Sanders, William Hasker, and David
Basinger, *The Openness of God: A Biblical Challenge to the Traditional Understanding of God*
(Downers Grove, Ill.: InterVarsity, 1994), 103-104.

[3] A parallel is made to divine omnipotence. Classical theism has affirmed, broadly, that
omnipotence should be defined in terms of God's ability to do all that it is logically possible to do.
So, for example, God cannot make round squares, but this does not count against his
omnipotence, since it is logically impossible to make a round square. In like manner, openness
proponents argue, God's omniscience is "limited" to that which is logically knowable. It should
not count against God, they say, nor should it count against the openness definition of a divine
omniscience devoid of knowledge of the future, to say that God knows all that is logically
knowable, and it just is the case that knowledge of the future is logically unknowable.

[4] John Sanders (*The God Who Risks: A Theology of Providence* [Downers Grove, Ill.:
InterVarsity, 1998], 198) writes, "Though God's knowledge is coextensive with reality in that God
knows all that can be known, the future actions of free creatures are not yet reality, and so there
is nothing to be known." And Greg Boyd (*God of the Possible: A Biblical Introduction to the
Open View of God* [Grand Rapids, Mich.: Baker, 2000], 16) writes, "If God does not foreknow
future free actions, it is not because his knowledge of the future is in any sense incomplete. It's
because there is, in this view, *nothing definite there for God to know!*" (emphasis in original). Cf.

The Bible, open theists claim, supports just this understanding. That is, while some passages teach that God determines specific future events, several more indicate, they say, that God learns from and changes his mind due to the unfolding of historical events. As such, while the Bible supports the view that God knows a *portion* of the future (i.e., God knows those aspects of the future which are logically entailed by the present, and in which human free will is excluded altogether and over which he exerts unilateral control and determining influence), it is clear that God does not have *comprehensive* knowledge of the future (i.e., God does not know any individual instances of, nor the complex totality of, the whole range of future free choices and actions of his moral creatures).[5]

This redefinition of omniscience and, with it, its departure from Christian orthodoxy's (including classical Arminianism's[6]) commitment to God's comprehensive knowledge of the future has elicited strong reaction. Perhaps the most notable to date is the forthright claim by Arminian/Wesleyan theologian Thomas Oden that this denial of the divine foreknowledge constitutes nothing short of "heresy."[7] In light of such criticism, why do openness advocates insist on an "open" future,

---

David Basinger, *The Case for Freewill Theism: A Philosophical Assessment* (Downers Grove, Ill.: InterVarsity, 1996), 39-40; W. Norris Clarke, *God, Knowable and Unknowable* (New York: Fordham University Press, 1973), 65; William Hasker, *God, Time and Knowledge*, Cornell Studies in the Philosophy of Religion (Ithaca, N.Y.: Cornell University Press, 1989), 64-74; and Richard Swinburne, *The Coherence of Theism*, rev. ed. (New York: Oxford University Press, 1993), 181-183.

[5] Boyd (*God of the Possible*, 13-15) establishes at the beginning of his defense of open theism the notion that the Bible is best understood as teaching two motifs, one of future determinism and the other of future openness. "On this basis," Boyd writes, "I arrive at the conclusion that the future is to some degree *settled* and known by God as such, and to some degree *open* and known by God as such" (15). In this statement, Boyd is reflecting normative openness understanding. Rice (*God's Foreknowledge and Man's Free Will*, 59), for example, writes: "The open view of God, then, views the future as partly definite and partly indefinite from God's perspective."

[6] Carl Bangs (*Arminius: A Study of the Dutch Reformation* [Grand Rapids, Mich.: Zondervan, 1971, 1985], 219) discusses Arminius's belief in God's comprehensive foreknowledge in the context of where he agreed and disagreed with Calvinists. Bangs writes that Arminius raised the question of "divine foreknowledge of future faith or unbelief. . . . Both Perkins [a Calvinist] and Arminius, along with the overwhelming majority of theologians up to their time, assume such a foreknowledge. The issue between them turns on the relation of foreknowledge to predestination." Cf. James Arminius, *The Writings of James Arminius*, 3 vols. (Grand Rapids, Mich.: Baker, 1956), III, 482-483; and H. Orton Wiley, *Christian Theology*, 3 vols. (Kansas City, Mo.: Beacon Hill, 1941), I, 357-360.

[7] Thomas Oden ("The Real Reformers Are Traditionalists," *Christianity Today* [February 9, 1998], 46) writes, "The fantasy that God is ignorant of the future is a heresy that must be rejected on scriptural grounds ('I make known the end from the beginning, from ancient times, what is still to come'; Isa. 46:10a; cf. Job 28; Ps. 90; Rom. 8:29; Eph. 1), as it has been in the history of exegesis of relevant passages."

that is, a future that is unknown[8] even to God? Consider the following two broad areas: the first pointing to perceived inadequacies in the Arminian heritage within which open theism develops and from which it, in some significant respects, departs (discussed here in chapter 2); and the second signaling reasons offered by open theists to commend the openness proposal as a more fruitful model (discussed more fully in chapter 3).

PERCEIVED INADEQUACIES OF THE CLASSICAL ARMINIAN VIEW OF DIVINE PROVIDENCE

The Question of the Ontological Grounding for Simple Foreknowledge

Openness advocates see several fundamental inadequacies in the classical Arminian doctrine of divine providence, particularly as this doctrine is impacted by the question of divine foreknowledge. First, according to open theists, the Arminian notion of God's comprehensive knowledge of the future as a "simple foreknowledge" lacks ontological grounding. How *can* God know the future comprehensively, they ask, when much of that future will be constituted by future free choices and actions of humans and other free moral agents?[9] The problem comes about because genuine freedom of will in the Arminian tradition is thought to be "libertarian freedom," or "contra-causal freedom."[10] This conception of freedom proposes that a moral agent is free so long as, for whatever choice he makes, he could

---

[8] When I speak of "a future that is unknown" to God as descriptive of the openness view, I understand the fuller and more precise statement would require something along the lines of, "that portion of the future that includes the entirety of future free decisions and actions that will be made by God's moral creatures is fully unknown" to God. I may use this shorter version for two reasons: 1) simplicity and brevity; and 2) the simple fact is that the discussion centers around the *God-human relationship* (as opposed, for example, to God's future ordering of stars and galaxies in the distant universe), and as such the vast majority of *this* future, for open theists, is fully unknown to God, so much so that the shorter statement comes close to the truth about *this* particular future. Argumentation will be given below to suggest that, since human choice and action pervade the future God-human relationship, the degree to which God could determine unilaterally and hence know aspects of this particular future is next to nil.

[9] While openness advocates speak most often about the future free choices and actions of *human beings*, they would generally agree that such freedom has also been granted to *spiritual beings* (angels, Satan, and demons) whose future choices and actions, when free, are also impossible for God to know in advance. See Gregory A. Boyd, *God at War: The Bible and Spiritual Conflict* (Downers Grove, Ill.: InterVarsity, 1997), who stresses the importance of this dimension of creaturely freedom in relation to divine providence and the problem of evil.

[10] For a clear and helpful definition of libertarian or contra-causal freedom, see Bruce Reichenbach, "God Limits His Power," in David Basinger and Randall Basinger, eds., *Predestination and Free Will: Four Views of Divine Sovereignty and Human Freedom* (Downers Grove, Ill.: InterVarsity, 1986), 102-104.

have chosen differently. That is, given all the conditions that are true of the situation in which he makes his choice, the agent is free so long as he could have chosen differently within that identical situation in which he makes the choice. Since this is the case, it is impossible to predict, for any and every free choice, just what choice *will* be made. And so, since all future free choices and actions are, strictly speaking, unpredictable, it is literally impossible for these future free choices to be known—and therefore not even God can know them. There is, then, no ontological basis for God's knowing what future free choices and actions will occur and, therefore, God cannot and does not know this portion of the future.

Arminians may respond to this critique by claiming that, since God is *eternal* and therefore exists outside of time, it is possible for God to "see" all of time as one eternal and non-sequential "now." Or, some may say, it simply is part of God's perfection to know everything that is and will be; we may not be able to comprehend just how it is that God can know what are to us future free choices and actions, but we must not limit God simply because we cannot grasp his fullness. Scripture's assertions that God's knowledge is infinite and that God knows the future teach this truth which we must affirm, even if *how* God knows future free actions is something of a mystery.[11]

These responses, of course, are not new. They represent a long-standing Arminian viewpoint on the doctrine of God's comprehensive foreknowledge. Given this, it may seem a bit odd, perhaps even unnecessary, for openness advocates to insist as they do that God *cannot* know future free choices and actions. Perhaps the objection that there is no ontological basis for comprehensive divine foreknowledge can be answered, or dismissed anyway, simply by an appeal to divine mystery. Why openness proponents disagree with this assessment may be seen by the relationship they understand as necessitated between such comprehensive foreknowledge and future free choices, to which we turn next.

Simple Foreknowledge and the Impossibility of Future Free Choices

Second, while open theists dismiss God's foreknowledge of future free choices and actions because of the lack of ontological grounding, they

---

[11] Wiley, *Christian Theology*, I, 335-339. Cf. the helpful summary discussion by Richard Rice, "Divine Foreknowledge and Free-will Theism," in Clark H. Pinnock, ed., *The Grace of God, The Will of Man: A Case for Arminianism* (Grand Rapids, Mich.: Zondervan, 1989), 123-126.

also claim that, if such divine foreknowledge were true, genuine freedom would be impossible in regard to all future choices and actions. That is, openness thinkers really see two related problems (two sides of a coin, as it were) in the classical Arminian juxtaposition of libertarian freedom and comprehensive divine foreknowledge. As discussed above, the first of these two perceived problems has to do with *how God can know* future (libertarian) free choices since, for any choice made, the person might have chosen differently. Now the second problem asks *how humans can be free* if, as is claimed in classical Arminianism, God knows precisely just what choices (and no others) *will* be made.[12]

For example, if God knows that later today Carl will take his family to the Oyster Bar restaurant for dinner and order a shrimp salad, then it must be the case that Carl will do just this and he may not choose differently. That is, because God knows this to be the case, and because God's knowledge is by definition infallible, it follows that Carl will choose and do precisely and only as God knows he will. But if this is so, then Carl is not in a position in which he could choose contrary to God's foreknowledge. That is, he is not in a position in which he could choose instead to eat by himself, or to take his family to Rose's, or to eat leftovers at home and save the money. In other words, it appears that Carl is not able to choose differently than he will in fact choose, and if this is the case, Carl clearly does not choose freely. True freedom in the classical Arminian model requires the ability, all things being just what they are, to choose differently than one does. But all things being just what they are, including God's foreknowledge being just what it is, Carl must choose what God knows he will choose. Hence, he is not able to choose differently. And hence, he is not free. The challenge from open theism to other Arminians is simple: Comprehensive divine foreknowledge and libertarian freedom are mutually exclusive notions. You cannot have both together. So, if you value libertarian freedom (as classical Arminianism clearly does), then you must be willing to give up your commitment to comprehensive divine foreknowledge.

---

[12] See the extended argument for the incompatibility of comprehensive divine foreknowledge and human freedom in William Hasker, "Foreknowledge and Necessity," *Faith and Philosophy* 2, no. 2 (April 1985), 121-157. Hasker asserts that "those who seek to maintain the compatibility of free will and foreknowledge are in the end forced to abandon, implicitly if not explicitly, the libertarian conception of freedom . . ." (154).

Simple Foreknowledge and the Lack of Providential Control

Third, according to open theists, the classical Arminian notion of comprehensive divine foreknowledge offers no benefit for divine providential control. To be sure, many Arminians have suggested that God's knowledge of all future choices and actions puts him in a far better position to regulate the future than if he had no such knowledge.[13] Openness proponents disagree. In their view, since God simply knows in eternity past, in one eternal "now," what free creatures (and he himself) will do; and since this knowledge includes *everything* that free creatures (and God himself) will choose and do; there is no opportunity for God to influence or respond to any free choices or actions that take place in the future. Knowledge of the future is simply a given, as it were, in the mind of God. By simple foreknowledge, says open theism, God knows and accepts what free creatures will do but he is not in a position to use such knowledge in a providentially beneficial way.[14] David Basinger writes:

> Since there can never be a time when a God who possesses complete SFK [simple foreknowledge] does not know all that will occur, and since foreknowledge can be utilized in a providentially beneficial manner only if there is a time at which what is foreknown can influence a divine decision that is itself not also already foreknown, there can exist no conceivable context in which SFK would enable God to make providentially beneficial decisions that he would not be able to make without this knowledge.[15]

Consider the force of the preceding objections: Open theists argue

---

[13] For example, Arminian theologian Jack Cottrell (*What the Bible Says about God the Ruler* [Joplin, Mo.: College Press, 1984], 208) writes, "For if God foreknows all the choices that every person will make, he can make his own plans accordingly, fitting his purposes around these foreknown decisions and actions."

[14] Interestingly, David Basinger ("Middle Knowledge and Classical Christian Thought," *Religious Studies* 22 [1986], 420) argues that, regarding the God of simple foreknowledge and the God of present knowledge (i.e., presentism) alike, each "is basically a cosmic *gambler* who must *react* to that which occurs in his creation" (emphasis in original). Basinger maintains this view against opposition. See, David Basinger, "Divine Knowledge and Divine Control: A Response to Gordon and Sadowsky," *Religious Studies* 26 (June 1990), 267-275.

[15] Basinger, *Case for Freewill Theism*, 55. Cf. David Basinger, "Simple Foreknowledge and Providential Control: A Reply to Hunt," *Faith and Philosophy* 10, no. 3 (July 1993), 421-427; and Sanders's extended discussion in a section titled, "The Uselessness of Simple Foreknowledge for Providence," in *God Who Risks*, 200-206.

that the classical Arminian notion of comprehensive divine foreknowledge, 1) lacks ontological grounding and hence renders *knowledge* of
future free choices and actions strictly impossible; 2) would render, if
true, genuine human freedom illusory; and 3) does not offer, contrary
to popular perceptions, any providential benefit to the God of classical
Arminianism. Is there not warrant, then (they say), to consider whether
alternate understandings of God, God's knowledge, and God's relation
to the world may be preferred?

Excursus on the Openness Response to the Middle Knowledge
Variant of Arminianism

Before turning in the next chapter to a consideration of some positive theological commitments put forth in open theism, it is necessary to examine briefly a variation within Arminianism that attempts to overcome the
above problems without giving up comprehensive divine foreknowledge.
The "middle knowledge" position or "Molinism" (named for its founder,
Luis de Molina)[16] argues that God possesses knowledge not only of what
could be, i.e., knowledge of all bare possibilities (which Molina calls "natural knowledge") and knowledge of what *will* be, i.e., knowledge of all
future actualities (which Molina calls "free knowledge"), but he also possesses knowledge of what *would* be if circumstances were different from
what they in fact will be in the actual world, i.e., knowledge of those possible states of affairs which would have become actual had circumstances
other than those in the real world obtained (which Molina calls "middle
knowledge"). According to this theory, God knows all possible states of
affairs, and he also knows what free creatures *would* do in various possible sets of circumstances. Although God does not and cannot control what
free creatures do in any set of circumstances (they retain libertarian freedom), he is able to control certain aspects of the circumstances themselves
and by this he can regulate which choices and actions *actually* obtain from
among all those that are possible. Now (according to this theory), while
God can control these sets of circumstances, he cannot necessarily guar-

---

[16] Luis de Molina, *On Divine Foreknowledge,* Part IV of the *Concordia,* trans. Alfred J. Freddoso
(Ithaca, N.Y.: Cornell University Press, 1988). For contemporary defenses of the middle
knowledge view, see especially William Lane Craig, *The Only Wise God: The Compatibility of
Divine Foreknowledge and Human Freedom* (Grand Rapids, Mich.: Baker, 1984); and Thomas
Flint, *Divine Providence: The Molinist Account* (Ithaca, N.Y.: Cornell University Press, 1998).

antee that the choice or action he wants a free creature to perform will be done. For example, it just may be the case, although God wants Carl to eat leftovers at home, that in no set of circumstances in which he envisions Carl deciding his dinner plans will Carl freely choose to eat leftovers. But there are many, many other cases in which God knows that, while in some sets of circumstances Carl will not freely do what God wants, there is at least one (or more) other set of circumstances which, if God were to actualize it, would result in Carl choosing freely to do as God wishes. So, by middle knowledge God exerts massively more providential regulative influence over the world than is the case if God possesses only simple foreknowledge, yet he does so in a manner in which libertarian freedom is retained for God's moral creatures.

Despite the advantages for divine providence that Molinism offers, openness proponents generally[17] see two problems that lead them to reject it. The first objection leveled by openness proponents might be called the "over-determination objection." Essentially this is the complaint that, while God's use of middle knowledge, if true, renders future human choices free in a strict formal (i.e., libertarian) sense, to the extent that God regulates just what choices are made by controlling and determining the circumstances within which he knows that just those exact choices and no others will be made, Molinism leads inevitably to a subtle form of indirect determinism. Granted, human beings are still free, technically, in the choices they make. But the fact that as often as possible God selects the precise sets of circumstances that will achieve just the results he wants means that he exerts a kind of meticulous determinative control over much (most?) human choosing. While advocates of middle knowledge see this as one of the great strengths of the position,[18]

---

[17] David Basinger has supported middle knowledge quite vigorously over several years, but he has evidently modified his view substantially, so much so that his more recent writing argues for God's "present knowledge." See David Basinger, "Divine Omniscience and Human Freedom: A 'Middle Knowledge' Perspective," *Faith and Philosophy* 1, no. 3 (July 1984), 291-302; "Middle Knowledge and Classical Christian Thought," 407-422; "Middle Knowledge and Human Freedom: Some Clarifications," *Faith and Philosophy* 4, no. 3 (July 1987), 330-336; "Middle Knowledge and Divine Control: Some Clarifications," *Philosophy of Religion* 30 (1991), 129-139; "Divine Control and Human Freedom: Is Middle Knowledge the Answer?" *Journal of the Evangelical Theological Society* 36, no. 1 (March 1993), 55-64; "Can an Evangelical Christian Justifiably Deny God's Exhaustive Knowledge of the Future?" *Christian Scholar's Review* 25 (1995), 133-145. Cf. an analysis of the beginnings of this shift in Basinger's thinking, in William Hasker, "How Good/Bad Is Middle Knowledge? A Reply to Basinger," *Philosophy of Religion* 33 (1993), 111-118.

[18] See William Lane Craig, "Middle Knowledge: A Calvinist-Arminian Rapprochement?" in Pinnock, ed. *Grace of God, Will of Man*, 141-164; and Flint, *Divine Providence*, 11-21.

openness proponents are distressed by its association with determination and meticulous providence, calling into question the genuineness of human freedom and human moral accountability, even if such freedom is still accounted for formally.[19]

Second, even if one accepts the indirect determinist implications of Molinism, it is not at all clear *how* God can know by middle knowledge just what choices free creatures would make in various sets of possible circumstances. Sometimes called the "grounding objection," the problem here is that, since freedom in the libertarian sense is defined as the ability, *all things being just what they are,* to choose differently, it is impossible to know what decision will be made simply by controlling the circumstances within which it is made. Because all conditions being just what they are, one can choose otherwise (e.g., Carl could choose a shrimp salad *or* fish and chips), control of the conditions exerts no regulative power over the actual choice made within those conditions (e.g., Carl's choice of a shrimp salad when he *could have* chosen fish and chips). Therefore, it is impossible to know what decision *would* be made just by knowing the conditions within which it is made. In short, nothing grounds God's knowledge of what free creatures would do in various possible sets of circumstances; and hence, God cannot know what middle knowledge advocates claim he knows, that is, what free creatures *would* do in any and all possible sets of circumstances.

ASSESSING THE OPENNESS CRITIQUE OF CLASSICAL AND MOLINIST ARMINIANISM

Open theists share much in common with their classical Arminian and even Molinist Arminian friends. All share in common deep commitments to God's impartial love for all and to the necessity of libertarian freedom to account truly for human moral responsibility, genuine love

---

[19] Basinger, "Divine Omniscience and Human Freedom: A 'Middle Knowledge' Perspective," 301, states that a God with middle knowledge "obviously has a great deal of control over which possible free actions will in fact be actualized. He might, in fact, possess so much control that the concept of meaningful human freedom is greatly damaged." In a later article ("Middle Knowledge and Divine Control: Some Clarifications," 138), however, Basinger minimizes this problem by stating: "There are similarities between a God with MK [middle knowledge] and the God of Theological Determinism. But, generally speaking, the providential capacities of a God with MK have been greatly overstated. A God with MK is simply not as powerful as has been thought."

for God and others, and the meaningfulness of human volition in a world created and ruled by God.

It is also clear, however, that open theists are deeply and fundamentally dissatisfied with *all* versions of the Arminian tradition for their uniform adherence to the doctrine of God's comprehensive knowledge of the future. Like it or not, says the open theist, this commitment to exhaustive divine foreknowledge undermines much of what Arminianism cherishes most. If God knows all future choices and actions, then it follows that those choices and actions are not free, that the meaningfulness of human behavior is destroyed, that genuine providential governance of the world is undermined, that real relationship with God is rendered only apparent and illusory, and that in the end a fundamentally determinist model of the God/creature relation, much like that advocated in versions of Calvinism, cannot be avoided.

Ironically, the openness critique at this point strongly resembles the long-standing kind of criticism that many Calvinists have given to the classical Arminian model. In this case, open theists and these Calvinists agree on one fundamental conviction, namely, that classical Arminianism is seriously flawed in at least two of its major tenets: 1) that exhaustive divine foreknowledge is compatible with libertarian freedom; and 2) that exhaustive divine foreknowledge gives God providential regulative power over the unfolding shape of the future.

Arminianism may more easily escape the force of the first objection (by appeal to God's timeless eternity or divine mystery), but the second objection is especially troubling. Open theism has made clear that, for one to affirm genuine divine providential regulative power, one must abandon classical Arminianism. What options does one then have? Basically three.

First, versions of Calvinism offer the most robust and comprehensive conception of divine providence, with their commitment to the notion that Scripture teaches God's ultimate control over *all* that occurs. And while Calvinism claims and defends the idea that God's meticulous providence and comprehensive decree are compatible with human freedom (i.e., non-libertarian, compatibilist freedom), open theists (and other Arminians) deny that compatibilist freedom is *genuine* freedom, and so they deny that God's comprehensive sovereignty allows humans *actually* to be free. Arminians troubled by the weaknesses of their own position may find in Calvinism a wonderful affirmation of God's glorious sovereignty, but it will require adopting significant changes. Ultimately, the teaching of Scripture itself must take the lead in this debate in order to commend a fundamentally Calvinist perspective and persuade that such changes must be made.

Second, Arminians concerned to ground the genuineness of God's providential regulative power might consider Molinism. Here, through middle knowledge, God is able to control *much* of what occurs in history, yet the full reality of libertarian freedom is also affirmed. Few Arminians have been attracted to this view, however, because of the indirect determinist implications connected with it. Furthermore, if it is true that middle knowledge of future free actions is impossible if the kind of freedom we have is libertarian freedom, even fewer Arminians will want to move toward Molinism—for fear of threatening their commitment to libertarian freedom.

This leaves open theism as the third and only other model in which genuine providential regulative power is asserted and grounded. As will be increasingly evident, the extent of God's providential oversight in open theism is greatly curtailed when compared to the Calvinist or even Molinist models of divine providence. Yet, the open theist appeal is simple: Here is an Arminian model in which 1) God does actually and genuinely regulate providentially much of what occurs in the unfolding of future events, and 2) the possession and exercise of genuine libertarian freedom is fully grounded, real, and not jeopardized by theological commitments (e.g., exhaustive divine foreknowledge and middle knowledge) elsewhere held.

Open view advocates, then, propose that, in the end, the only really viable Arminian contender among the available Arminian models of divine providence is open theism. Because both classical and Molinist versions falter, open theism offers the most compelling Arminian version. What is it about open theism more specifically that commends it? To this we now turn.

3

The Perceived Benefits of
Open Theism

The term "presentism"[1] has recently been used to express open theism's commitment to the notion that God is really and presently involved in the unfolding of history in such a way that *present free actions,* both creaturely and divine, really do *together shape the future.* No divine blueprint or decree determines what shall be,[2] according to this view, nor does God know with certainty the future free choices of his volitional creatures. Rather, the future is genuinely open, that is, undetermined and even (in large part) unknown. God's present involvement with his people—he and they together—direct the future of human history. God learns from what happens, responds to what happens, and plans, as best he can, based on his comprehensive knowledge of the past and present (i.e., all that can be known). Consider the following five central commitments of open theism or presentism.

REAL RELATIONSHIP BETWEEN GOD AND HIS PEOPLE

At the heart of the openness proposal is the desire to uphold the *real* relationship that exists between God and others. Certainly classical theism's insistence on a comprehensive decree, made in eternity past and apart from real historical interaction with creatures, must be rejected, say openness proponents. Such a theory makes a mockery of human choice

---

[1] John Sanders, *The God Who Risks: A Theology of Providence* (Downers Grove, Ill.: InterVarsity, 1998), 12.

[2] See Gregory A. Boyd, *God at War: The Bible and Spiritual Conflict* (Downers Grove, Ill.: InterVarsity, 1997), 141-142; and Sanders, *God Who Risks,* 73.

and action. We may live under the illusion of acting freely, but in fact we merely carry out the divine "script" like players on a stage repeating lines they were directed to say.[3] Open theists show great disdain for this classical decretal model of divine providence. If, for example, a believer's response of faith in conversion is the result of God's effectual drawing of this blind sinner to see the glory of Christ and to respond (as the doctrine of irresistible grace advocates[4]), God is guilty, in the words of John Sanders, of "divine rape because it involves nonconsensual control; the will of one is forced on the will of the other."[5] With a decretal model, say open theists, real relationship is precluded, genuine freedom is an illusion, human moral action and responsibility have no foundation, and the problem of evil must rest squarely and only on God's shoulders.

But, according to these openness advocates, even classical Arminianism's commitment to God's comprehensive foreknowledge, though devoid of the determinist elements described above, still renders *real* God-human interaction and *real* human freedom illusory. For reasons described in chapter 2, if God knows all that humans will choose, say, and do, the genuineness of the interaction between God and humans *at a point in time* is lost. There are no surprises, and humans always and only do what God knows they will do. Even here, then, real relationship that requires learning from one another, listening to each other, responding spontaneously to new situations, is greatly diminished if not altogether removed.

Only when God is understood as one (albeit the supreme) historical player along with all his temporally located creatures in the unfolding of an unscripted history is it possible for such real God-human relationships to occur. God's never-beginning and never-ending (i.e., everlasting or temporally eternal) temporal nature locates him in the temporal succession of historical unfolding along with all of his creation. His comprehensive knowledge of all past and present actualities assures him that he uniquely possesses all that can be known, yet he awaits the next moment, along with the rest of his intelligent creatures, to learn what in fact occurs. God's knowledge is conditioned by creaturely free

---

[3] Sanders, *God Who Risks*, 210-211.
[4] See my defense of the doctrine of irresistible grace in Thomas R. Schreiner and Bruce A. Ware, eds., *Still Sovereign* (Grand Rapids, Mich.: Baker, 1999), 203-227.
[5] Sanders, *God Who Risks*, 240.

decisions, and he must respond to new, perhaps even unanticipated, situations moment by moment. He listens to his people, learns, reevaluates his plans, and acts—all based on his growing, historically unfolding knowledge. In short, for real God-human relationship to occur, there can be no previous divine script (even one merely undeterministically foreknown), and God must be in a position in which he learns moment by moment what unfolds through time.

Consider a few biblical examples where openness proponents claim that God learns and may even be taken by surprise by what develops in his relation with humans:

1) In Genesis 22:10-12, God halts Abraham at the last moment with knife in hand ready to be raised above Isaac's tethered body and says, "Do not stretch out your hand against the lad, and do nothing to him; for now I know that you fear God, since you have not withheld your son, your only son, from Me" (v. 12). Commenting on this text, Sanders first quotes approvingly Walter Brueggemann, who writes, "God genuinely does not know. . . . The flow of the narrative accomplishes something in the awareness of God. He did not know. Now he knows."[6] Then, Sanders himself explains further:

> If the test is genuine for both God and Abraham, then what is the reason for it? The answer is to be found in God's desire to bless all the nations of the earth (Gen. 12:3). God needs to know if Abraham is the sort of person on whom God can count for collaboration toward the fulfillment of the divine project. Will he be faithful? Or must God find someone else through whom to achieve his purpose? God has been faithful; will Abraham be faithful? Will God have to modify his plans with Abraham? In [Gen.] 15:8 Abraham asked God for assurance. Now it is God seeking assurance from Abraham.[7]

This account, according to Sanders, is illustrative of the fact that God does not know what free creatures will do until they act. Will Abraham obey God? God does not know, but he learns here and now that

---

[6] Walter Brueggemann, *Genesis* (Atlanta: John Knox, 1982), 187, quoted in Sanders, *God Who Risks*, 52.
[7] Sanders, *God Who Risks*, 52-53.

Abraham will. We rob the passage of its natural meaning, says Sanders, when we strip from it its simple message contained in God's own words: "For *now* I know."

2) An earlier episode in the biblical narrative, according to Sanders, shows clearly not only that God learns moment by moment as humans freely choose and act, but that at times he may even be genuinely surprised by what occurs. Future free actions may not only be unknown by God; they may also be unanticipated. Sanders suggests that the first sin of the woman and man in the garden of Eden constitutes such a case. He writes:

> God, in freedom, establishes the context in which a loving and trusting relationship between himself and the humans can develop. God expects that it will, and there is no reason to suspect, at this point in the narrative, that any other possibility will come about. A break in the relationship does not seem *plausible* considering all the good that God has done.[8]

Yet, says Sanders, "the implausible," "the totally unexpected happens."[9] That is, not only does God learn that the man and woman have sinned; God is, as it were, taken aback by this occurrence. Although God always knew that sin was possible, it was not at all probable, or plausible, or expected that his human creatures would turn their backs on him. It is impossible to know how often this may be the case in the unfolding of human history, but here we have one concrete example where God's beliefs about the future (i.e., what he thought most likely to occur) were strikingly wrong. The "totally unexpected happens," God is taken aback, and so God corrects his mistaken beliefs as he learns this surprising truth that the man and woman have sinned.

3) Another example from Sanders is especially significant due to the central importance of this event in all of human history. For Sanders, it simply is not and cannot be the case that God *knew* in advance of the cross that Christ would in fact choose to be given over to be crucified. Christ's decision to go to the cross was made, *not* in eternity past (it was not foreknown by God) but in the historical moment when, in prayer to the Father, Christ determined *then* to take this path. The fact that

---

8 Ibid., 45-46 (emphasis in original).
9 Ibid., 46.

Jesus prays to the Father, "If you are willing, let this cup pass from me," evidences the fact, according to Sanders, that the future was open, no decision had been made, and Christ's death on the cross was not inevitable. Sanders writes:

> Is the path [to the cross] set in concrete? Must Jesus go this route even if he has misgivings? . . . Although Scripture attests that the incarnation was planned from the creation of the world, this is not so with the cross. The path of the cross comes about only through God's interaction with humans in history. Until this moment in history other routes were, perhaps, open. . . . In Gethsemane Jesus wonders whether there is another way. But the Father and Son, in seeking to accomplish the project, *both come to understand* that there is no other way.[10]

Only then, at that moment in the garden of Gethsemane, says Sanders, was the decision made for Christ to be crucified, because *only then*, at that moment, was it clear to both the Father and the Son that this path alone would succeed. The Father along with his Son *learn here and now* that Christ's death on the cross will be necessary. As Sanders puts it, "Together they [Father and Son] determine what the will of God is for this historical situation."[11]

RISK IN THE CREATION PROJECT

If there is no divine script for human history, if the future is genuinely unknown and open, and if God has created volitional creatures who are genuinely free, then it follows that God does not control much of what occurs in human history and, to the extent that this is the case, God takes *significant risks* in his creation of this world.[12] Let us be clear on what open theists mean by "risk." At one level, any view that rejects the doc-

---

[10] Ibid., 100-101 (emphasis added).

[11] Ibid., 100.

[12] As openness advocates are quick to grant, God could have created a different world with no inherent risks. He could, for example, have created a world with no free creatures, one in which he controlled each and every action his creatures performed. Risk, then, is a function of the fact that God, in *this* world (i.e., the real world) has limited his control of what unfolds in history by granting creatures genuine freedom. See, e.g., David Basinger, *The Case for Freewill Theism: A Philosophical Assessment* (Downers Grove, Ill.: InterVarsity, 1996), 32-36; and Sanders, *God Who Risks,* 170-173.

trine of meticulous providence or exhaustive divine sovereignty (the notion, as in Calvinism, that God has ultimate control over every facet of creation and every action and event in history) and holds instead that God limits his control over creation by granting libertarian freedom to a portion of his creatures, must affirm the reality of divine risk-taking in the creation of the world.

But how can this be, say, for classical Arminianism, in which God creates a world in which he foreknows with complete accuracy and precision *exactly* what will occur in *every moment* of history? For in such a view, as Sanders describes it, "God is never caught off guard, never surprised by any event and never forced to make any ad hoc decisions."[13] Where is the risk in *this* view? Sanders continues, "Yet God remains a risk taker in the sense that God allows libertarian freedom and does not control what the creatures do with it."[14]

So, there is a sense in which God takes a risk in his creation of the world in *any* nondeterministic model of divine providence. The granting of libertarian freedom is a sufficient (and also, of course, a necessary) condition for genuine risk-taking.

But there is a sense in which the level of risk for the God of open theism is unmistakably greater.[15] In all other Arminian (i.e., nondeterministic) models, at least you can say that before God creates the world he knows exactly what he is getting, so to speak, when he brings the world into existence. He can foresee just what will happen and he knows every aspect of history and its outcome from the start. Every detail of the future, including every future free creaturely choice and action, is foreknown by God with exact precision before he acts to bring the world into existence. And importantly, in all of these other Arminian models, from all eternity God knows with certainty *that* and precisely *how* he will reign victorious in the end in accomplishing *all* his purposes and fulfilling *all* his promises. Not so with the God of open theism. At the very moment I

---

[13] Sanders, *God Who Risks*, 196-197.

[14] Ibid., 197.

[15] This distinction, in which a greater sense of risk is attached to the openness model than is the case with other forms of Arminianism (i.e., models employing libertarian freedom), is supported by a comment made by David Basinger. In discussing middle knowledge, Basinger (*Case for Freewill Theism*, 47) writes, "A God with MK [middle knowledge], unlike the God of theological determinism, must rely on luck, may experience the divine equivalent of disappointment and may need to intervene significantly in earthly affairs. However, like the God of theological determinism, a God with MK knows exactly what will happen (including how he will react to a given state of affairs) before he begins to actualize any creative option. Thus creation is in one sense not a gamble or risk in any way."

write or you read these words, God himself can only speculate what the next moment, much less the distant future, will hold. Who knows what unanticipated twists or turns lay ahead in the course of a contingently unfolding history? This is a rhetorical question, whose answer is, "no one knows, not even God." Surely God is able to conjecture far better than anyone else as to what *may* occur and what *may* be the outcome, but it simply is the case that every aspect of the future of human history that is, in any respect whatsoever, affected by future free choices of moral creatures, cannot, according to this view, be known to God. Prior to creation it was true, every bit as much as it is true at this moment, that God cannot know the ultimate outcome. This risk, it seems, is qualitatively greater than the risk of the non-openness yet nondeterministic versions of Arminianism. God waits, as do we, to see how it all comes out.

Some might consider it demeaning to think of God risking greatly in his creating a world with free creatures. Boyd suggests, however, that taking responsible risks is a virtue and so is appropriate for God. Boyd writes,

> Everyone who is psychologically healthy knows it is good to risk loving another person, for example. You may, of course, get hurt, for people are free agents. But the risk-free alternatives of not loving or of trying to control another person is evidence of insecurity and weakness, if not sickness. Why should we abandon this insight when we think about God, especially since Scripture clearly depicts God as sometimes taking risks?[16]

Furthermore, the only alternative to God being a risk-taker is that God has *everything* under his control, that all that happens is as God wants it to be. But Boyd suggests that, "if God is truly 'above' taking risks, then, we must accept that things such as sin, child mutilations, and people going to hell are all in accordance with God's will."[17] Though some affirm this, says Boyd, most Christians "reject it in horror."[18] Clearly, God doesn't always get his way, but because God is wise, God's risks are always "worth it."[19]

---

[16] Gregory A. Boyd, *God of the Possible: A Biblical Introduction to the Open View of God* (Grand Rapids, Mich.: Baker, 2000), 57-58.
[17] Ibid., 58.
[18] Ibid.
[19] Ibid.

Where in Scripture do we see God taking such risk? From the examples given above, it is clear from an openness perspective that God took a big risk simply in giving humans libertarian freedom. Although God wanted them to use their freedom to love and obey him, God knew such a capacity could be used for evil, destructive purposes. When the man and the woman first sinned, it showed how big was the risk that God took—that although he fully expected them to obey, they failed the test and brought the beginnings of extensive human sin into the world. This risk is all the more amazing when we realize that God would have known (yes, he did *know* his own nature and what was required by that nature) that his holiness would *require* sin's penalty to be paid. The possibility of hell and the necessity of redemption, were he to attempt salvation, were part of the risk he took in creating humans with such freedom. And to think that this sin, though a possibility in God's mind, was fully unanticipated! What a risk, indeed! What consequences and what divine responses would be required. And all of these (the consequences and the divine responses) were unknown, because the sin that was to occur was both unknown and unexpected.

Or consider again God's test of Abraham. Since he did not know how Abraham would respond, God took a big risk. Suppose Abraham had refused to offer Isaac as God required. What would God do then? Would he, could he, find another who *would* obey him and be the one through whom his blessing to the nations could be brought? Is it possible that his promise might fail? After all, he had already specified that his blessing would come *through Abraham* (Gen. 12:1-3), so what would he do if Abraham refused? Would his word and promise be broken? But must he not *always* keep his word? Clearly, God risked greatly in Abraham's test, knowing that his very covenant promise to and through Abraham might remain unfulfilled.

Despite numerous expressions of hope, in open theism, that God will surely and certainly fulfill his purposes in the end,[20] it must be seen here

---

[20] See, e.g., Sanders, *God Who Risks*, 42: "If God has brought new things out of nothing or has conquered chaos in the past, then we may have confidence in God for establishing new and greater things (for example, the new heaven and earth) and triumphing over the forces of death and disorder in the future"; or 129: "Though the Spirit may not get everything he desires, we have reason to hope because we have a God with a proven track record of successfully navigating the vicissitudes of human history and redeeming it. We have confidence that God will bring his project to the fruition he desires because God has proven himself faithful time and again." The question of the basis for optimism and eschatological hope in open theism will be discussed further, below.

just how significant is this sense of risk that God accepts when he chooses to create the kind of world he has created. The fact is, the God of open theism brings into existence a kind of world in which he exercises largely a power of love and persuasion toward his volitional creatures. All their free decisions, unknown in advance by him, have the potential of either advancing or violating his purposes. The success of these purposes rests, to a significant degree, in others' hands. At this very moment, according to open theism, not even God *knows* whether his purposes will be fulfilled.[21] The God of open theism truly is the God who risks.

REPENTANCE OF GOD IN LIGHT OF NEW INFORMATION

It follows from the previous two points that the God of open theism must face the real possibility that he should change his plans or even reassess what he has done or believed in the past, based on new information presented to him. We will consider separately the issues of the divine repentance (i.e., God's change of mind) and of God's self-reassessment, beginning here with God's repentance.

At times, according to open theism, God may receive new information in the form of the prayers of his people, who plead with him to act in a particular way. Since God adjusts his plans to fit changing situations, and since he values greatly the hopes, fears, longings, and pleadings of his people, he may reevaluate what he was planning to do and change his mind because of these urgent, sincere prayers. In other cases, it simply may be the case that some unexpected situation develops that affects the outworking of God's purposes. So, because of prayers and unforeseen situations, God must be open to changing his mind about what he has planned to do.

Boyd develops at some length the two statements in 1 Samuel 15:11, 35, that God regretted making Saul king. Though God would have established Saul's throne long-term (1 Sam. 13:13), because of Saul's sin,

---

[21] William Hasker ("Providence and Evil: Three Theories," *Religious Studies* 28 [1992], 91-105) argues at length that open theism (which he calls "free will theism") handles the problem of evil far better than either Calvinism or Molinism, simply because of God's lack of control over human actions (i.e., God's risk). He ends by saying: "So if one can find excellence in the vision of a creation which, wholly dependent every moment on the sustaining and energizing power of its Creator, nevertheless contains beings which possess under God unprogrammed freedom and creativity of their own—if such a case can be made, then it will be possible to claim that the God of free will theism is indeed the being than which nothing greater can be conceived" (p. 105).

God now changes his mind about the good he was going to bring Saul and instead removes the throne from him and his house. Concerning this, Boyd writes:

> We must wonder how the Lord could truly experience regret for making Saul king if he was absolutely certain that Saul would act the way he did. Could God genuinely confess, "I regret that I made Saul king" if he could in the same breath also proclaim, "I was certain of what Saul would do when I made him king"? I do not see how. Could I genuinely regret, say, purchasing a car because it turned out to run poorly if in fact the car was running exactly as I knew it would when I purchased it? Common sense tells us that we can only regret a decision we made if the decision resulted in an outcome other than what we expected or hoped for when the decision was made.[22]

One of Sanders's most developed biblical examples of God changing his mind is the situation recorded in Exodus 32. Israel has been impatient in waiting for Moses to return from the mountain. At Aaron's direction, they gather their gold jewelry, craft a molten calf, and proclaim this to be their god. God (the true God) is deeply angered and tells Moses he plans to destroy the people. Beginning at 32:11, Moses entreats the Lord with the result that "the LORD changed His mind about the harm which He said He would do to His people" (32:14). Concerning this episode, Sanders writes:

> Apparently, Moses has a relationship with God such that God values what Moses desires. If Moses interprets God's intentions in an unfavorable way and God values his relationship with Moses, then God must either persuade Moses or concede his request. It is unlikely that Moses presents God with new information.
>
> The real basis for the change in God's decision comes from a forceful presentation by one who is in a special relationship with God. With Moses' prayer, the decision-making situation is now altered for God. Being in relationship to Moses, God is willing to allow him to influence the path he will take. God permits human

---

[22] Boyd, *God of the Possible*, 56.

input into the divine future. One of the most remarkable features in the Old Testament is that people can argue with God and win.[23]

Here, according to Sanders, is a clear example of God changing his mind. He said he would do one thing, but something occurs (in this case, it is Moses' prayer) that leads God to do something different. Appeals to anthropomorphism, in which it is claimed that it only *appears* that God changes his mind (as proposed in classical theism), only betray the presence of "control beliefs" which deny, from the outset, any sense of God's changeability or conditionality. Such an approach, says Sanders, is disingenuous in the hands of those who claim to follow the Bible's authorial and intended meaning. If the passage does not mean that God changed his mind, it leaves us with no real meaning at all. "Thus classical theists," says Sanders, "are left with the problem of misleading biblical texts, or, at best, meaningless metaphors regarding the nature of God."[24] How much better to take the text at face value and realize that God, in dynamic relationship with humans, has not pre-planned the future and "reserves the right to alter his plans in response to human initiative."[25]

REASSESSMENT BY GOD IN LIGHT OF NEW AND UNFORESEEN DEVELOPMENTS

In addition to repenting and changing plans for the future, according to open theists, God may also, upon learning how the future *actually* unfolds, and upon gaining new and additional knowledge from this, change his assessment of his own actions or beliefs regarding some past situation. One example of this has already been discussed above, when Sanders tells us that the first sin was, in God's estimate, unexpected and implausible. So, when the man and woman sin, God realizes that his previous belief (i.e., that in all probability they would *not* sin) was mistaken. Openness advocates offer other examples.

In a nearly breathtaking analysis, John Sanders suggests that evidently God radically reassessed his own past action after bringing a

---

[23] Sanders, *God Who Risks,* 64.

[24] Ibid., 69.

[25] Ibid., 70. Cf. Clark H. Pinnock, "From Augustine to Arminius: A Pilgrimage in Theology," in Clark H. Pinnock, ed., *The Grace of God, The Will of Man: A Case for Arminianism* (Grand Rapids, Mich.: Zondervan, 1989), 25-26.

flood upon the whole world. Upon learning what he did through seeing the entire human race and animal kingdom killed (save Noah, his
family, and the collected animals), God promises never again to send a
flood on the whole earth. Why is this so? Sanders writes, "It may be
the case that although human evil caused God great pain, the destruction of what he had made caused him even greater suffering. Although
his judgment was righteous, God decides to try different courses of
action in the future."[26] Here, then, God second-guesses his prior decision. *Perhaps this is not after all the best way to deal with despicable
human evil*, God apparently reasons. *Although just, perhaps this is not
best*. And given that God promises never again to act in this manner,
on Sanders's reading of this account, God must have felt very badly
about what he had done.[27]

Consider another example of God's reassessment, in this case
another reassessment of his own past beliefs. Jeremiah 3:6-7 reads:

> Then the LORD said to me in the days of Josiah the king, "Have
> you seen what faithless Israel did? She went up on every high hill
> and under every green tree, and she was a harlot there. I thought,
> 'After she has done all these things she will return to Me'; but
> she did not return, and her treacherous sister Judah saw it."

Texts like this (cf. Jer. 3:19-20; 32:35) indicate that, as events unfold,
God is faced with the necessity to reevaluate whether what he thought
would happen actually has come about. According to Jeremiah 3:7, God
had certain beliefs about Israel and her future. He believed that her sin-
fulness would not continue indefinitely and that after she had sinned for
a season she would return to the Lord. But as time progressed, it became
apparent that Israel did not do what God believed she would do. The
unfolding of this future reality resulted, then, in God realizing and
admitting that he had been wrong. Concerning this, Sanders writes, "In
these texts [Jer. 3:7; 32:35] God is explicitly depicted as not knowing the

---

[26] Sanders, *God Who Risks*, 50.

[27] Other open theists may differ with Sanders on his interpretation of this text and on this exact
point. However, it is clear that Sanders's view here is fully consistent within the broader model of
open theism; in fact, something like Sanders's proposal is called for by the model. After all, since
God does not know what will be until it happens, it stands to reason that there may be times
(perhaps many times?) when he looks back on his own past actions and regrets what he chose to
do. Knowing what he *now* knows, he may well wish he had acted differently.

specific future. God himself says that he was mistaken about what was going to happen."[28]

Some statements by openness advocates seem to deny what Sanders so clearly and honestly claims here, that is, that God can be so surprised by what occurs that he reassesses what he has done and believed in an acknowledgment that he has been wrong. Boyd, for example, says that God "is never caught off guard or at a loss for options"[29] and that "[h]e is certain about everything that could be and thus is never caught off guard."[30] Yet, in other places, Boyd speaks of God as being surprised by what occurs. Commenting on Jeremiah 3:6-7, 19-20, he writes,

> Since God is omniscient, he always knew that it was remotely possible for his people to be this stubborn, for example. But he genuinely did not expect them to actualize this remote possibility. He authentically expected that they'd be won over by his grace.[31]

So God *was* surprised by what happened and realized that his beliefs about what the Israelites likely would do were wrong. Boyd clarifies what God not being "caught off guard" means when he says, "God wasn't caught off guard (for he knew this stubbornness was possible), but he was genuinely disappointed (for he knew the possibility was improbable and hoped it wouldn't come to pass)."[32] Open theists hold, then, that because God knows *all possibilities,* nothing can be *absolutely* unforeseen or can *absolutely* take God by surprise. Yet, God can clearly be wrong about what he thinks will *probably* occur, leading him to reassess both his own beliefs and his past decisions and actions.

In the openness view, then, God must constantly reassess both the appropriateness of his past choices and actions and the correctness of his past beliefs. In both cases, he may conclude that he simply did not get things quite right. The divine repentance and divine self-reassessment, then, are literally true of God. For the sake of the genuineness of human relationship and the integrity and efficacy of prayer, and based

---

[28] Sanders, *God Who Risks,* 74.
[29] Boyd, *God of the Possible,* 51.
[30] Ibid., 150.
[31] Ibid., 61.
[32] Ibid.

on the reality of God's moment-by-moment growth in knowledge, God may and does change his plans and reassess his past actions and beliefs.

RESPONDING TO SUFFERING IN OPEN THEISM

When human tragedy, injustice, suffering, or pain occurs, open theists stand ready with their words of comfort and pastoral counsel: God is as grieved as you are about the difficulties and heartache you are experiencing, and he, too, wishes that things had worked out differently. However, because God does not (and cannot) know, much less control, much of what the future holds, and because many things occur that are contrary to his good and loving desires, we must not blame God for the evil things that happen in our lives. Instead, we can be assured of his love for us and we must know that he feels the pain we feel. Also, he stands with us to provide strength to rebuild our lives out of whatever unpredictable and unforeseen tragic events have occurred. God is love; never doubt this. Suffering often is pointless; learn to accept this. And be consoled with the realization that God cares deeply about our pain even as he watches tragic events unfold, helpless and unable[33] to prevent the suffering he so deeply bemoans and regrets.

Two accounts from openness advocates will suffice to illustrate the basic lines of response open theism offers to much of human suffering. First, Greg Boyd tells of being approached by an angry young woman after having preached a sermon on how God directs our paths.[34] In brief, this woman (whom he calls "Suzanne") had been a committed Christian single person with a zeal for missions. She prayed fervently for God to bring to her a missions-minded young man who shared her burden, in particular, for Taiwan. In college, she met such a man, spent rich times

---

[33] Of course, the God of open theism is not in any absolute sense helpless or unable to prevent any specific occurrence of suffering or suffering in general. After all, God chose to create a world with creatures possessing libertarian freedom (though he did not have to do this), and he has chosen in the vast majority of cases not to interfere with their use of that libertarian freedom (though he retains the right and power to violate that freedom in any instance he so chooses). So, any given instance of suffering could be prevented by God, and suffering in general could have been precluded, had God chosen to create a different kind of world or to regulate this one more meticulously. The statement that God is helpless and unable to prevent suffering has in mind, then, the open theist's commitment to the notion that God values libertarian freedom so much that he rarely will interfere with its operation. By self-constraint, then, God is faced with the reality of being helpless to stop suffering that he wishes did not happen.

[34] Boyd, *God of the Possible*, 103-106.

of prayer and fellowship with him over three and a half years, and after a prolonged period of seeking God's will—including a lengthy period of fasting and seeking much godly counsel—they married, fully confident that God had brought them together. Following college, and two years into their missionary training, Suzanne learned that her husband was involved in an adulterous relationship. He repented (or so it appeared), but several months later he returned to his involvement in this affair, began treating Suzanne very badly, and eventually divorced her to move in with his lover. Within weeks of the divorce, Suzanne learned that she was pregnant, leaving her, now at the end of this horrible ordeal, emotionally and spiritually empty. Boyd writes:

> Understandably, Suzanne could not fathom how the Lord could respond to her lifelong prayers by setting her up with a man he *knew* would do this to her and her child. Some Christian friends had suggested that perhaps she hadn't heard God correctly. But if it wasn't God's voice that she and everyone else had heard regarding this marriage, she concluded, then no one could ever be sure they heard God's voice.[35]

Confronted with this agonizing situation, and seeking to help this hurting and angry woman deal with her pain, loss, and sense of divine betrayal, Boyd offered his pastoral counsel:

> Initially, I tried to help Suzanne understand that this was her ex-husband's fault, not God's, but her reply was more than adequate to invalidate my encouragement: If God *knew* exactly what her husband would do, then he bears all the responsibility for setting her up the way he did. I could not argue against her point, but I could offer an alternative way of understanding the situation.
> I suggested to her that God felt as much regret over the confirmation he had given Suzanne as he did about his decision to make Saul king of Israel (1 Sam. 15:11, 35; see also Gen. 6:5-6). Not that it was a bad decision—at the time, her ex-husband was a good man with a godly character. The prospects that he and Suzanne would have a happy marriage and fruitful ministry

---

[35] Ibid., 105 (emphasis in original).

were, at the time, very good. Indeed, I strongly suspect that he had influenced Suzanne and her ex-husband toward this college with their marriage in mind.

Because her ex-husband was a free agent, however, even the best decisions can have sad results. Over time, and through a series of choices, Suzanne's ex-husband had opened himself up to the enemy's influence and became involved in an immoral relationship. Initially, all was not lost, and God and others tried to restore him, but he chose to resist the prompting of the Spirit, and consequently his heart grew darker. Suzanne's ex-husband had become a very different person from the man God had confirmed to Suzanne to be a good candidate for marriage. This, I assured Suzanne, grieved God's heart at least as deeply as it grieved hers.

By framing the ordeal within the context of an open future, Suzanne was able to understand the tragedy of her life in a new way. She didn't have to abandon all confidence in her ability to hear God and didn't have to accept that somehow God intended this ordeal "for her own good." Her faith in God's character and her love toward God were eventually restored and she was finally able to move on with her life. . . . This isn't a testimony to his [God's] exhaustive definite foreknowledge; it's a testimony to his unfathomable wisdom.[36]

A second pair of related stories comes from John Sanders. In the introduction to *The God Who Risks*, Sanders tells the stories of two tragic deaths, first of his brother.[37] As Sanders relates it, he was driving home one evening when he saw a terrible accident. A semitrailer blocked the road and a motorcycle lay on its side. A white sheet covered what he later learned was the body of his brother, Dick. After arriving home, Sanders says he went to his room and prayed, "God, why did you kill my brother?" Now, skip forward to about fifteen years later. Sanders tells of attending the funeral service of the young child of two of his close friends. When a few weeks had passed, he spoke with them about their grief. They asked him a question very similar to his own question some

---

[36] Ibid., 105-106 (emphasis in original).
[37] Sanders, *God Who Risks*, 9-10.

fifteen years earlier. "Why did God kill our baby girl?" they inquired. As Sanders recalls the incident, he tells us the counsel he gave these grieving parents as set within the context of his overall view of the openness of God. Sanders writes:

> They were angry with God but did not feel safe enough to cry out in lamentation at church. They had always been told that God's ways are best and that questioning God is a sin. In answering their question, I sought to provide them with a different model of God—the one that is explained in this book. Many people, both churchgoers and non-churchgoers, feel anger and even hatred toward God. But their anger is directed at a particular model of God.[38]

And for Sanders, the model of God he commended to these parents and now, through this book, commends to his readers, is the "risk model of providence." Sanders explains:

> [I]f God is in some respects conditioned by his creatures, then God takes risks in bringing about this particular type of world. According to the risk model of providence, God has established certain boundaries within which creatures operate. But God sovereignly decides not to control each and every event, and some things go contrary to what God intends and may not turn out completely as God desires. Hence, God takes risks in creating this sort of world.[39]

For Sanders, such a view of God's relation to the world does not mean that God exercises no providential control whatsoever. Rather, it simply means that God's providential control is general and broad, not comprehensive and meticulous. That is, God providentially chooses to grant moral creatures freedom but he does not control the specific uses they make of that freedom. As this relates to tragedy and suffering in human life, Sanders explains:

---

[38] Ibid., 10.
[39] Ibid., 10-11.

The overarching structures of creation are purposed by God, but not every single detail that occurs within them. Within general providence it makes sense to say that God intends an overall purpose for the creation and that God does not specifically intend each and every action within the creation. Thus God does not have a specific divine purpose for each and every occurrence of evil. The "greater good" of establishing the conditions of fellowship between God and creatures does not mean that gratuitous evil has a point. Rather, the possibility of gratuitous evil has a point but its actuality does not. . . . When a two-month-old child contracts a painful, incurable bone cancer that means suffering and death, it is pointless evil. The Holocaust is pointless evil. The rape and dismemberment of a young girl is pointless evil. The accident that caused the death of my brother was a tragedy. God does not have a specific purpose in mind for these occurrences.[40]

Here we have, then, a fair sampling of the openness response to human tragedy, suffering, and pain. Consider this listing of the most important facets of open theism's approach:

1. God does not know in advance the future free actions of his moral creatures.
2. God cannot control the future free actions of his moral creatures.
3. Tragic events occur over which God has no control.
4. When such tragedies occur, God should not be blamed, because he was not able to prevent them from occurring, and he certainly did not will or cause them to occur.
5. When such tragic events occur, God feels the pain of those who endure its suffering.
6. God is love, and he may be trusted always to do his best to offer guidance that is intended to serve the well-being of others.
7. At times, God realizes that the guidance he gave may have inadvertently and unexpectedly led to unwanted hardship and suffering.

---

[40] Ibid., 261-262.

8. At times, God may repent of his own past actions, realizing that his own choices have not worked out well and may have led to unexpected hardship (e.g., 1 Sam. 15:11).
9. Some suffering is gratuitous and pointless, i.e., some suffering has no positive or redeeming quality to it at all, so that not even God is able to bring any good from it.
10. Regardless of whether our suffering was gratuitous, or whether God may have contributed inadvertently to our suffering, God always stands ready to help rebuild our lives and offers us further grace, strength, direction, and counsel.

This summary of the openness position on responding to suffering pulls together all the previous four themes discussed in this chapter. In our suffering, according to openness theology, God is in *real relationship* with us, intimately involved in our lives and interacting with us in the unfolding of life's events. But, because much of the future is unknown, God, and we, face genuine *risks*. Unexpected tragedies can occur, people can choose to resist God's gracious prompting, and as a result great injury can come to ourselves and others. The God who risks creates a world in which all of creation, of necessity, joins in on the risks, meaning that even deeply injurious and gratuitous suffering can occur. And because of life's surprises, some good but others bad, God may see things afresh and so *repent* of his previous intentions or *reassess* his own past beliefs and actions. At times this may include God's recognition that the good he intended resulted in unanticipated pain. In such cases God will work in *new* ways on behalf of those whom he loves. And when he does so, one can be confident that God will always seek to bring good out of whatever pain or tragedy one faces. Life may have many hardships, some unforeseen by God, some that serve no good purpose, even some to which God inadvertently contributed. But, says open theism, be assured of God's constant love and presence with us. His love will never fail. He is supremely resourceful. So, hope in God.

CONCLUSION

At its heart, open theism understands the relation between God and the world as being dynamic, interactive, and mutually engaging. The open-

ness of the future is not so much a value in itself; its value lies in secur-
ing the reality of this genuinely spontaneous and dynamic creator/crea-
ture relationship. God values freedom because he values *relationship*
with free creatures. Therefore, he chooses *not* to determine all things or
to know everything future but to enter into his own creation "project,"
attempting to lead creation forward to his desired ends. Along the way,
he wins and loses; free creatures sometimes obey and sometimes rebel.
But God is magnified, say open theists, precisely by demonstrating his
resourcefulness, expressing his love, and charting the course of the
unknown and unfolding future not by himself but together with us.

PART TWO

What's Wrong with Open Theism's View of God?

ASSESSING GOD'S LESSER GLORY

4

Assessing Open Theism's Denial of Exhaustive Divine Foreknowledge

Open theism's denial of exhaustive divine foreknowledge provides the basis for the major lines of difference between the openness view and all versions of classical theism, including any other version of Arminianism. The implications of denying that God knows what the future holds are enormous. It is incumbent upon us to take this proposal seriously and weigh the evidence. In this chapter, consideration will be given to the positive evidence openness proponents offer for their denial of divine foreknowledge as seen in the proposed divine growth-in-knowledge texts and divine repentance texts. Chapter 5 will then turn our attention to biblical evidence supporting God's exhaustive knowledge of the future.

OPEN THEISM'S "STRAIGHTFORWARD" READING OF DIVINE GROWTH-IN-KNOWLEDGE TEXTS

One of the initial appeals of the openness proposal is its challenge that we take the text of Scripture simply for what it says. Stop making it say the opposite of what it so clearly and plainly does say, openness proponents argue. When the Lord says to Abraham, as we saw earlier, "for now I know that you fear God" (Gen. 22:12), we should allow these words to speak and mean exactly what normal conversational speech would convey. That is, God truly and literally learned what he previously had not known; this was a real test, openness advocates insist, and God learned the results only when Abraham acted.

Behind this insistence, of course, is an underlying hermeneutic.

Openness defenders propose that the "straightforward" or "literal" or "face value" meaning of these passages is the correct meaning. Throughout *God of the Possible*, for example, Greg Boyd commends his interpretation of text after text by affirming that his understanding takes these passages in a straightforward fashion. Here are a few sample statements: "The open view," says Boyd, "is rooted in the conviction that the passages that constitute the motif of future openness should be taken *just as literally* as the passages that constitute the motif of future determinism."[1] In reference to Isaiah 5:1-5, he states, "If we take the passage *at face value*, does it not imply that the future of Israel, the 'vineyard,' was not certain until they settled it by choosing to yield 'wild grapes'?"[2] Commenting on Exodus 4:1-9, Boyd bemoans the fact that many interpreters fail to acknowledge God's ignorance of how many miracles it might take to convince the people of Israel that Moses has been sent by God. He writes, "If we believe that God speaks *straightforwardly*, however, it seems he did not foreknow with certainty exactly how many miracles it would take to get the elders of Israel to believe Moses."[3] Interpreting 2 Peter 3:12 ("as you look forward to the day of God and speed its coming"—NIV), Boyd says, "If *taken at face value*, the verse is teaching us that how people respond to the gospel and how Christians live affects the timing of the second coming."[4] And, in a summary statement of his position, Boyd writes, "All the evidence indicates that the verses signifying divine openness should be *interpreted every bit as literally* as the verses signifying the settledness of the future."[5]

As a general rule, I believe it is wise to adopt Boyd's hermeneutical reflex, if I might use this term. Generally, he is right that we ought to take the straightforward meaning of the text as the intended meaning, even when that straightforward meaning is not culturally acceptable; and we ought to be very reticent to deny any straightforward reading unless there is compelling reason to think that such a straightforward reading is not the intended meaning of the text. Lutherans and Zwinglians, for example, disagree over whether we ought to take the words of Jesus, "This is

---

[1] Gregory A. Boyd, *God of the Possible: A Biblical Introduction to the Open View of God* (Grand Rapids, Mich.: Baker, 2000), 54 (emphasis added).
[2] Ibid., 60 (emphasis added).
[3] Ibid., 67 (emphasis added).
[4] Ibid., 71-72 (emphasis added).
[5] Ibid., 120 (emphasis added).

my body," in a straightforward manner. Luther felt strongly that the literal meaning of Jesus' statement was the intended meaning, whereas
Zwingli believed that there were good biblical reasons for seeing this
statement as *metaphorical* and *representational*. For Zwingli, "This *is* my
body" must be interpreted like "I *am* the good shepherd," "I *am* the
bread from heaven," "I *am* the living water," and "I *am* the door." While
I agree with Zwingli on this issue, I also affirm that we should only deny
the literal meaning that Luther had insisted on *if*—and what an important *if* this is—the reasons are compelling that Jesus *actually meant* his
statement to be understood in a metaphorical, not literal, fashion. So,
while I am very sympathetic with the openness insistence on respecting
Scripture's straightforward meaning, this openness hermeneutic raises the
question—an extremely important question for the outcome of the issues
at hand—whether *in this particular case,* regarding these so-called openness passages, we should rightly accept the straightforward meaning as
the authorially intended meaning of these texts.

Genesis 22:12 Reconsidered

Let's test this hermeneutic by beginning with Genesis 22:12, one of the
favorite passages of the defenders of the open view of God. Recall that
in this text, God says that he learns the state of Abraham's heart ("for
now I know that you fear God") as he observes Abraham's willingness
to offer Isaac on the altar. Without any question, the most straightforward and literal meaning of these words is just as openness advocates
say it is. God *now* learned what previously he had not known. When
Abraham actually raised the knife, *then and only then* was God able to
say, "now I know" that you fear me. God learned something he had not
known before, and this demonstrates that he does not have exhaustive
knowledge of the future—so argues the open theist.

But, probing this understanding and the Scriptures a bit deeper, how
does this straightforward interpretation of Genesis 22:12 fare? There are
at least three problems raised by this openness interpretation. First, if
God must test Abraham to *find out what is in his heart* (recall that the
text says, "for now I know that you fear God"), then it calls into question God's *present knowledge* of Abraham's inner spiritual, psychological, mental, and emotional state. Consider that 1 Chronicles 28:9 ("for

the LORD searches all hearts, and understands every intent of the thoughts") and 1 Samuel 16:7 ("God sees not as man sees, for man looks at the outward appearance, but the LORD looks at the heart") teach us that God knows fully the thoughts and intentions of the hearts and inner lives of people. So, doesn't God know Abraham fully? In fact, doesn't God know the state of Abraham's heart better than Abraham himself does? Is there any facet of Abraham's inner thoughts, feelings, doubts, fears, hopes, dreams, reasonings, musings, inclinations, predispositions, habits, tendencies, reflexes, and patterns, that God does not know absolutely, fully, and certainly? Does not God understand Abraham perfectly? Cannot God read Abraham exactly? Because the openness interpretation of Genesis 22:12 claims that only when Abraham raises the knife to kill his son does God know Abraham's heart, this open view interpretation cannot avoid denying of God at least *some* knowledge of the present. As such, this straightforward interpretation ends up conflicting with Scripture's affirmation that God knows all that is, and it contradicts open theism's own commitment to God's exhaustive knowledge of the past and present.

Second, the even more interesting and important question is this: Does God need this test to know specifically whether Abraham *fears God*? That is, while it is significant that the openness interpretation implicitly denies God's present knowledge (the first point), even more telling here is the implicit denial of the *specific content* of this present knowledge, that is, knowledge that Abraham fears God. For we are told that only at the point that Abraham raises the knife over his son does God *then* learn that Abraham in fact fears God. But is it reasonable to think that God really does not know *until this moment* whether Abraham is God-fearing?

Granting that God knows Abraham's inner life perfectly, it seems highly doubtful, even by openness standards,[6] that God actually and truly learns at this moment that Abraham is God-fearing. In general, open theists are sympathetic with this argument. They respect and even appeal to God's intimate and perfect knowledge of his creatures' inner states of mind and heart. Consider on this issue how convenient Boyd

---

[6] Boyd (ibid., 152) writes, "He [God] knows the thoughts and intentions of all individuals perfectly and can play them out in his mind like an infinitely wise chess master anticipating every possible combination of moves his opponent could ever make."

finds it to appeal exactly to God's perfect knowledge of people's inner lives in his explanation of Jesus' prediction of Peter's three denials of Christ. Boyd writes:

> Sometimes we may understand the Lord's foreknowledge of a person's behavior simply by supposing that the person's character, combined with the Lord's perfect knowledge of all future variables, *makes the person's future behavior certain.* As we know, character becomes more predictable over time. The longer we persist in a chosen path, the more that path becomes part of who we are. . . . Our omniscient Creator knows us perfectly, far better than we even know ourselves. Hence we can assume that he is able to predict our behavior far more extensively and accurately than we could predict it ourselves.[7]

Amazingly, Boyd uses this line of reasoning to explain how Jesus could predict accurately that Peter would deny him *three times.* More will be said on Peter's denials later in this chapter, but suffice it here to suggest that if one compares the two cases, Abraham's heart seems far more predictable than Peter's three denials. That is, it seems apparent that Abraham's past conduct provides a better basis for knowing the state of his heart than Peter's past expressions of character would have

---

[7] Ibid., 35 (emphasis added). Strangely enough, later in Boyd's defense of open theism, he has a section titled, "God Tests People to Know Their Character" (*God of the Possible*, 63-66). Here he offers, for example, God's test of Abraham (Gen. 22:12) and God's test of Hezekiah (2 Chron. 32:31), and several others, all as illustrations of God learning what is in the hearts of these individuals. That Boyd has earlier stated in such strong and definitive terms God's intimate and exhaustive knowledge of our inner lives and characters leaves one to wonder both why God needs to test people to know what is in their hearts (presuming that God knows this already), and why Boyd would say in one place that God knows us perfectly and in another place that God only learns what is in our hearts by testing us. Boyd tries to alleviate this problem a bit, it appears, by a subtle shift in that of which God is actually ignorant. Consider one statement, his treatment of Hezekiah: "Similarly, the Bible says that God tested Hezekiah 'to *know* all that was in his heart' (2 Chron. 32:31). If God eternally knew how Hezekiah would respond to him, God couldn't have *really* been testing him in order to come to this knowledge" (64, emphasis in original). Notice that, where 2 Chronicles says that God sought to know "*all that was in his heart,*" Boyd says God sought to know "*how Hezekiah would respond.*" Within Boyd's open view framework, God must have exhaustive present knowledge, including perfect knowledge of people's psychological, mental, and emotional states. Given this, God really cannot fail to know what is in someone's heart at any point. But, for Boyd, God can be (and is) ignorant of future free actions. So, it is only by changing "know what is in his heart" to "know how he will respond" that Boyd can try to make his case that these texts support his view that God grows in knowledge. The fact is, however, that this text and others Boyd cites speak of God knowing *what is in their hearts.* From what Boyd says on page 35, God needs no help in knowing this. The tests, then, contrary to Boyd's bravado in this section, simply cannot reveal to God the state of these people's hearts, whose hearts he knows perfectly already.

provided for predicting that he would deny Christ *specifically three times*. And yet, with Abraham, we are told that until he raised the knife over Isaac's body, *God did not know whether he feared him.*

Consider this: Romans 4:18-22 tells us that Abraham had such strong faith in God that even when both he and Sarah grew old and so moved past their ability to parent children, year after year Abraham believed that God would keep his promise and give Sarah and him a son! "In hope against hope," and "without becoming weak in faith," and "giving glory to God" are phrases in this account which reveal that Abraham truly, faithfully, and lastingly *feared God* and he did so all these years, *long before* the Genesis 22 test of sacrificing Isaac. Abraham's faith in God, in fact, is so notable that the apostle Paul uses it in Romans 4 as a supreme illustration of the nature of true faith. *Clearly God knows this about Abraham.*

Consider this also: Hebrews 11:8-12, 17-19 is devoted to the faith of Abraham, charting his faith all the way from his call in Ur of the Chaldeans through the episode of the near-sacrifice of Isaac. Through each of these instances in the lives of Abraham and Sarah, a consistent pattern of faith in God is evident. And the writer to the Hebrews chooses to emphasize particularly Abraham's consistent and commendable heart of faith. *Clearly God knows this about Abraham.*

One more observation is especially important. Hebrews 11:19 says of Abraham and his choice to obey God's command to sacrifice Isaac, that "he [Abraham] considered that God is able to raise people even from the dead, from which he also received him [Isaac] back as a type." My question is this: *When* did Abraham "consider that God is able to raise people even from the dead"? Was this *after* God had stopped Abraham from killing Isaac? Obviously not. Why would he *afterward* think of this and put his hope in God for it, for now he *knows* God is not going to demand the life of Isaac after all.

The point of this statement in Hebrews 11:19 is that Abraham was prepared to obey God's command to kill his beloved son, knowing that God could raise Isaac even from the dead if he so chose. It was this confidence that Abraham had in God that led him to obey God's command, to travel to Mt. Moriah, build the altar, fetter his son atop its wood, and raise his knife to plunge it into Isaac's flesh. No doubt, the writer to the Hebrews is reflecting here on Abraham's own words of hope, when to his helper he said, "Stay here with the donkey, and I and the lad will go over there; and we will worship and return to you" (Gen. 22:5). What confidence in God in the face of such an enormous test! But if Abraham had this confidence in God *prior to* his action, if Abraham was praying, reflecting, and contemplating in his own heart and mind, trusting that God would be able even to raise Isaac from the dead, if Abraham was even planning to return with Isaac, and if Abraham was doing this prior to raising his knife, then does this not demonstrate that Abraham truly has a heart that fears God, and that he has this God-fearing heart before (and as) he lifts the knife? *Yes, and clearly God knows this about Abraham.*

Because Abraham has such a God-fearing heart before the actual attempted sacrifice takes place, and since God knows Abraham's heart perfectly, then it simply cannot be the case that only when Abraham raised his knife, only then and not before, does God learn that Abraham fears him. If Hebrews 11:19 (as reinforced by Genesis 22:5) makes anything clear on this issue, it demonstrates without any doubt that Abraham had a God-fearing heart leading up to his sacrifice of Isaac. Since God knows this, it is absolutely wrong to interpret Genesis 22:12 as saying that only when Abraham lifted the knife did God "learn" that Abraham feared God. The openness interpretation, then, stumbles over Scripture's clear warrant for denying, in this case, the literal, straightforward interpretation proposed. Both the pattern of Abraham's faith commended in Romans 4 and Hebrews 11, and the specific reference in Hebrews 11:19 to Abraham believing, before the attempted sacrifice, that God could raise Isaac from the dead, give clear biblical warrant for taking Genesis 22:12 anthropomorphically and analogically, not literally and at face value.

Third, given the openness commitment to the nature of libertarian freedom, God's test of Abraham simply cannot have accomplished what open theists claim it has. Notice carefully the interpretive comments on this text made by Sanders and Boyd. Sanders writes, "God needs to know if Abraham is the sort of person on whom God can count for collaboration toward the fulfillment of the divine project. *Will he be faithful?* Or must God find someone else through whom to achieve his purpose? God has been faithful; *will Abraham be faithful?*"[8] And Boyd's comment on Genesis 22:12 reads: "The verse clearly says that it was

---

[8] John Sanders, *The God Who Risks: A Theology of Providence* (Downers Grove, Ill.: InterVarsity, 1998), 52-53 (emphasis added).

because Abraham did what he did that the Lord *now* knew he was a faithful covenant partner."[9]

According to these openness advocates, Abraham's testing proved to God *now* that Abraham was a faithful covenant partner who, therefore, could be trusted to be faithful in working with God in the fulfillment of God's covenant purposes. But since Abraham possesses libertarian freedom, and since even God can be taken aback by improbable and implausible human actions, what assurances could God have that Abraham would remain faithful in the future? One realizes how transient the "now I know" is for God. As soon as the test is over, another test would seemingly be required.[10]

And notice, too, an interesting dilemma faced in the openness understanding of Abraham's testing. At best, what God could come to know, on openness grounds, is whether or not Abraham's passing the test demonstrated the continuation of a *pattern of behavior* that would render Abraham's future faithfulness more probable. But of course, on the one hand, if Abraham's passing of this test confirms further a pattern of faithfulness Abraham had already demonstrated in his life of trust and obedience, then it could not be literally true that in *this* test (i.e., the test of the sacrifice of Isaac) God learned *now* that Abraham feared him. On the other hand, if Abraham passed this test in striking contrast to a pattern of his previous unfaithfulness, why would God then conclude that Abraham would remain faithful in the future, even when he had passed *this* test, given his previous pattern of disobedience? Either way, whether Abraham had previously demonstrated a pattern of faithfulness or not, the singular and transient nature of this specific test demonstrates that what openness proponents claim God learned simply could not have been gained.

It is clear, then, that the openness interpretation fails. Because God knows our hearts intimately, he knew previously every hope and fear, every thought and inclination of Abraham's heart as Abraham ascended Mt. Moriah and proceeded to bind his son. Further, there is strong and compelling biblical warrant from Genesis 22:5, Romans 4, and Hebrews 11 for affirming God's previous knowledge of Abraham's deep trust and fear of God. It is biblically untenable to claim that only when Abraham

---

[9] Boyd, *God of the Possible*, 64 (emphasis in original).

[10] I am grateful to Ardel Caneday for sharing the above insight with me in e-mail correspondence.

raised the knife did God *then, and not until then,* learn that Abraham feared God. And, given the nature of Abraham's ongoing libertarian freedom (as understood in open theism), God simply could not have known from this test whether Abraham would be faithful in the future. What open theists claim God gained from this was, on openness grounds, either already known to God (so he did not learn something new in this test) or at best was a transient and passing truth (which could give no real assurance of how Abraham would act in the future). The straightforward meaning open theists commend simply cannot be the intended meaning of this text.

Yet, clearly this text (and all others cited in support of the openness view) has an intended meaning. It simply will not do to say, in response to the openness proposal, that when Genesis 22:12 says, "for now I know" it means, "for I have eternally known." Openness advocates are right to point to something that takes place *in relation to God* when Abraham lifts his knife. But if this statement cannot refer to a literal acquiring of knowledge that Abraham fears God—knowledge of which God was ignorant until Abraham raised the knife to kill Isaac—what can this statement mean?

I have argued elsewhere[11] that the divine immutability is best understood as involving God's unchangeable nature (ontological immutability) and promise (ethical immutability), but that Scripture does not lead us to think of God as unchangeable in every respect (absolute immutability). Importantly, God is changeable *in relationship* with his creation, particularly with human and angelic moral creatures he has made to live in relationship with him. In this relational mutability, God does not change in his essential nature, purposes, will, knowledge, or wisdom; but he does interact with his people in the experiences of their lives as these unfold in time. God actually enters into relationship with his people, while knowing from eternity all that they will face.

Therefore, when God observes Abraham bind his son to the altar he has crafted and raise his knife to plunge it into his body, God literally sees and experiences in this moment what he has known from eternity. When the angel of the LORD utters the statement, "for now I know that you fear God," this expresses the idea that *"in the experience of this*

[11] Bruce A. Ware, "An Evangelical Reformulation of the Doctrine of the Immutability of God," *Journal of the Evangelical Theological Society* 29, no. 4 (1986), 431-446.

action, I (God) am witnessing Abraham demonstrate dramatically and afresh that he fears me, and I find this both pleasing and acceptable in my sight." Through Abraham's action of faith and fear of God, God sees and enters into the experience of this action of obedience, which action and heart of faith he has previously known fully and perfectly. What this kind of interpretation offers is a way to understand the text as communicating a *present and experiential reality that is true of God* at the moment of Abraham's act of faith, while it also safeguards what Scripture elsewhere demands, the *previous full and perfect knowledge God had of Abraham's fear of him.* Open theists are right to say that this text demands that we understand something happening *in relation to God* at this moment, but they are wrong on Scriptural grounds to take the straightforward reading of this text and say that what happened in God is that he literally learned at this moment that Abraham feared him. Rather, God has witnessed and experienced in this moment what he had always known, and it is this that is communicated by the phrase, "for now I know."

Genesis 3:8-13

A little reflection on similar passages exposes further problems with this straightforward approach to such texts. I begin with Genesis 3:8. Several features of this verse are peculiar on a straightforward reading. The man and woman "heard the sound" of God in the garden, the sound they heard was of God "walking" in the garden, and the man and woman "hid themselves from the presence of the LORD." On a straightforward reading, God has physical characteristics such that he can make sounds, his physical (bodily?) nature can be heard as he walks in the garden, and most significantly, God can be hidden from, thus indicating that he is spatially located and delimited. All this raises the question whether one ought to read such texts in a straightforward manner. If the open theist also denies that we should, then the obvious question becomes, where is a straightforward reading legitimate and where is it not? Certainly, then, it won't work to commend the openness interpretation of various texts simply by asserting that the openness understanding respects the straightforward meaning of these passages. We all agree that the straightforward meaning sometimes cannot be the correct meaning. We will explore this further below, but consider first some even more directly relevant features of this text.

In Genesis 3:9, with the man and woman hiding among the trees of the garden following the first sin, we read: "Then the LORD God called to the man, and said to him, 'Where are you?'" Now, what would a straightforward reading here yield? It appears 1) that God *does not presently know* where the man is, and 2) that God is *spatially located* (i.e., not everywhere present) so that he is unaware of where the man is hiding until the man reveals himself. In other words, to read this text in the same manner many other texts are read by openness proponents would result in a denial of God's exhaustive *present* knowledge and a denial of his *omnipresence*.

The problem only gets worse as we read on in the Genesis 3 narrative. In verse 11, God asks the man, "Who told you that you were naked? Have you eaten from the tree of which I commanded you not to eat?" Here we add another doctrinal denial to the above two. God's second question ("Have you eaten . . . ?") implies, on a straightforward reading, that God does not know what has happened in the *past*. His question to the man, taken at face value, serves the purpose of informing God as to whether the man had violated God's prohibition. And, as we continue reading, God's similar question to the woman in verse 13 ("What is this you have done?") likewise indicates God's ignorance of the woman's *previous* action. Altogether, then, if we apply the openness hermeneutic to this passage, we are forced to deny God's exhaustive knowledge of the *past*, God's exhaustive knowledge of the *present*, and God's *omnipresence*.

Clearly open theists are unwilling, by their own stated commitments, to deny any of these doctrines. But how can they avoid doing so? If the hermeneutic applies to Genesis 22:12 (as open theists understand it), should it not also apply to Genesis 3:8-13? It appears that the only way to avoid the undesirable doctrinal implications of this straightforward reading of the problematic statements in Genesis 3 is to deny the so-called straightforward reading itself. Surely openness advocates will agree. Given their doctrinal commitments, their response will be that there are a number of biblical passages which inform us that God has comprehensive knowledge of the past and present, and many passages teach that God is omnipresent, so in this passage, we need to understand statements such as, "Where are you?" and "What is this you have done?" as rhetorical and anthropomorphic (i.e., as understood in common human ways of speaking that should be taken in a non-literalistic, non-straightforward manner). But if that is so here, why not also in Genesis 22:12? That is, even apart from the reasons raised above for denying a straightforward reading of Genesis 22:12, would not a comparison with Genesis 3:8-13 raise the question of whether the former is being interpreted correctly? *Is not the issue, then, whether Scripture elsewhere teaches, with sufficient clarity and fullness, that God has exhaustive knowledge of the past, present, and future so as to see other purposes served in these texts than that of teaching us that God has just learned something new?*

Genesis 18:9-21

Consider another "growth-in-knowledge" text.[12] In Genesis 18, three men visit and dine with Abraham. While eating, the men (who apparently represent, at least in one of the members, a theophany, since "the LORD" is used following this) inquire of Abraham in verse 9, "Where is Sarah your wife?" Apparently they do not know, so they ask where Sarah is. But does not "the LORD" know at this moment where Sarah is? Apparently not. Perhaps this by itself could be set aside (wrongly, in my view) by appeal to the "three *men*" of the account. Reading on, however, much larger problems arise. Just before leaving for Sodom, "the LORD" speaks to Abraham. Genesis 18:20-21 reads, "And the LORD said, 'The outcry of Sodom and Gomorrah is indeed great, and their sin is exceedingly grave. I will go down now, and see if they have done entirely according to its outcry, which has come to Me; and *if not, I will know'*" (emphasis added).

Again, a moment's reflection on this text reveals the severe doctrinal implications that would follow were one to employ here the openness hermeneutic of Genesis 22:12. By God's own admission, first, *he does not presently know* whether the sin of Sodom is as great as its outcry. Second, *he does not know the past* sin of Sodom fully, since he must see if they *have done* according to its outcry. Third, *he is not omnipresent*, since he

---

[12] So far as I can tell, Genesis 18:21 is not dealt with in Sanders's *The God Who Risks* or Boyd's *God of the Possible*. I may have missed the discussion, but neither a careful reading of both books nor a search of these books' Scripture indexes turned up any coverage of this critical verse. Given the direct relevance of this verse to the central claims of the open view of God, and its close proximity to the much-favored openness text of Genesis 22:12, one is only left to wonder why this discussion was omitted by both authors.

needs to travel there and only then will be able to *see* what the status of their sin is; when he arrives and looks, *then* (and only then) he will "know." Hermeneutical consistency, it would seem, requires that if Genesis 22:12 means that God learned something new, as open theists claim, then Genesis 18:21 means that God does not know all of the past or present and that he is spatially confined. So which should it be? Shall we follow the openness approach consistently and deny *even more* of God's attributes than have already been trimmed away?[13] Or shall we, with great caution and care, consider whether Scripture elsewhere teaches, with sufficient clarity and fullness, that God in fact knows the past, present, and future and is everywhere present, in order then to reconsider the narrative and personal dialogue form of these Genesis texts (and others), to discern in them their proper and intended meanings? We shall return to this question below after consideration of some other texts relating to the question of God's knowledge of the future.

"Entering-God's-Mind" Texts

An intriguing line of defense for the openness position comes from a handful of texts (e.g., Jer. 7:31; 19:5; 32:35) in which God says that *it has never entered his mind* that Israel would act as they have. Here, it appears, God is totally ignorant of some particular kind of behavior until it occurs. When Israel performs this behavior, then, presumably, knowledge of the behavior "enters" God's mind. Commenting on these verses, Boyd states:

> Three times the Lord expresses shock over Israel's ungodly behavior by saying that they were doing things "which I did not command or decree, *nor did it enter my mind*" (Jer. 19:5; see also 7:31; 32:35). However we understand the phrase "nor did it enter my mind," it would at the very least seem to preclude the possibility that the Israelites' idolatrous behavior was eternally certain in God's mind. If the classical view is correct, we have to be will-

---

[13] I have sometimes wondered whether some open theists might respond to these arguments by affirming their implications and thus denying of God exhaustive knowledge of the past and present. A consistent hermeneutic would, in some ways and at one level, be more defensible than the *ad hoc* and special pleading sort that results in open theism as currently practiced. Of course, at another level, such a move would even more greatly distort and diminish the true and living God and would signal an even greater departure from a fully biblical understanding of God.

ing to accept that God could in one breath say that the Israelites'
behavior "did not enter my mind," though their behavior "was
eternally in my mind." If this is not a contradiction, what is?[14]

Two responses are in order. First, since open theists affirm God's
awareness of all possibilities (i.e., omniscience is defined as God's comprehensive knowledge of everything past and present, of everything logically entailed from the past or present, and of all possible states of
affairs), it cannot literally be the case that "it never entered God's mind"
that Israel would behave as she did. God has known from eternity that
this could happen, even on openness criteria.

Second, and more important, Jeremiah 19:5, from which Boyd cites
his phrase "nor did it enter my mind," reads: "[Judah and Jerusalem]
have built the high places of Baal to *burn their sons in the fire* as burnt
offerings to Baal, a thing which I never commanded or spoke of, *nor did
it ever enter My mind*" (emphasis added). Jeremiah 7:31 says essentially
the same thing, but 32:35 should be noted: "They built the high places
of Baal that are in the valley of Ben-hinnom to cause their *sons and their
daughters to pass through the fire to Molech,* which I had not commanded them *nor had it entered My mind* that they should do this
abomination, to cause Judah to sin" (emphasis added).

The specific "ungodly behavior" that Jeremiah points to is the horrible act of Israel burning their sons and daughters on the altars of the
high places. Since this is the sin the prophet has in mind, it is especially
important to note that God warned Israel against committing *this specific evil act* hundreds of years earlier. Deuteronomy 12:31 warns Israel
not to follow after the gods of the nations, "for they even burn their sons
and daughters in the fire to their gods." Similarly, Deuteronomy 18:10
warns, "There shall not be found among you anyone who makes his son
or his daughter pass through the fire. . . ." And in light of the reference
to Molech in Jeremiah 32:35, it is especially noteworthy that Leviticus
18:21 says, "You shall not give any of your offspring to offer them to
Molech . . . ."

Can we rightly take these statements in Jeremiah as indicating that
God had not thought about or known in advance about this kind of hor-

---

[14] Boyd, *God of the Possible,* 61-62 (emphasis in original).

rible behavior? Clearly not, since he several times warned them against committing *this specific sin*. Or can we even take these statements to mean that he had never conceived of Israel performing such actions? This also cannot be, since the warnings were given to Israel. Clearly neither of these interpretations is possible in light of the texts we have seen from Deuteronomy and Leviticus. God not only had known of this kind of behavior far in advance, he had furthermore warned Israel herself not to enter into such behavior. Therefore, these ideas simply *could not literally have entered God's mind for the first time* at the point when Israel actually acted in such a despicable way. Apparently we are to understand by these phrases the extreme disapproval God has for his people in this vile activity: God expresses his disapproval by saying that it is a kind of behavior so vile, so wicked, so detestable that he does not want even to consider such a thing as happening—although, as we have seen, he in fact does know about such behavior. Once again, it is apparent that the underlying issue in the interpretation of these Jeremiah texts, as with all the proposed "openness" texts here considered, is whether Scripture gives us sufficient warrant for looking beyond the straightforward understanding of these texts in order to discern their intended meanings.

Divine Remembrance (Forgetfulness?) Texts

Another biblical theme that strains the openness hermeneutic involves God being reminded of, or seeking to remember, certain things about the past. For example, in Genesis 9:13-17, God sets the rainbow in the sky in order "to remember the everlasting covenant" he made with Noah. Given the openness hermeneutic, why should a straightforward reading not be given of this text? Or in Isaiah 62:6, God says that he has appointed watchmen (likely angels) on the walls of the new Jerusalem whose job it is, night and day, "to remind the LORD" of his pledge. Many more such examples could be given, but what is especially interesting about these two instances is that God actually *establishes a mechanism* for being reminded. God puts the rainbow in the cloud so that when he sees it, he will remember the covenant with Noah. God appoints watchmen whose constant purpose it is to remind God of his gracious pledge to Israel. Why would readers of the openness proposal not also naturally think that these passages indicate, by a straightforward reading, that God has a faulty memory? At least God knows this about himself (!), they might reason, and surely that is commendable, perhaps even more commendable, due to its greater difficulty, than would be true of God in the traditonal view.[15] He purposely puts reminders in place so that he won't forget—a sort of divine version of a string tied to one's finger. But the fact is, on a straightforward reading, God is at least potentially forgetful. What confidence can open theism give that this interpretation is wrong, and that this is not true about God, apart from sheer assertion that it is not? Does not their hermeneutical appeal lead to such a possible reading of these texts? Again we face the pivotal question of the basis by which we might understand whether God's knowledge of the past, present, and future is exhaustive. Appeal to the so-called openness texts on their own, saying that a straightforward reading of them requires the view that God lacks knowledge of the future, is simply not convincing.

Conditional Future Texts

A number of passages present God as saying, often through his prophets, that some future possible situation *may* occur, thus indicating for open theists that God does not know whether it will or will not occur.[16] In Exodus 4, for example, when Moses worries that the people will not believe that the Lord has sent him, God gives him several attesting miracles to perform so that if they don't believe after one miracle, they *may* believe after another. Also, passages such as Exodus 13:17, Jeremiah 26:3, and Ezekiel 12:3 use words such as "perhaps" and "may" to indicate that whether the people will obey or not is evidently not known, even to God. Do these texts, then, indicate God's ignorance of the future actions of his people?

First, one should be extremely hesitant to draw this conclusion in light of many *other* texts in which God declares just what his people *will* do. In chapter 5 we will explore the substantial biblical support for God's knowledge of future free actions. For now, let it simply be noted

---

[15] I can hear the triumphalism even now! God is even more glorious here than in the traditional view, so it would go, because rather than just remembering everything by nature (the easier and hence less praiseworthy option), he must strategize, plan, and work at remembering what he does (the harder and hence more praiseworthy option).

[16] See Boyd's discussion of these texts in *God of the Possible*, 66-71.

that every reference to God's knowing in advance of some future free choice would give one great pause in thinking that, in these "conditional future" texts, God literally does not know what his people will do. For example, when God declares in Deuteronomy 31:21, "for I know their intent [Israel's spurning God and turning to other gods—see 31:20] which they are developing today, before I have brought them into the land," and when the song of Moses in the next chapter assumes their rebellion, God's judgment, Israel's captivity by other nations, and then God's merciful deliverance, it is clear that these aspects of the future are not "open" in God's sight; he knows what innumerable freewill agents will do, and he tells them in advance precisely how the future will unfold. Or consider God's predicting the very name of Cyrus, the rise and fall of nations not yet in existence, the words that come off our lips moment by moment, specific actions such as Jesus being pierced (the other two men crucified with him were not pierced) or the bartering for his clothing or his being buried in the grave of a rich man instead with the criminals, or Peter's three denials of Christ—all of these accurately predicted events and many more (see chapter 5) should give one great reluctance to conclude that "conditional future" texts are really intended to teach us that God honestly and literally does not know what will happen.

Second, there is another reason why God may use such language as "perhaps," "may," and "if." Although he knows what will occur, he may be purposely withholding this information from others. Now, granted, God sometimes tells people precisely what will occur (as stated above). But in other cases God may think it best that they do not know. Take the situation with Moses, for example. God might have said to Moses, "When you tell the people that I have sent you, and when you perform one miracle, at that point they *will believe*" (in a way comparable to Jesus telling Peter that before the cock crows he *will deny* him three times). But, had God said this to Moses, Moses would not have had to trust God through the whole experience in the same way he did, not knowing how the people might respond. So, the "perhapses" and "maybes" may be for our sake; they do not necessarily indicate that God does not know.

Third, from our human standpoint, the conditionality is real. *If you obey me, I will bless you; if you disobey me, I will judge you.* From *our* standpoint it is absolutely true that perhaps we may obey or perhaps we may not, and depending on what we do, God will respond in an appropriate measure.

Questions-about-the-Future Texts

Some texts portray God as musing over the future, even asking questions that would appear to reflect his uncertainty about how things will develop. Numbers 14:11 records, "The LORD said to Moses, 'How long will this people spurn Me? And how long will they not believe in Me, despite all the signs which I have performed in their midst?'" And Hosea 8:5 says concerning God, "He has rejected your calf, O Samaria, saying, 'My anger burns against them!' How long will they be incapable of innocence?" Shall we adopt a straightforward interpretation of these texts and affirm that God honestly puzzles over why and how long his people will remain disobedient?

Commenting on these passages, Boyd denies that the questions of these texts are parallel to the question God asks in Genesis 3:8-9. You will recall that there, God asked the man, "Where are you?" Actually, though Boyd does not mention it, God's questions continue through 3:13. In these verses, God also asks the man, "Who told you that you were naked? Have you eaten from the tree of which I commanded you not to eat?" (3:11); and he inquires of the woman, "What is this you have done?" (3:13). As seen above, a straightforward reading of "Where are you?" (3:9) would deny God's omnipresence primarily while also questioning God's exhaustive knowledge of the present, whereas a straightforward understanding of the other three questions (not mentioned by Boyd) would deny God's exhaustive past and present knowledge. Boyd argues as follows:

> Some suggest that in these verses [Num. 14:11 and Hos. 8:5] the Lord was asking rhetorical questions, just as he had done when he asked Adam and Eve where they were (Gen. 3:8-9). This is a possible interpretation, but not a necessary one. Unlike God's question about location in Genesis, *there is nothing in these texts or in the whole of Scripture that requires these questions to be rhetorical.* Moreover, the fact that the Lord continued for cen-

turies, with much frustration, to try to get the Israelites not to
"despise" him and to be "innocent" suggests that the wonder
expressed in these questions was genuine. The duration of the
Israelites' stubbornness was truly an open issue.[17]

A few responses are needed. First, to say that the Numbers and
Hosea questions are *unlike* the Genesis question about location means
that Boyd is employing, albeit implicitly, a mechanism for distinguish-
ing when and when not to take texts at their face value. Evidently the
"Where are you?" question qualifies to be interpreted non-literally and
rhetorically because there is something "in these texts or in the whole
of Scripture" that "requires" this to be the case. Therefore Boyd's
repeated complaint that classical theists fail to take the straightforward
meaning of the text seriously is a shallow, empty criticism. Boyd does
the same thing himself here, and in this particular case he surely is right
to do so.

Second, omitting the other questions in Genesis 3:8-13 makes it
easier to maintain the supposed contrast between the question of 3:8-
9 and the questions of Numbers and Hosea. But actually, the other
three Genesis questions all have to do with God's knowledge of the past
and present. Might not someone argue from this Genesis text and many
others that a straightforward reading of these texts shows that God has
limited knowledge of the past and present? It begins to look a bit like
special pleading when *only those texts* which have to do with God's
limited knowledge of the *future* are considered literally true, but *all of*
the rest of those which speak of his limited knowledge of the *past and*
present are ignored or taken to be obviously non-straightforward in
their meanings. But, to account for a passage such as Genesis 3:10-13
in a way that upholds God's comprehensive knowledge of the past and
present, the open theist must acknowledge the principle of appealing
to other, broader scriptural teachings about God's exhaustive knowledge of the past and present, on the basis of which we can rightly set
aside the straightforward and literal meaning of these texts as their
intended meaning.

Third, regarding the questions recorded in Numbers and Hosea,

---

[17] Boyd, *God of the Possible*, 59 (emphasis added).

how can Boyd say so dogmatically that "there is nothing in these texts or in the whole of Scripture that requires these questions to be rhetorical"? This assertion proves nothing but only begs the question. The very question at hand is just this: whether the whole of biblical teaching justifies taking texts such as these in Numbers and Hosea in some way other than a straightforward manner. Certainly Boyd has done just this with Genesis 3:8-9. Is not this debate with him (and with other open theists) precisely whether the *same principle* he uses to avoid a straightforward reading of Genesis 3:9 ("Where are you?") should also be employed in interpreting Numbers 14:11 ("How long will this people despise me?")?

Fourth, Boyd comments on how long God must endure the disobedience of his people and states his view that "the duration of the Israelites' stubbornness was truly an open issue." I wonder how this is the case with a God who is capable of so working in his people's hearts that he causes them to obey him? Both Jeremiah 31:31-34 and Ezekiel 36:26-36 stress God's new covenant promise that in the time that God chooses, he will so transform his people that they will fully and completely walk in his statutes and obey his ordinances. They will fully know the Lord! The new covenant, says Jeremiah, will not be like the old covenant that Israel violated. In contrast, this covenant will be unbreakable! Admittedly, such immeasurable power and lavish grace to accomplish unconditional and comprehensive transformation of God's people is a concept sadly foreign to open theists, but it is what these two new covenant texts teach. The God of the Bible, the God who establishes his new and unbreakable covenant with his people, is simply not frustrated (in the sense with which Boyd speaks) with how long they disobey. Boyd's claim that "the Israelites' stubbornness was truly an open issue" is wrong because both Jeremiah and Ezekiel disagree.

Conclusion

As often noted, the question arises of whether all these so-called "openness" texts should be interpreted at face value, that is, by their straightforward and literal meanings. While this is always the interpretive starting point, as it were, one can often be led astray if one insists that the straightforward meaning is in fact the intended and correct meaning. In principle, open theists agree with this line of reasoning.

For example, openness proponents agree that references to God's eyes, arms, hands, etc., should not be taken in a straightforward manner.[18] Because Scripture gives us strong reason for thinking that God is an infinite spiritual and omnipresent being, nearly all have believed that there is ample justification to deny the straightforward meaning of these bodily ascriptions to deity. So the real issue here is not whether these "openness" texts *when interpreted in a straightforward manner* yield the conclusion that God lacks exhaustive knowledge of the future. Many of these texts do yield such a conclusion when interpreted in that way! And most classical theists would agree. The real issue is whether the intended and correct understanding of these passages is uncovered when they are taken simply at face value. Stated differently, the issue is whether the authorially intended meaning is the straightforward meaning. And, as shown above, open theists must acknowledge this hermeneutical question as legitimate, because openness advocates affirm that there are *other* categories of texts (e.g., texts concerning God's bodily parts, God's limited knowledge of the past and present, and God's spatial locatedness) where, if a straightforward understanding were taken, we would clearly arrive at wrong conclusions.

Along the same lines, I suspect that openness advocates would yield to their classical theist colleagues in admitting that a straightforward reading of Genesis 18:21 would indicate that God lacks exhaustive *past* knowledge, *present* knowledge, and *omnipresence* (if they do not agree with us here, I surely would like to know why).[19] But of course, on openness criteria alone, such a straightforward interpretation would be unacceptable. We know, the open theist would say, that God knows

---

[18] Sanders, *God Who Risks*, 20, writes that "just about everyone takes the biblical references to the 'eyes,' 'arms,' and 'mouth' (anthropomorphisms proper) of God as metaphors for divine actions, not assertions that God has literal body parts."

[19] I see evidence of this in Greg Boyd's dismissal of any lack of God's present knowledge that might be reflected in the question of Genesis 3:8-9. Boyd (*God of the Possible*, 59) simply asserts without argument that this question is rhetorical, whereas other questions from God that Boyd points to in other texts should be taken straightforwardly. As argued earlier, the only difference between the two sets of questions is that the "literal" questions reflect God's ignorance of the future (acceptable in open theism), whereas the questions in Genesis 3:8-13 reflect God's ignorance about the present and past (unacceptable in open theism).

everything past and present and that he is omnipresent. So, in this case, a straightforward reading must not reflect the correct and intended meaning of the passage. But of course, the critical question is precisely this: Why here, but not with Genesis 22:12? Why this text, but not some other so-called "openness" texts? As examination is given now to the openness handling of the divine repentance texts, this hermeneutical question will be addressed further.

OPEN THEISM'S "STRAIGHTFORWARD" READING OF DIVINE REPENTANCE TEXTS

In a similar fashion, openness proponents take the divine repentance texts in a straightforward manner. So when we read, for example, "So the LORD changed His mind about the harm which He said He would do to His people" (Ex. 32:14), openness proponents believe we should understand this to indicate that God was confronted with a previously unknown situation that resulted in his reassessing his plans and changing his mind about what he intended to do. Granted, the simplest and most straightforward reading of this passage, and others like it, would lead one to this interpretation. But as we have seen above, the simplest and most straightforward reading may not be the correct reading. How can we know?

Part of the answer, I have argued elsewhere,[20] is to inquire as to whether it is possible that such divine repentance statements may best be understood as anthropomorphic. Consider this working definition: "A given ascription to God may rightly be understood as anthropomorphic when Scripture clearly presents God as transcending the very human or finite features it elsewhere attributes to him."[21] In relation to the question of the divine repentance, two texts in particular describe God as *not* capable of repenting, and if these biblical statements represent a broad and comprehensive teaching about God's nature, then we have here a case in which Scripture presents God as transcending (i.e., in some sense he does *not* repent because he, as God, transcends human repentance) the very human or finite feature it elsewhere

---

[20] Ware, "Immutability of God," 441-444.
[21] Ibid., 442.

attributes to him (i.e., in some sense he *does* repent).[22] Consider briefly these texts.[23]

Numbers 23:19, expressed by Balaam in his second oracle, reads:

> God is not a man, that He should lie, nor a son of man, that He should repent; has He said, and will He not do it? Or has He spoken, and will He not make it good?

There is no question but that the purpose of this statement is to reinforce the certainty with which God pledges to accomplish the blessing (not cursing!) on Israel stated in Balaam's first oracle. God's will is set; he will not be deterred from performing his will as already declared. But it simply will not do to turn this declaration *merely* into a statement concerning God's pledge in this particular, concrete, historical situation *alone*. Consider two reasons.

First, if, as open theists understand this text, it is taken as *generally* true that God *can repent*, but that in this *particular* case he chooses not to, then does it not follow from this text that, while it is *generally* true that God *can lie*, in this *particular* case he chooses not to? That is, the parallelism of lying and repenting indicates that just as God cannot lie, he cannot repent. The question becomes, then, can God *ever* lie? Second Timothy 2:13, Titus 1:2, and Hebrews 6:18 state explicitly not only that God *does not* lie; they declare that he *cannot* lie. It appears, then, that the parallel relation of God's repentance with lying would lead one to conclude that this passage is teaching more than simply that in this particular historical situation God chooses not to lie or repent. Rather, just as God *can never* lie, so He *can never* repent.

Second, notice the contrast made between God and man. God is not like a man who, presumably, both lies and repents. Does not the force

---

[22] In responding to my definition of anthropomorphism, along with similar discussion on the divine repentance from John Calvin and Paul Helm, John Sanders (*God Who Risks*, 68) asks, "On what basis do these thinkers [Calvin, Helm, Ware] claim that these biblical texts do not portray God as he truly is but only God as he appears to us? How can they confidently select one biblical text as an 'exact' description of God and consign others to the dustbin of anthropomorphism?" In what follows, I propose to demonstrate why Numbers 23:19 and 1 Samuel 15:29 should, in fact, be understood as "exact" descriptions of God. I hope to do so, however, while sustaining the real and substantive meanings of the divine repentance texts and so avoid the charge of consigning them to the "dustbin of anthropomorphism."

[23] A third text, Hosea 11:8-9, also supports the understanding I am developing here. Because its interpretation is disputed, I will treat it after these two, attempting to demonstrate that it also fits the same pattern.

of this claim evaporate the instant one reads it to say, *in this particular situation* God is not like a man and so does not repent? Do men (i.e., human beings) *always* repent of what they say they will do? If so, the contrast can be maintained. But if human beings *sometimes* carry out what they say and *sometimes* repent and do otherwise, and if God, likewise *sometimes* carries out what he says and *sometimes* repents and does otherwise, then how is God different from humans? The only way the contrast works is if God, unlike men, *never* repents. It is generally true, not merely situationally true, that God does not repent.

First Samuel 15:29 makes its claim for God's non-repentance, strikingly, in a context in which it is twice affirmed (1 Sam. 15:11 and 35) that God does repent. Samuel says, "the Glory of Israel will not lie or change His mind; for He is not a man that He should change His mind" (1 Sam. 15:29). One may immediately notice that both arguments developed above to support the general truth of God's non-repentance from Numbers 23:19 apply here as well. That is, the parallelism with lying (also in 1 Sam. 15:29) would suggest that, just as God never lies, he likewise never repents. The two need to be treated alike. To say that God sometimes repents (e.g., 1 Sam. 15:11, 35) and sometimes doesn't (1 Sam. 15:29) would be to argue that he sometimes lies and, in the same sense as with "repent," sometimes doesn't. But the truth is that God never lies, and so this text requires also that he never repents. In addition, the contrast with men who change their minds (also in 1 Sam. 15:29) would suggest that, since men sometimes do what they say and sometimes change their minds, God, *unlike men,* never changes his mind. Again, God cannot be different from men if it turns out that his behavior is *just like* theirs. So, unlike men, God never changes his mind. Amazingly, Numbers 23:19 and 1 Samuel 15:29 argue in parallel fashion, both excluding from God the possibility of any true change of mind.

It has been suggested that Hosea 11:8-9 actually teaches something quite to the contrary of what I have been arguing here. These verses, it is argued, should be taken to say that God *changes his mind* because he is *not* like a man. The text of Hosea 11:8-9 reads:

> How can I give you up, O Ephraim?
> How can I surrender you, O Israel?
> How can I make you like Admah?

How can I treat you like Zeboiim?
My heart is turned over within Me,
All My compassions are kindled.
I will not execute My fierce anger;
I will not destroy Ephraim again.
For I am God and not man, the Holy One in your midst,
And I will not come in wrath.

In responding to an earlier discussion I offered of the divine non-repentance texts,[24] and commenting on this text, Sanders writes,

> ... Ware's own criterion [definition of anthropomorphism given above] becomes problematic when put into use because Hosea 11:8-9 says God repents because he is *not human*. According to Ware's own criterion, when the Bible predicates something of God and this predication is accompanied by the "transcendent" ground that God "is not human," then we have the literal truth about God. Following Ware we have a real problem on our hands because the Bible teaches both (1) that God cannot change his mind because he is not human and (2) that God literally does change his mind because he is not human.[25]

Unfortunately for Sanders's criticism, Hosea 11:8-9 does *not* teach that God has changed his mind, and certainly it does not teach that *unlike* humans God *does* change his mind! Rather, it affirms that God, unlike humans, is absolutely faithful to his covenant promises. As God says through the prophet, "I am God and not man, the Holy One in your midst, and I will not come in wrath" (Hos. 11:9b). The point is that, unlike humans, God will faithfully do what he previously pledged to Israel. He will not ultimately destroy them ("come in wrath"); he will be merciful (see Malachi 3:6 for a similar pledge based on God's immutable promise). So, contrary to Sanders's interpretation, Hosea 11:8-9 does not teach that "God repents because he is not human," but rather that God will not judge them utterly because, unlike

---

[24] Ware, "Immutability of God," 441-444.
[25] Sanders, *God Who Risks*, 68-69.

humans, he always keeps his promises. Concerning this text, Thomas McComiskey writes that:

> [t]he emphasis is on the fact that God will not destroy his people a second time. Yahweh's refusal to execute his wrath must mean that he will not execute it to its fullest intensity. . . . Such an action [full or final judgment] would vitiate the ancient promise given to Abraham (Gen. 12:1-7; see Lev. 26:44). . . . The reason that Yahweh will not give up his people is that he is God, not man. This contrast between the divine and human is not one of power, but of moral purity. This verse describes Yahweh as the Holy One; it is thus similar to Numbers 23:19 which states that "God is not like man in that God does not lie."[26]

Far from conflicting with 1 Samuel 15:29 and Numbers 23:19, this reassuring promise in Hosea 11:8-9 agrees fully with those passages. All three actually contribute a varied yet uniform testimony to the fact that the Creator God, who is not a man, is, in himself and his own actions, above the moral lapses and changeability of character and purpose that characterize the world of humanity. Scripture, then, does in fact present God as transcending the human and finite qualities of changeability that it elsewhere attributes to him. We have a legitimate basis for interpreting the divine repentance texts as fundamentally anthropomorphic, and we would be wrong not to do so, just as we would be wrong to think of God as having eyes and hands.

But what do the divine repentance statements of Scripture mean? If they are anthropomorphic, they nonetheless convey a meaning, albeit not the meaning that God literally changes his mind. I believe it is best to see all of these texts as expressing two related notions, and in many cases, a third idea is also present.

First, when God is said to repent, it indicates 1) his awareness that the human situation has altered and 2) his desire to act in a way fitting to this changed situation. In Exodus 32:14, God was aware of and took into account the urgent prayer of Moses. In 1 Samuel 15:11 and 35, God was aware of and took into account the failure of Saul. In no cases of

---

[26] Thomas Edward McComiskey, "Hosea" in T. E. McComiskey, ed., *The Minor Prophets: An Exegetical and Expository Commentary* (Grand Rapids, Mich.: Baker, 1992), 191-192.

the divine repentance is it necessary to go further than this and say that God *learned* something new *by* this changed situation. Rather, these expressions of repentance may indicate more narrowly that God was aware of what had changed and chose to act in accordance with this new situation. His awareness and choice to act accordingly *may have been from eternity,* yet he interacted in the temporal and existential flow of developing and changing human situations.

Although all human analogies ultimately fail, this may be thought of as being like the situation in which an engaged couple anticipates and plans for the moment when they are officially joined in matrimony. Although both have "known" (i.e., both have had strong, even compelling, beliefs regarding their upcoming marriage to each other) for months where, when, and whom they would marry, and likewise both have "known" the changed situation that will result the moment they are declared husband and wife, yet in the actual moment of their marriage union, their thoughts toward each other "change." Though their union as husband and wife was anticipated fully and "known in advance," as it were, the changed situation (i.e., now being actually married to each other) results in "changed" thoughts and attitudes toward each other. The point of the analogy, simply, is to indicate that although God can know and anticipate some future changed situation (e.g., Moses' prayer, Saul's failure) and can know and plan how he would correspondingly respond (e.g., forestall judgment, remove Saul as king), in the moment these changes take place, he may be said to "change" in respect to that situation as he relates to it differently than he previously indicated he would.

Second, when God is said to repent, it indicates his real experience, in historically unfolding relationships with people, of changed dispositions or emotions in relation to some changed human situation.[27] Just because God knows in advance that some event will occur, this does not preclude God from experiencing appropriate emotions and expressing appropriate reactions when it actually happens. So, although God may have known that the world would become morally corrupt (Gen. 6:5-6), that Nineveh would repent (Jonah 3:5-10), that Moses would plead for

---

[27] See Ware, "Immutability of God," 444-446, for discussion of real changeable emotions of God which, rightly understood, do not threaten at all the immutability of God's nature or ethical commitments.

his people (Ex. 32:11-14), and that Saul would fail as king (1 Sam. 13:8-14; 15:1-9), nonetheless God may *experience internally* and *express outwardly* appropriate moral responses to these changed situations *when they occur in history.* That is, he may literally change in emotional disposition and become angry over increasing moral evil and flagrant disobedience, or he may show mercy in relation to repentance or urgent prayer. And, this may occur in historical interaction with his human creatures even though he knows, from eternity past, precisely what would occur and what his response would be.

Again, analogies fail. Nevertheless, this situation is like the experience of a mother who takes her eight-year-old daughter to the dentist's office for her first filling. The mother, with her vast experience of such procedures, may "know" exactly what will happen and anticipate each step of the process. Yet, as she sits beside her daughter, who is reclining fearfully and tearfully in the dentist's chair, and as she observes the dentist intensely at work, she may feel distress, anguish, even pain as she stares into the frightened and confused eyes of her precious little girl. The fact that she "knew" previously everything that would occur did not preclude her from entering into the existential situation, feeling genuine and heartfelt pity. So too with God. While he can know everything about some future situation, he also may enter fully into the existential unfolding of that situation and respond appropriately, changing in emotion and disposition in a way fitting the changed situation itself.[28]

Third, some texts also display a very important interpersonal dynamic that utilizes the concept of the divine repentance.[29] There are many cases where one wonders why God even *told* his prophet or the people what he intended to do. For example, with Nineveh, in light of its wickedness, why did God not simply destroy the city without giving Nineveh a forty-day period of suspended judgment, and without sending Jonah to *tell* them that they had these forty days? Or in Exodus 32, when God observed the people of Israel worshiping the golden calf, why did God not simply destroy the people instead of first *telling* Moses concerning both their great sin and his intent to vent his anger against them? Since God surely could

---

[28] See also the discussion in chapter 5 on Deuteronomy 31:16-21, where we see that God knows precisely the sins that Israel will commit in the future and yet he also says that, when they sin in just the ways he has predicted they will sin, he will be extremely angry at them for what they do.

[29] I am indebted to Thomas Schreiner for sharing this insight with me.

have acted directly and unilaterally, he purposely chose to involve others in the situation, thus purposely postponing the action he otherwise would have taken. What this allows for, perhaps even invites, is the response of the people who become informed of God's stated intentions. So, when the people of Nineveh hear, they repent. When Moses hears, he earnestly prays. It appears, then, that God's purpose is to involve others, planning that he will "change" *when they have acted in the ways he anticipated they would and gave opportunity for them to do.*

The change, then, is a real change in the narrow sense but not in the broad sense. That is, in the narrow sense, God really does do something different than he first said. Nineveh is shown mercy when they repent, which is a change from God's stated intention to destroy them. God postponed the destruction he stated he would bring on Israel when Moses interceded earnestly for them. In both cases (and in other similar cases), the specifically stated intention of God changed, without question. But, the fact that God *told them* of his stated intention suggests that he was inviting them to respond. As they responded, God carried out the broader purposes he had planned from the outset. The *broader* purposes include *God telling others in order to elicit their response.* Since the response of the people is part of what God intends, it appears that his "changed" course of action is the one he intended all along.

Perhaps the situation is a bit like a father who decides to surprise his teenage son with an outing to see his favorite baseball team play an early-evening game. His son has been hard at work since early morning preparing their garden for planting and getting their lawn in shape, and by this point in the day, he is obviously very tired and ready for some rest. As the father approaches his weary son, he grabs a few lawn tools from the garage and says with enthusiasm, "I thought I would join you back here so we could get in three or four more hours of good work!" Upon hearing this, the son responds by telling his dad that, although he's pretty worn out and hungry from laboring so hard, he'd be happy to keep on working for a few more hours, if this is what his father wants. In response, the father looks back at his son, and with a smile says, "How about instead you and I head for the baseball stadium? We'll catch the evening game and get some hot dogs and peanuts as soon as we get to the park!" The much relieved and deeply grateful son thanks his dad and the two of them get ready to head to the game. The father clearly has "changed" what he had just stated that he and his son would do. Instead of staying home and working together in the yard, they go to the game. Yet inwardly the father's intention from the outset was to take his hard-working son to the game. The manner in which he accomplished this goal, however, involved his son's willing response to continue working as part of the background for announcing his real intention of taking his son to the game. So, in the *narrow* sense, the father changed course from his stated intention. But in the *broad* sense, he fulfilled exactly what he had secretly intended all along. But notice: The father only fulfilled this broad intention in the way that he chose *by involving his son and through the response of his son.*

While the above story is only an analogy, nonetheless it appears that the book of Jonah gives us a clue that something akin to the situation described above is occurring here. In Jonah 4:2 we learn that the reason Jonah did not want to obey God's call and go to Nineveh in the first place is because he feared that God would be merciful. How odd, one might think, when the message God gave Jonah was, "Yet forty days and Nineveh will be overthrown" (Jonah 3:4). Given that Jonah wanted calamity to come on the city, one would have thought that he would be delighted to bring this message of impending doom to the despised Ninevites. But, he wasn't. And why is this? Evidently Jonah suspected from the outset that God had a *secret* intention that was different from his *stated* intention. That God would send Jonah to tell them of this coming destruction, and that God would give them forty days' warning—all of this together indicated to Jonah that God's *real* intention was to save the city. Only this will explain Jonah's reluctance to go, given that the message he proclaimed to them was one, formally, with which he would have been quite happy. On this reading, God surely did change in the narrow sense, in that God's *explicitly stated intention* ("forty days and Nineveh will be overthrown") changed as God had mercy on the repentant Ninevites. But, given Jonah's reluctance to go in the first place, it appears we are to understand that God did not change at all in the broad sense. God's *secret intention* was to show mercy to Nineveh (which Jonah suspected), and God accomplished this intention exactly as he had purposed, but he accomplished it *through* Jonah's warning of the Ninevites and the repentance that the warning elicited.

It may be helpful to consider one other repentance text. A favorite example among open theists of God's supposed literal change of mind is the lengthening of Hezekiah's life, recorded in 2 Kings 20.[30] We read that Hezekiah became mortally ill, and the Lord said to him, "Set your house in order, for you shall die and not live" (2 Kings 20:1). At this news, and with tears and great earnestness, Hezekiah fervently prayed, and the Lord responded, saying, "I have heard your prayer, I have seen your tears; behold, I will heal you. . . . I will add fifteen years to your life" (2 Kings 20:5-6). Consider a few factors in regard to this remarkable account.

First, here is another example in which God simply could have acted directly and in accordance with his *stated intention* ("You shall die and not live") without a word to Hezekiah. By simply not healing Hezekiah, God would thereby bring him to a speedy death. He did not have to *tell* Hezekiah that this would occur, but he did! So, one must wonder why God purposely spoke through Isaiah to let Hezekiah know his stated intention. Is it not entirely conceivable that God's purpose behind these words to Hezekiah was in fact to elicit from him such earnest, heartfelt dependence on God in prayer? After all, would it not be natural and expected for anyone, upon hearing that he was about to die, to plead with God to spare his life? And might God not have known and expected that Hezekiah would respond in just this way? Would not this give God an opportunity to demonstrate to Hezekiah his love for him by granting his earnest request? But cannot all of this be true while conceiving that God *used his stated intention* through Isaiah ("you shall die and not live") in order to accomplish his *real intention* ("I will heal you [and] add fifteen years to your life") by eliciting Hezekiah's prayer and then granting him this longed-for extended life?

Second, God granted to Hezekiah *fifteen years* of extended life—not two, not twenty, and certainly not "we'll both see how long you live," but *fifteen years exactly*. Does it not seem a bit odd that this favorite text of open theists, which purportedly demonstrates that God does not know the future and so changes his mind when Hezekiah prays, also shows that God *knows precisely and exactly how much longer Hezekiah will live?* On openness grounds, how could God know this? Over a fifteen-year time span, the contingencies are staggering! The number of

---

[30] Boyd (*God of the Possible*, 7-8) begins the preface of his book referring to this particular text and noting that this text was among the first biblical passages that led him to begin challenging the classical commitment to exhaustive divine foreknowledge.

future freewill choices, made by Hezekiah and by innumerable others, that relate directly to Hezekiah's life and well-being, none of which God knows (in the openness view), *is enormous.* As we shall see in a discussion on divine guidance later in the book, open theists are quite honest and forthright about *not* recommending that we ask God's guidance for the distant future.[31] Because, in the openness view, there are so many variables, so much of which God is absolutely ignorant, so few things God can know for sure of human lives and situations the further one projects into the future, it is inconceivable that God could know and predict *exactly* this fifteen-year extension of life to Hezekiah—inconceivable, that is, so long as God keeps the libertarian freedom of Hezekiah and innumerable others with whom he relates intact over the span of these years. Yet, God says, "I will add fifteen years to your life, and I will deliver you and this city from the hand of the king of Assyria; and I will defend this city for My own sake and for My servant David's sake" (2 Kings 20:6). With absolute confidence and assurance, God promises and predicts. Does not this expression of God's certain knowledge of the future cause one to question whether the openness interpretation of the added fifteen years is correct? Surely the most compelling overall understanding of this story is to see God's earlier statement that Hezekiah would die as a tool he uses to bring great joy to Hezekiah, as God now does what he intended all along. Fifteen years exactly, no fewer, no more. God has *not* literally changed his mind, for he knows the future and carries out his purposes.

Third, it appears that even if we grant an openness perspective, it is highly doubtful that God's granting Hezekiah fifteen additional years actually constituted a literal change of mind for God. Recall the theme in open theism that God knows us better than we know ourselves, that he knows every detail of our inner lives, and that he can predict with amazing accuracy the kinds of ways we will act and react. Certainly, knowing Hezekiah as God did (i.e., perfectly), and knowing, as mentioned above, how almost *anyone* would greet the news of his or her impending death, even on openness grounds it is hard to see how Hezekiah's response could have taken God by surprise. And if the

---

[31] E.g., David Basinger, "Practical Implications," in Clark Pinnock, Richard Rice, John Sanders, William Hasker, and David Basinger, *The Openness of God: A Biblical Challenge to the Traditional Understanding of God* (Downers Grove, Ill.: InterVarsity, 1994), 163.

response didn't taken him by surprise, then it is also hard to see how God really changed his mind when he added the fifteen years to Hezekiah's life. Would not God have fully anticipated Hezekiah's agonizing plea? And if so, would not God have already planned and known what he would do next? It is highly doubtful, then, even on openness grounds, that this constituted a literal change of mind on God's part.

It seems clear that the divine repentance, in such cases, functions as part of a tool for eliciting a dynamic relationship with people, a means of drawing out responses which God uses, then, to accomplish his ultimate purposes. These texts are wrongly used to indicate that God learned something new. Since we have strong biblical basis by which to affirm of God that he cannot change his mind ("the LORD is not a man who should change his mind . . ."), and since the purposes of these repentance texts can be fully explained apart from attributing to God what Scripture elsewhere denies of him (literal change of mind), we have compelling reason to deny that these texts teach that God literally changes his mind.

But if all this is true, can what these passages describe about God really be called "repentance"? Yes, it can be true repentance, of a sort, while it differs altogether from ways in which humans may often repent (remember, God is not a man that he should repent). Commenting on repentance texts such as 1 Samuel 15:11, John Piper offers this helpful explanation:

> So my alternative way of thinking about these texts is: God foreknows the grievous and sorrowful effects of some of his own choices—for example, to create Adam and Eve, and to make Saul king. These effects are genuinely grievous to God as he sees them in themselves. Yet he does not regard his choices as mistakes that he would do differently if only he foreknew what was coming. Rather, he wills to do some things which he then genuinely grieves over in part when the grievous effect comes to pass.
>
> Now if someone should say, This does not sound like what we ordinarily mean by "regret" or "repentance," I would respond that this is exactly what Samuel said: God "will not lie or repent; for he is not a man, that he should repent" (1 Sam. 15:29). In other words, Samuel means something like this: when

I say "[God] repented that he made Saul king" (or when Moses said that God repented that he created Adam and Eve), I do not mean that God experiences repentance precisely the way ordinary humans do. He is not a man to experience "repentance" this way. He experiences it his way—the way one experiences "repentance" when one is all-wise and foreknows the entire future perfectly. The experience is real, but it is not like finite man experiences it.[32]

CONCLUSION

We have endeavored to demonstrate that neither the divine growth-in-knowledge texts nor the repentance texts imply that God has learned something he did not previously know. All of the passages put forth by open theists as support for God's limited knowledge, particularly of future contingencies and future free actions, can be explained in entirely reasonable and more compelling ways which show that their "straight-forward" meanings are not the intended and correct meanings of those passages. In addition, we have seen that, in several cases, if the straight-forward hermeneutic of open theism were to be applied to other growth-in-knowledge texts, we would be required to deny God's exhaustive knowledge both of the past and of the present, as well as his omnipresence. Clearly, the openness approach is deeply troubled, and we have serious reason to question it.

Next, however, we must turn to address a question repeatedly raised above, that is, whether Scripture teaches, with sufficient clarity and fullness, that God in fact has exhaustive knowledge of the future. If the open view interpretations are problematic in their own rights, as we have endeavored here to demonstrate, and if it can be shown that in fact there is more than ample warrant to affirm God's exhaustive knowledge of the future, it will be clear that the doctrinal foundation of the openness position is indeed unstable.

---

[32] John Piper, "Why the Glory of God Is at Stake in the 'Foreknowledge' Debate," *Modern Reformation* 8, no. 5 (September/October 1999), 43.

5

Scriptural Affirmation of Exhaustive Divine Foreknowledge

Having examined the range of biblical texts and arguments advanced by open theists to support their denial of exhaustive divine foreknowledge, we turn now to the positive case that can be made for this cardinal, orthodox doctrine. One thing in this debate is clear: Open theism collapses as a comprehensive model of divine providence if it can be demonstrated that God does in fact know all of the future, including all future contingencies and all future free choices and actions of his moral creatures. If it can be established that the openness denial of God's comprehensive foreknowledge is dubious while the case for affirming exhaustive divine foreknowledge is strong, then it renders the open view position untenable. Chapter 4 offered reason to challenge and reject the openness claim that the Bible is best interpreted as supporting God's limited knowledge of the future due to his supposed growth in knowledge and genuine change of mind. In this chapter we turn our attention to scriptural evidence for exhaustive divine knowledge of the future. Is the Bible best understood as affirming that God's omniscience encompasses comprehensive knowledge of the past, present, *and future?*

Because open theists affirm God's exhaustive knowledge of the past and present, and because they affirm God's omnipresence (despite the hermeneutical difficulties raised earlier), I will focus exclusively here on the issue of whether the Bible teaches, with sufficient clarity and fullness, that God has exhaustive knowledge of the future, i.e., that God knows everything—including but not limited to every free choice and action of volitional creatures—that will occur temporally future to any given moment in time. Much has been written to support the claim that Scripture clearly teaches that God knows all that will occur in the future.[1] Furthermore, the scriptural evidence for this position, simply put, is overwhelming.[2] In this chapter we will consider a limited yet significant portion of the biblical evidence.

SELECT BIBLICAL EVIDENCE FOR EXHAUSTIVE DIVINE FOREKNOWLEDGE

In what follows, I have tried to give a sampling of the kinds of biblical data which support God's exhaustive foreknowledge. Some passages are more directly declarative, and others illustrate God's knowledge of the future in specific settings. In examining this evidence we must work hard neither to overstate nor to understate what conclusion the evidence might yield. Open theists have charged classical theists with overstating the force of the evidence for exhaustive divine foreknowledge, and no doubt there is at times validity to this criticism. But just as wrong is to understate the force of the evidence, by this failing to take seriously the full meaning and implication of certain scriptural teachings.

On this score, we will have to keep in mind the particular claim made regularly by open theists that biblical texts that speak of God's knowledge and/or determination of some future reality are always limited to specific situations and as such do not constitute general teachings that would support *comprehensive* divine foreknowledge. Boyd, for example,

---

[1] Support for comprehensive divine foreknowledge (comprising part of God's omniscience) comes equally strongly from Arminian and Calvinist writers. See, e.g., S. M. Baugh, "The Meaning of Foreknowledge," in Thomas R. Schreiner and Bruce A. Ware, eds., *Still Sovereign* (Grand Rapids, Mich.: Baker, 1999), 183-200; Stephen Charnock, *The Existence and Attributes of God* (1797; repr. Minneapolis: Klock and Klock, 1977), 196-220; William Lane Craig, *The Only Wise God: The Compatibility of Divine Foreknowledge and Human Freedom* (Grand Rapids, Mich.: Baker, 1984), 25-37; John Miley, *Systematic Theology*, 2 vols. (New York: Hunt and Eaton, 1892), I, 180-193; A. W. Pink, *The Attributes of God* (Grand Rapids, Mich.: Baker, 1975), 22-27; W. G. T. Shedd, *Dogmatic Theology*, 2nd ed. (1888; repr. Nashville: Thomas Nelson, 1980), I, 342-359; and H. Orton Wiley, *Christian Theology* (Kansas City, Mo.: Beacon Hill, 1952), I, 354-360.

[2] Steve Roy, a doctoral student and faculty member at Trinity Evangelical Divinity School, has conducted a comprehensive biblical survey of passages relating to divine foreknowledge. As categorized, the summary of results is as follows: 164 texts explicitly teach/affirm God's foreknowledge; 271 texts explicitly teach/affirm other aspects of God's omniscience (e.g., knowledge of past or present or possible states of affairs); 128 texts offer predictions of what God will do through human beings; 1,893 texts state predictively that God will do something or other in or through human beings; 1,474 texts state predictively what human beings will do, apart from God directly acting in or through them; 622 texts state predictively what unbelievers will do or have happen to them; 143 texts affirm God's sovereign control of human choices; 105 texts of apparent counter-evidence.

has argued that, while it is true that Scripture does speak of God's determination and foreknowledge, it never suggests that God determines *all* things or knows *everything* future. Boyd states that "the future is to some degree *settled* and known by God as such, and to some degree *open* and known by God as such. To some extent, God knows the future as *definitely* this way and *definitely* not that way. To some extent, however, he knows it as *possibly* this way and *possibly* not that way."[3]

We shall endeavor to let the evidence speak for itself and work to understand the authorially intended meanings of these passages. Where some speak of God's foreknowledge and/or determination explicitly in a restricted sense, we should accept this. But should we find in these very texts implicitly and in other passages explicitly that Scripture teaches God's comprehensive knowledge and oversight of all future contingencies and future free actions, we likewise should accept this. And of course, these two sets of truths are not in principle mutually exclusive. Some texts indeed may speak in explicit and restricted ways of God's knowledge and control of some specific and discrete future item(s). If so, this does not cancel out God's comprehensive foreknowledge that might be *implied* by these very texts and also *explicitly supported elsewhere.* Furthermore, one must consider with which overall model of divine providence these particularist-foreknowledge texts best fit. So, even if Scripture speaks in places of selective divine foreknowledge and control, unless we find that Scripture does this exclusively and in a way that leaves exhaustive divine foreknowledge completely unsupported, we should be open to the possibility of the broader understanding of God's full mastery of all future actions and events.

In what follows, primary attention will be given to the astonishing portrayal of God's foreknowledge as taught repeatedly in Isaiah 40–48. While open theists refer to this portion of Scripture and give some attention to a few of the relevant passages and their implications,[4] there is a need to display in summary fashion the fullness of the case Isaiah makes for God's foreknowledge throughout these chapters. Following this, we will sketch some of the case that can be made from select passages else-

---

[3] Gregory A. Boyd, *God of the Possible: A Biblical Introduction to the Open View of God* (Grand Rapids, Mich.: Baker, 2000), 15.

[4] See, e.g., Boyd, *God of the Possible*, 24–25, where Boyd briefly discusses Isaiah 46:9-10 and 48:3-5; and John Sanders, *The God Who Risks: A Theology of Providence* (Downers Grove, Ill.: InterVarsity, 1998), 82 and 130, where Sanders deals briefly with Isaiah 45:7 and 46:9-11.

where to demonstrate what Scripture says about God's knowledge of the future, including knowledge of the future free actions of his creatures. As brief as this must be, consider the weight of these passages in support of exhaustive divine foreknowledge.

Isaiah Texts

The single richest and strongest portion of Scripture supporting God's knowledge of the future is Isaiah 40–48. There are no fewer than nine separate sections in these chapters[5] whose point is essentially the same: Yahweh, the God of Israel, is known as the true and living God in contrast to idols, whose pretense to deity is evident on the basis that *the true God knows and declares the future* (including future free human actions) before it occurs, *while those impostor rivals neither know nor declare any such thing*. Consider the force of these passages.

Isaiah 41:21-29 asserts:

> [21] "Present your case," the LORD says.
> "Bring forward your strong arguments,"
> The King of Jacob says.
> [22] Let them bring forth and declare to us
>   what is going to take place;
> As for the former events, declare what they were,
> That we may consider them, and know their outcome;
> Or announce to us what is coming.
> [23] Declare the things that are going to come afterward,
> That we may know that you are gods;
> Indeed, do good or evil,
>   that we may anxiously look about us and fear together.
> [24] Behold, you are of no account,
> And your work amounts to nothing;
> He who chooses you is an abomination.
> [25] "I have aroused one from the north, and he has come;
> From the rising of the sun he will call on My name;
> And he will come upon rulers as upon mortar,
> Even as the potter treads clay."

---

[5] Isaiah 41:21-29; 42:8-9; 43:8-13; 44:6-8; 44:24-28; 45:20-23; 46:8-11; 48:3-8; 48:14-16.

²⁶ Who has declared this from the beginning,
    that we might know?
Or from former times, that we may say, "He is right!"?
Surely there was no one who declared,
Surely there was no one who proclaimed,
Surely there was no one who heard your words.
²⁷ "Formerly I said to Zion, 'Behold, here they are.'
And to Jerusalem, 'I will give a messenger of good news.'
²⁸ But when I look, there is no one,
And there is no counselor among them
Who, if I ask, can give an answer.
²⁹ Behold, all of them are false;
Their works are worthless,
Their molten images are wind and emptiness."

In 41:22-23, God challenges the idols to prove their deity: "Let them bring forth and declare to us what is going to take place; as for the former events, declare what they were that we may consider them, and know their outcome; or announce to us what is coming. Declare the things that are going to come afterward, *that we may know that you are gods.*" Notice that the challenge is general in nature. "Declare to us what is going to take place," and "announce to us what is coming." This is highly significant in light of the openness claim that, at best, God knows about and can predict just selective future events. God's challenge to the idols is, rather, declare *what is going to take place*, announce *what is coming*.

And note that God's revelation of specific future items (of which Isaiah has numerous examples) does not cancel out but rather illustrates the general claim. It is ridiculous to think that God would reveal every specific future occurrence. So his general claim is, of necessity, supported by specific cases of predictive revelation. But we dare not miss the point that it is the general claim of announcing "what is coming" to which God here appeals. The test, then, is not whether some specific event on its own can be foretold, though God does foretell specific events, but whether the future can be declared and announced generally before it occurs.

Furthermore, the test is a test of true deity. Verse 23 gives the purpose as, "that we may know that you are gods." Right away in our examination of these Isaiah references we are faced with the claim that true deity can announce generally what is coming, can declare what is going to take place, and so *true deity must know the future generally and not merely in isolated, particular, and selective elements.*

Following the challenge, Yahweh specifies exactly how he has fulfilled the challenge himself. He declared from the beginning, from former times, things that would come, so that we might say, "He is right" (v. 26). Concerning this passage, Charnock comments:

> He [God] puts his Deity to stand or fall upon this account, and this should be the point which should decide the controversy whether he or the heathen idols were the true God. The dispute is managed by this medium: he that knows things to come is God; I know things to come, *ergo* I am God: the idols know not things to come, therefore they are not gods.[6]

Since God himself declares the criterion by which the question of his deity is to be evaluated and established, and since that criterion is the possession of a knowledge of the future that can be declared and its truthfulness verified (or falsified) by the unfolding of future events, how utterly impertinent and presumptuous to deny of God divine foreknowledge and so deny *the very basis by which God himself has declared that his claim to deity shall be vindicated and made known.*

What of those who follow these supposed gods who are unable to declare and announce the future? Concerning these impostor deities (who lack knowledge of the future) and those who follow them, 41:24 offers some very sobering words: "Behold, you [idols] are of no account, and your work amounts to nothing; he who chooses you is an abomination." In similarly strong language regarding these pretender deities, 41:29 states, "Behold, all of them are false; their works are worthless, their molten images are wind and emptiness." This language indicates that it is a very, very serious matter to deny of God that he knows and can declare broadly what the future holds. Since open theism does just this, it falls under the charge of folly, and it shows that the "God of openness" is not in this respect the God of the Bible.

---

[6] Charnock, *Existence and Attributes of God*, 203.

Isaiah 42:8-9 states:

[8] "I am the LORD, that is My name;
I will not give My glory to another,
Nor My praise to graven images.
[9] Behold, the former things have come to pass,
Now I declare new things;
Before they spring forth I proclaim them to you."

What is most striking about 42:8 is God's absolute refusal to give his glory to any pretender deity. Yahweh is the true God, and no other. He will receive all the glory, for he alone is truly God. Given this, it appears that the connection with 42:9 is this: Yahweh as the only true God is known as God and deserving of glory as God precisely *because* he has brought to pass what has happened and *because* he now declares new things that will come to be. God's claim to deity and his right to unsurpassed and exclusive glory are founded on his knowledge and control of what occurs in history, *including his ability to declare what will take place in the future.* Before these new things come to be, God proclaims them—thus demonstrating his worth and excellence and the basis for his exclusive claim to glory.

As with 41:22-23, here again we see the general way in which God asserts his ability to "declare new things." God's claim to deity and glory rests, then, not on some specific item of knowledge about the future, nor on some particular event over which he has control, although he does reveal and control specific future occurrences to make his general claim good. Rather, God speaks in broad and comprehensive ways of knowing and declaring what is to come. The attempt to restrict these claims to merely specific items of future reality, thus leaving the bulk of the future outside of God's knowledge and prior declaration, denies the full meaning of these texts and in so doing undermines God's claims to exclusive deity and glory. God as God and God as glorious has chosen to found his reputation on his knowledge and declaration of what comes to pass. Those who wish to honor God as the only true and glorious God must likewise affirm, not deny, his broad and comprehensive foreknowledge. Isaiah 43:8-13 asserts:

[8] Bring out the people who are blind,
  even though they have eyes,
And the deaf, even though they have ears.
[9] All the nations have gathered together
So that the peoples may be assembled.
Who among them can declare this
And proclaim to us the former things?
Let them present their witnesses that they may be justified,
Or let them hear and say, 'It is true.'
[10] "You are My witnesses," declares the LORD,
"And My servant whom I have chosen,
So that you may know and believe Me,
And understand that I am He.
Before Me there was no God formed,
And there will be none after Me.
[11] I, even I, am the LORD;
And there is no savior besides Me.
[12] It is I who have declared and saved and proclaimed,
And there was no strange god among you;
So you are My witnesses," declares the LORD,
"And I am God.
[13] Even from eternity I am He;
And there is none who can deliver out of My hand;
I act and who can reverse it?"

Again we see clearly the contrast between the true God and these false substitutes on the basis of whether they have indeed proclaimed things that have now occurred so that all could see and say, "It is true!" (43:9), thus confirming that they are true gods. Of course, they have not so declared, and therefore they are not true gods. In contrast, and proving then to be the only true God and Savior, the Lord says, "It is I who have declared and saved and proclaimed" (43:12). The false gods fail to proclaim and thus they cannot save; I have proclaimed and so I prove myself to be the true Savior, says the Lord. This is the logic of this text: God links not only his deity and glory but now his rightful role as *Savior* to the proof he offers of declaring the future.

Further, God's role as Savior is manifest in acting on behalf of Israel in ways that simply cannot be thwarted or reversed, for God declares, "I act and who can reverse it?" (43:13). So, where 42:8-9 linked God's foreknowledge to his glory, this passage links God's foreknowledge to his rightful sovereignty as Israel's invincible Savior. If we care not only about God alone receiving all glory but also about having a Savior who cannot fail or be resisted in his saving work, we must care that he is the true God! And on what basis shall we tell if he is? Answer: The true God declares and proclaims what will take place.

Isaiah 44:6-8 says:

> 6 "Thus says the LORD, the King of Israel
> And his Redeemer, the LORD of hosts:
> 'I am the first and I am the last,
> And there is no God besides Me.
> 7 'Who is like Me? Let him proclaim and declare it;
> Yes, let him recount it to Me in order,
> From the time that I established the ancient nation.
> And let them declare to them the things that are coming
> And the events that are going to take place.
> 8 'Do not tremble and do not be afraid;
> Have I not long since announced it to you and declared it?
> And you are My witnesses.
> Is there any God besides Me,
> Or is there any other Rock?
> I know of none.'"

In keeping with previous texts, God's claim here again is his general knowledge of "things that are coming" and "events that are going to take place" (44:7). So again, God's claim to deity is not based on his specific control over some specific future event or even a select number of events taken in isolation from the whole of what is coming, but incredibly it is based on all the events that have taken place in Israel's history, as the Lord says, "from the time that I established the ancient nation" (44:7).

What outcome is designed for the people of God as they consider that God is known as the true God precisely because he has spoken in advance everything that has occurred in their history? The effect on God's people, in brief, is to *hope and trust in God*. Isaiah 44:8 declares with such comfort and confidence, "Do not tremble and do not be afraid; have I not long since announced it to you and declared it? And you are My witnesses. Is there any God besides Me, or is there any other Rock? I know of none." The intrinsic argumentation of this verse is clear: God has announced and declared what has happened in their history. They are witnesses of his declarations and of the accuracy of what he has said. This proves that God alone is God, and that there is no other Rock than the God of Israel. Therefore, they are to take heart and have hope (another way of saying, "Do not tremble and do not be afraid"), *because the same God who has known and declared all of their prior history now declares what will occur in the future.* He knows and is in control, and he is their Rock. So, Israel, hope in God!

One is faced again with the debilitating and harmful effects on the people of God if they lose confidence that God knows and can declare accurately what the future holds. The logic of this text would lead us to say that *confidence in God is based on God's sure and certain grasp of all that occurs in history.* Without this, we soon wonder whether things are spinning out of control and whether God truly is God over history. The reassurance God gives is simple: From the beginning and throughout all of your history I have known and declared what will be. I can do this because I am God. Therefore, do not fear.

Isaiah 44:24-28 declares:

> [24] Thus says the LORD, your Redeemer,
> And the one who formed you from the womb,
> "I, the LORD, am the maker of all things,
> Stretching out the heavens by Myself,
> And spreading out the earth all alone,
> [25] Causing the omens of boasters to fail,
> Making fools out of diviners,
> Causing wise men to draw back,
> And turning their knowledge into foolishness,
> [26] Confirming the word of His servant,
> And performing the purpose of His messengers.
> It is I who says of Jerusalem, 'She shall be inhabited!'
> And of the cities of Judah, 'They shall be built.'
> And I will raise up her ruins again.

²⁷ It is I who says to the depth of the sea, 'Be dried up!'
And I will make your rivers dry.
²⁸ It is I who says of Cyrus, 'He is My shepherd!
And he will perform all My desire.'
And he declares of Jerusalem, 'She will be built,'
And of the temple, 'Your foundation will be laid.'"

Here, specific divine predictions are stressed, rather than the general and sweeping claims to "declare what is to come" that we have seen earlier. And yet, what this text has in common with others is its contrast between the true God and the pretender gods whose omens fail and whose purported knowledge is mere foolishness (44:25). The true God, the One who alone created all that is, demonstrates his power over all by confirming the word his servant has spoken (i.e., demonstrating its accuracy and truthfulness) and by performing the purpose his messengers have announced (i.e., accomplishing what his word promised). Both by validating the truthfulness of his previous word and by performing precisely what he said he would, God makes a mockery of the false gods who can do neither of these things. God is God, because God knows and performs what will occur (vv. 24-26).

Specifically, what does God claim here to declare and perform? Verse 26 specifies that God will reinhabit the city of Jerusalem and rebuild the cities of Judah. As one considers the magnitude of this promise, it becomes clear that God claims to have prior knowledge and oversight of enormous numbers of future free decisions and actions. How much is involved in reinhabiting and rebuilding cities? Just imagine the numbers of people involved, whose every free action to move, build, plant, establish their homes, etc., God depends on for this promise to be fulfilled. And in light of God's judgmental dismissal of the "boasters" and "diviners" in verse 25, *God cannot afford for his word not to come true.* It simply won't do to get a lot of things right but miss on several points! The contrast with these pretender deities requires that these things occur *just as God has said.* His reputation and his exclusive claim to deity, set in contrast to the false gods, demands that God *as God* get *everything* right, where "everything" includes innumerable future free choices and actions. The only conclusion one can rightly draw, then, is that God *knows* that he will accomplish his predicted purposes. And he *knows precisely* all the conditions that are necessary (including a multitude of free choices) for those predictions to come to be—conditions without which God could not be confident that what he planned would occur. For God *as God* will do exactly as he has said.

Even more remarkable is the prediction of a future king to whom God gave the name Cyrus nearly 200 years before his parents gave him that exact name. So, not only will God rebuild Jerusalem but he will use this pagan king whom God calls "My shepherd" who will "perform all My desire" (44:28). Again, consider the vast array of attending circumstances God must know about in advance for this prediction to be given. At the time Isaiah prophesies this, God must already know about the fall of Assyria, the rise and fall of Babylon, the rise of Medo-Persia, the fall of Israel, the fall of Judah, the birth and naming of Cyrus, the life and growth of this particular king, his ongoing life into adulthood, his selection as king, his willingness to consider helping the Israelites, his decision to assist in rebuilding Jerusalem, and on and on. This list hits a very few of the most significant items. Within each of these items is hidden a multitude of freewill choices that would affect everything about the outcome for that particular piece of human history. It simply is incredible that God can say through Isaiah such a long time prior to Cyrus's reign, "It is I who says of Cyrus, 'He is My shepherd! And he will perform all My desire.'"

Boyd explains God's predictive naming of Cyrus (and of Josiah in 1 Kings 13:2), saying, "This decree obviously set strict parameters around the freedom of the parents in naming these individuals. . . . It also restricted the scope of freedom these individuals could exercise *as it pertained to particular foreordained activities.*"[7] Two brief responses are needed. First, Boyd here acknowledges that if such remarkable predictions are to be accounted for, one must at these points leave behind general openness commitments to the unrestrained exercise of libertarian freedom and to God's ignorance of the future. *These* events require, admits Boyd, God's *curtailing libertarian freedom* and his *knowing exactly* that these names will be chosen. Second, as argued above, what seems to be absent here is an awareness of the multitude of factors that

---

[7] Boyd, *God of the Possible*, 34 (emphasis in original).

relate to the naming of these individuals, their upbringing, their rise to power, their rulership over their kingdoms, and the exact activities they perform. It appears that if libertarian freedom is curtailed *"as it pertained to particular foreordained activities,"* this would include such a vast number of items that the whole structure of moral creatures making their choices with libertarian freedom, so commended in open theism, would be jeopardized if not fully obliterated. Boyd's tacit admission that such divine predictions simply do not fit with a robust model of libertarian freedom is telling.

I passed over 44:27, but it is worth a brief comment. It reads, "It is I who says to the depth of the sea, 'Be dried up!' And I will make your rivers dry." What a seemingly odd statement to be tucked between God's pledge to rebuild Jerusalem (44:26) and his raising up of Cyrus to accomplish this very promise (44:28). What purpose does this statement about drying up seas and rivers serve? If verses 27 and 28 are taken together, I believe the point becomes clear. God claims to be the one, in each of these verses and in parallel fashion, who accomplishes precisely what he wants to happen. So, verse 27 essentially says, "It is I who dries the sea," and verse 28, "It is I who works through Cyrus." Raising up, naming, and using Cyrus in exactly the ways God intends is no more to me, says the Lord, than is the drying of the sea or a river bed. I have just as much control over one as over the other. Surely God is able to foretell the naming and using of Cyrus "to perform all his desire" precisely because he has as much control over Cyrus as he has over whether water does or does not fill the rivers and the sea.

Isaiah 45:1-7 states:

¹ Thus says the LORD to Cyrus His anointed,
Whom I have taken by the right hand,
To subdue nations before him
And to loose the loins of kings;
To open doors before him so that gates will not be shut:
² "I will go before you and make the rough places smooth;
I will shatter the doors of bronze,
    and cut through their iron bars.
³ I will give you the treasures of darkness
And hidden wealth of secret places,

So that you may know that it is I,
The LORD, the God of Israel, who calls you by your name.
[4] For the sake of Jacob My servant,
And Israel My chosen one,
I have also called you by your name;
I have given you a title of honor
Though you have not known Me.
[5] I am the LORD, and there is no other;
Besides Me there is no God.
I will gird you, though you have not known Me;
[6] That men may know from the rising to the setting of the sun
That there is no one besides Me.
I am the LORD, and there is no other,
[7] The One forming light and creating darkness,
Causing well-being and creating calamity;
I am the LORD who does all these."

Here again we see very specific predictions by God of how he will raise up and use Cyrus to fulfill his purposes. He predicts that Cyrus will destroy other nations, often going easily to victory, taking great treasures from conquered lands and by this becoming wealthy and prosperous. Amazingly, all this will occur despite the fact that Cyrus will not even know God (45:4b, 5b) and hence will not even be aware that *God* has named and anointed Cyrus, *God* has taken him by the right hand, *God* has subdued nations before him, and *God* has smoothed the rough places in his path. In the end, though, God will make it clear to Cyrus and others that it is he (God) who has called Cyrus by name and has done all these things through him (45:1, 3b), so that glory and praise will be given to God from Cyrus himself and from all the nations (45:6-7).

While this passage has direct bearing on the subject of chapter 6, where we assess the openness notion of God as a risk-taker, it also relates here. Clearly God predicts and then fulfills a multitude of future actions and events, all of them exactly as he so designs. But consider again here how much of what God predicts involves massive numbers of future free choices and actions of God's moral creatures. How can God predict and guarantee such things as the naming of a future king, his ascendancy to power, his leadership ability and disposition to conquer, his sure victories in battles, the plundering of others' treasuries, the shattering of bronze doors and iron bars, etc., unless God *knows and regulates* precisely what will in fact occur in the future? In the openness model, with the bulk of these future events dependent on future free choices, none of which God can either know or regulate, it becomes impossible to account for the certainty and exactness of these predictions and their fulfillment. So, while this text stops short of explicitly asserting God's exhaustive knowledge of all future actions and events, it does claim of God massive future knowledge, the vast majority of which is simply impossible to account for on openness grounds. An important question (to which we will return), then, becomes: In which overall model of divine providence do these data most naturally fit? Clearly the openness model fails while the classical model succeeds in making sense fully of these realities.

Isaiah 45:18-25 says:

¹⁸ For thus says the LORD, who created the heavens
(He is the God who formed the earth and made it,
He established it and did not create it a waste place,
But formed it to be inhabited),
"I am the LORD, and there is none else.
¹⁹ I have not spoken in secret,
In some dark land;
I did not say to the offspring of Jacob,
'Seek Me in a waste place';
I, the LORD, speak righteousness,
Declaring things that are upright.
²⁰ Gather yourselves and come;
Draw near together, you fugitives of the nations;
They have no knowledge,
Who carry about their wooden idol,
And pray to a god who cannot save.
²¹ Declare and set forth your case;
Indeed, let them consult together.
Who has announced this from of old?
Who has long since declared it?
Is it not I, the LORD?
And there is no other God besides Me,

A righteous God and a Savior;
There is none except Me.
²² "Turn to Me, and be saved, all the ends of the earth;
For I am God, and there is no other.
²³ I have sworn by Myself,
The word has gone forth from My mouth in righteousness
And will not turn back,
That to Me every knee will bow,
     every tongue will swear allegiance.
²⁴ They will say of Me, 'Only in the LORD are
     righteousness and strength.'
Men will come to Him,
And all who were angry at Him shall be put to shame.
²⁵ In the LORD all the offspring of Israel
Will be justified and will glory."

As we have seen before, God chooses to contrast himself with the "wooden idol," with the "god who cannot save" (45:20). The basis of this contrast, he says, is revealed by this challenge: "Declare and set forth your case" (45:21). Since the idol can say nothing, he continues, "Who has announced this from of old? Who has long since declared it? Is it not I, the LORD? And there is no other God besides Me, a righteous God and a Savior; there is none except Me" (45:21). Then, in what follows, God tells us that it is on the basis of "the word" that has gone forth from his mouth that every knee will bow and every tongue will swear allegiance to him and to him alone (45:23). The point is so very clear: *The "Godness" of God and his worth before which all will bow are proven and demonstrated by his word.* His word and character are righteous (45:19, 21, 23, 24) and so God's word reflects who God is in his very nature. Furthermore, God did not have to speak this word publicly; he could have spoken it in secret. But he went public (45:19, "I have not spoken in secret, in some dark land") precisely because he wanted people to hear and testify that *God and his word are altogether righteous.*

Given this depiction of the righteous word and character of God, and given that his word and character jointly are the unified basis by which all people will bow and swear allegiance to him alone, it is altogether unfitting and dishonoring to God to imagine that God's word may be wrong!

God's word reflects his character. And he declares his word, not in some far-off secret place but in full hearing *so that* all will hear and give him honor. His word is true, upright, faithful, and righteous. How utterly wrong it is to claim of God that his word is mistaken. How dishonoring to God to say that God tried his best to get things right, but missed. The God of Isaiah speaks, and he swears by himself. He declares, "The word has gone forth from My mouth in righteousness, and it will not turn back." God speaks the truth. He never, never, never gets it wrong. Isaiah 46:8-11 says:

[8] "Remember this, and be assured;
Recall it to mind, you transgressors.
[9] Remember the former things long past,
For I am God, and there is no other;
I am God, and there is no one like Me,
[10] Declaring the end from the beginning,
And from ancient times things which have not been done,
Saying, 'My purpose will be established,
And I will accomplish all My good pleasure';
[11] Calling a bird of prey from the east,
The man of My purpose from a far country.
Truly I have spoken; truly I will bring it to pass.
I have planned it, surely I will do it."

That the sweeping claim here ("declaring the end from the beginning") involves *future* actions and events is evident by the repeated affirmation, "My purpose *will* be established," "I *will* accomplish all My good pleasure," "I *will* bring it to pass," and "I *will* do it" (46:10-11). But, do these future actions and events, foreknown by God, concern only aspects of the determinate future of God alone, or do they involve also future free decisions of others? The reference to "a bird of prey" or "the man of My purpose" (46:11a) indicates that another volitional agent is involved in this foreknown future. God claims to know and accomplish a future reality that includes the decision of a man to fulfill this predicted outcome. The broad declaring of "the end from the beginning" is of a comprehensive past, present, and future known by God, including a future in which free volitional action other than God's alone takes place. Here, then, we have divine foreknowledge involving advance knowledge of free creaturely choice. This point is missed by Boyd in his discussion of this text.[8] Boyd rightly stresses God's promises to fulfill his plans and purposes ("My purpose will be established," and "I have planned it, surely I will do it," in 46:10-11), but he fails to mention that these purposes and plans include *centrally* "calling a bird of prey from the east, the man of my purpose from a far country" (46:11a). Likely a reference to Cyrus (from 44:28–45:7), God declares that his purpose is to call and use *this man* to accomplish *God's purpose*. Given this, even if Boyd is correct here that God "foreknows that certain things are going to take place because he knows *his own purpose and intention* to bring these events about,"[9] we dare not miss the point that *his own purpose and intention* includes a multitude of future free choices and actions both of this man himself and of all the surrounding network of individuals whose choices would relate to his being placed in the position where he then carries out specifically what God has intended that he do. Rice, Sanders, and Boyd[10] are all greatly mistaken, then, to give this text as an example of God's unilateral control of a portion of the future within which no other free creaturely decisions relate.

But does this text relate only to specific forecasted future realities? Again, Boyd asserts that God "declares that the future is settled to the extent that he is going to determine it, but nothing in the text requires that we believe that *everything* that will ever come to pass will do so according to his will and thus is settled ahead of time."[11] Great caution and further reflection are needed in addressing this issue. I will argue that, while this text does not state *explicitly* and *directly* that "*everything* that will ever come to pass" is foreknown by God and settled from eternity past, nevertheless a model of exhaustive divine foreknowledge is both *implied* here and is the *only model that can account for all that is explicitly taught here.* Boyd is correct that the focus of the text is on the purposes God has planned and will accomplish in the future. But Boyd's

---

[8] Ibid., 30.

[9] Ibid. (emphasis in original).

[10] Richard Rice, "Biblical Support for a New Perspective," in Clark Pinnock, Richard Rice, John Sanders, William Hasker, and David Basinger, *The Openness of God: A Biblical Challenge to the Traditional Understanding of God* (Downers Grove, Ill.: InterVarsity, 1994) 51; Sanders, *God Who Risks,* 130; and Boyd, *God of the Possible,* 30.

[11] Boyd, *God of the Possible,* 30 (emphasis in original).

interpretation and assessment of this passage falters by his neglect to consider *in this text* the broader context of God's expansive foreknowledge within which these specific purposes and plans for the future are placed. We must look further at what God declares here.

There is a theme in these verses that Boyd overlooks, a theme whose truth has the effect of placing these specific future purposes and plans of God in a much broader, richer, fuller context of the divine foreknowledge. Verses 8 and 9 call on God's people to "recall to mind" and "remember the *former things* long past." Now, why would God ask them to remember *former* things when the main point is God's accomplishment of *future* things? The answer is obvious, is it not? The confidence that God in fact will accomplish in the *future* what he here declares, is based on recalling the multitude of ways that God in the *past* has declared what will come to be and has then brought those things to pass just as he had said. This explains the chiastic declaration of verse 10: "declaring the end [i.e., the future] from the beginning [i.e., the past], and from ancient times [i.e., in the past] things which have not been done [i.e., in the future]." Confidence in the truthfulness of the declarations of God's *future* plans is rooted squarely in the accuracy with which God in the *past* declared precisely what would be and then accomplished it. So, while it is true that this one text in and of itself does not *explicitly* assert exhaustive divine foreknowledge, this text does place these specific new declarations of God within the long-standing pattern of God's truthful declarations and successful accomplishments. How broad is this pattern? The general nature of the "former things" of verse 9 and the "end from the beginning" of verse 10 would suggest a very large, broad, far-reaching pattern that encompasses the sweep of history, and within which God has so very, very often spoken of what will be—which then transpired just as he had said.

Given this, what implications can we draw about this passage's "fit" with either the classical or the openness models of divine foreknowledge? It appears quite clear that the teaching of this passage is at odds with open theism's model. From this text, as with so many others, we learn that God declares large portions of the future, portions which include a multitude of future freewill choices. He knows and oversees vast amounts of future reality, and his predictions at every point fit a sweeping, general, history-wide pattern in which his very Godness is on display in the accuracy of the predictions and the fulfillment of his purposes. That he is God and there is no one like him (46:9) is based exactly on this point: God knows the future; he declares it to be what it will be; others' free choices and actions form a necessary and integral part of the future God knows and declares; and as the future unfolds, all that God has said is accomplished. Open theism simply cannot accommodate such decisive knowledge and oversight of future free actions. Clearly, Isaiah 46:8-11 does not fit the openness model.

On the other hand, clearly the exhaustive foreknowledge model of classical theism fully accommodates these truths. While this one text on its own may not support the full weight of this classical doctrine, one must ask whether it is reasonable that God could have the extensive amount of foreknowledge that is here claimed of him did he not know all that will take place. Is not the interconnectedness of future events and actions such that, to know with accuracy such a large amount of that future, one would really have to know it all? At least this is clear: This text lends great weight toward the classical model while it conflicts absolutely with the openness proposal.

Isaiah 48:3-8 declares:

> 3 "I declared the former things long ago
> And they went forth from My mouth,
>   and I proclaimed them.
> Suddenly I acted, and they came to pass.
> 4 Because I know that you are obstinate,
> And your neck is an iron sinew
> And your forehead bronze,
> 5 Therefore I declared them to you long ago,
> Before they took place I proclaimed them to you,
> So that you would not say, 'My idol has done them,
> And my graven image and my molten image have
>   commanded them.'
> 6 You have heard; look at all this.
> And you, will you not declare it?
> I proclaim to you new things from this time,
> Even hidden things which you have not known.
> 7 They are created now and not long ago;

And before today you have not heard them,
So that you will not say, 'Behold, I knew them.'
[8] You have not heard, you have not known.
Even from long ago your ear has not been open,
Because I knew that you would deal very treacherously;
And you have been called a rebel from birth."

Because of the people's obstinacy and hard-heartedness, God declared things "long ago"; he proclaimed them "before they took place" in order that they would know that *God* has spoken and acted, not their molten images and idols. God removes any basis for thinking that any one of these false gods has legitimacy. God's proof? "I declared the former things long ago and they went forth from My mouth, and I proclaimed them. Suddenly I acted, and they came to pass" (48:3).

Again, what this passage asserts is nothing short of *massive fore-knowledge* and *absolute accuracy*, neither one of which can be accounted for in open theism. The general term "former things," as observed earlier, is purposely broad, encompassing a multitude of times that God has spoken and his word can be shown to have come true. And, because God wants Israel to come back to him, he now proclaims new things. God's purpose in this is to prove to this idolatry-oriented people that he alone is God. Once again we see God's heart and earnest desire. He longs for people to know from his constant and remarkably detailed and accurate declarations of the future that he alone is God. *God's designated authenticating sign of his deity is the reality and truthfulness of his foreknowledge.* To diminish this reality or to qualify its truthfulness is to make a mockery of God and the stated purpose for his futuristic declarations.

Summary of the Isaiah Texts

Before examining some other select passages relating to exhaustive divine foreknowledge, it will help to pull our thoughts together on some of the main observations from these texts in Isaiah. First, most of these passages have stressed God's claim to know and declare the future in purposely *sweeping* and *general* language. Phrases such as "the former things," "the things that will take place," "what is coming," "the end from the beginning," "new things," "the events that are going to take place," permeate these texts. They indicate that God intends his people to think of his foreknowledge as broad and comprehensive and not merely as selective, specifically focused, and occasional. Clearly, the *context* of any and all of the specific predictions within these texts is one of *general claims of broad foreknowledge.* What else does this rightly imply but God's comprehensive command of *all the future* within which *all these specific predictions* are purposely placed? That God has exhaustive foreknowledge appears to be the conclusion God intends us to draw from the breadth of the claims of these texts.

Second, as noticed several times, *all of the specific predictions* given by God in these texts (there are no exceptions, so far as I can tell) involve, for their fulfillment, the future free choices and actions of human agents. In many cases the numbers of these future freewill factors are staggeringly immense. How many freewill choices are involved in the rise and fall of nations, in the raising up and naming of a future king, and in so many other predictions and parts of predictions, God only knows (and he does know!). It simply will not do to say that God's predictions are highly selective and that they relate only to future actions over which God has unilateral control. Both of these claims, made by open theists and necessary for open theism, are refuted by these texts.

Third, how can we possibly state in sufficiently weighty language that *God has chosen to vindicate himself as God by declaring what the future will be,* so that when God's predictions come true, people will testify that he alone is God? What does God rest upon this claim to be able to declare and bring to pass what will be? A reading of all of these texts gives us an array of answers. By predicting and fulfilling what will be across the width and breadth of the unfolding future, God demonstrates: 1) his exclusive claim to deity; 2) his absolute rejection of all pretender deities as false gods; 3) the fullness of the glory that is his alone and that he will not share with any other; 4) the truthfulness of his promise that he alone is Savior; 5) the faithfulness of his pledge to be Israel's Rock and defender; 6) his ability to reign over a multitude of actions and events that will come to pass; 7) his ability to rule over nations, kings, and peoples; 8) the righteousness of the word that goes forth from his mouth; 9) the righteousness of his character from which this word proceeds; and 10) his demand that all bow before him and testify that he alone is God, that his word is true, and that "he is right!" I shudder to think of how God may judge any proposal that would deny of him his *self-chosen* and *self-proclaimed* means by which to demonstrate all of these truths. God is God and God is glorious, and God has said that we know this to be true *because* "I declare the end from the beginning." For the sake of the sole uniqueness of God and his matchless glory, we must magnify, not diminish, the Godness of God as we uphold, not call into question, his exact and sweeping foreknowledge.

Deuteronomy 31:16-21 with Isaiah 5:1-7

In Isaiah 5:1-7 God describes Israel metaphorically as his vineyard and himself as the vinedresser. Twice in this passage, God says that he is deeply disappointed because he *expected* his vineyard, Israel, to bear good grapes. Despite his loving care, they bore only worthless fruit. Commenting on this text, Boyd says:

> If everything is eternally certain to God, as the classical view of foreknowledge holds, how could the Lord twice say that he "expected" one thing to occur, only to have something different occur? How could the Lord expect, hope for, and even strive ("what more was there to do?") for something he knew from all eternity would never happen? If we take the passage at face value, does it not imply that the future of Israel, the "vineyard," was not certain until they settled it by choosing to yield "wild grapes?"[12]

Very little of my own response is needed to Boyd on this point. Some 700 years prior to Israel's rebellion of which Isaiah 5 speaks, and before Israel had entered the land God promised to give them, God, through Moses, had already predicted with complete understanding and foresight the future rebellion and idolatry of Israel. Notice in the following text God's dogmatic assertions of how Israel *will* act and that he *knows precisely* what they will do. Notice also that, despite the fact that God

---

[12] Ibid., 59-60.

knows exactly how Israel will rebel, he states how angry *he will become* with them at that time in the future. Deuteronomy 31:16-21 reads:

> The LORD said to Moses, "Behold, you are about to lie down with your fathers; and this people will arise and play the harlot with the strange gods of the land, into the midst of which they are going, and will forsake Me and break My covenant which I have made with them. Then My anger will be kindled against them in that day, and I will forsake them and hide My face from them, and they will be consumed, and many evils and troubles will come upon them; so that they will say in that day, 'Is it not because our God is not among us that these evils have come upon us?' But I will surely hide My face in that day because of all the evil which they will do, for they will turn to other gods. Now therefore, write this song for yourselves, and teach it to the sons of Israel; put it on their lips, so that this song may be a witness for Me against the sons of Israel. For when I bring them into the land flowing with milk and honey, which I swore to their fathers, and they have eaten and are satisfied and become prosperous, then they will turn to other gods and serve them, and spurn Me and break My covenant. Then it shall come about, when many evils and troubles have come upon them, that this song will testify before them as a witness (for it shall not be forgotten from the lips of their descendants); for I know their intent which they are developing today, before I have brought them into the land which I swore."

Consider especially the force of the concluding statement in verse 21. God says, "I know their intent which they are developing today, before I have brought them into the land which I swore." God *knows their future rebellion,* for he specifically predicts it with certainty and in some detail before it occurs. Furthermore, this passage helpfully illustrates a point made earlier: that God can know something fully in advance and yet express the appropriate emotion and ethical response to that situation when it actually arises in its historical unfolding. Knowing something in advance does not preclude real relational interaction. God knows fully what Israel will do and he enters fully into intimate relationship with them, hot with emotion and deeply involved in response to the wickedness of their sin.

Psalm 139

What great comfort Psalm 139 gives to God's people as it extols God's intimate acquaintance with all our ways. Within this psalm, consider first the amazing claim of verse 4: "Even before there is a word on my tongue, behold, O LORD, You know it all." How can one do justice to this text from the perspective that God does not know the future? When Psalm 139:4 declares that God *knows* the words we speak before we open our mouths, can this be reduced to God's informed guesses as to what we will say? If so, it simply is not true to say that God *knows* our words in advance. We all say surprising things—surprising sometimes even to ourselves. No amount of past and present knowledge of individuals could predict with complete accuracy the words they will speak next. But Psalm 139:4 declares that God *knows in advance* all the words we speak.

Furthermore, this declaration that God knows our every word before we utter it is merely an example of the general principle, stated in the early verses of the psalm, that God knows and oversees every aspect of our lives. The God who knows when we sit and rise (139:2), who understands our every thought (139:2), who scrutinizes our paths (139:3), who encloses us behind and before (139:5), is the God who also knows all our words before any are uttered. This psalm depicts meticulous providential oversight in a way that should inspire in God's people great confidence that all of their lives are under his supervision. While we marvel that God knows precisely and exactly every word before we speak, we see that this is stated as an example of how meticulous is his loving care and oversight of our lives.

Psalm 139:16 provides another glimpse into the extent of God's meticulous oversight of his creatures. The psalmist here declares, "Your eyes have seen my unformed substance; and in Your book were all written the days that were ordained for me, when as yet there was not one of them." Clearly this passage indicates that God ordained (literally "formed," from *yatsar*) the days of our lives before we even existed. But how can this be? How can God ordain or form all our days when (as the open theists would claim) he does not know any of the multitude of the future contingencies and future free actions of ourselves and of other people that may relate to our lives? The fact is that, without fore-knowledge of a contingent future, God could not even know *that* we would be (e.g., God could not know what individuals might be miscar-ried or die in childbirth), much less *know the days* that would occupy our lives, and much less again, *ordain* them all from the outset. Clearly we are intended to be comforted with the assurance that God knows *all that will happen to us.*

Consider this a bit further. For God to know all the days of our lives before there was yet one of them (139:16), God must *know about* and be in *command of* all the contingencies and future freewill choices that will happen in regard to our lives. To ordain the days of our lives is both to *know about* and to *have regulative power over* the host of innumer-able variables that go into making the substance of each and every one of those days. Consider just one day. Take today, for example. Think about the multitude of variables that affect your life this day. You are living, but could you have died? Might you have had a car accident? Did you get your exercise in, so that your good health will persist? How might your diet and level of stress affect your life, well-being, and longevity? How many other people made free decisions today that had potential impact on your life and well-being? *Consider all of these fac-tors and many, many more as they potentially affect just one single day!* The fact is that God cannot be subject to and limited by the libertarian free choices of people of which he has no prior knowledge and over which he has regulative control, and still be able to know and ordain all the days of our lives.[13] The fact is, then, that Psalm 139:16 faces us with a reality that simply cannot be accounted for in open theism. God knows our future days, all of them, from before there was one of them. No wonder the psalmist marvels and places unfailing confidence in this gen-uinely omniscient God.

Boyd[14] tries to escape the force of this text by appealing to the very odd King James translation of Psalm 139:16 which reads, in part, "and

---

[13] For this reason, I find Boyd's comment (*God of the Possible*, 40) that "even if this verse [Ps. 139:16] said that the exact length of our lives was settled before we were born, it wouldn't follow that *everything* about our future was settled before we were born" somewhat disingenuous. Certainly, even if absolutely everything were not foreknown, the amount of what must be foreknown, most of which includes future free choices and actions, to know *that* we will live a certain number of days, is staggering.

[14] Boyd, *God of the Possible*, 41.

in thy book all *my members* were written." While the KJV puts "my members" in italics, indicating that these words do not appear in the Hebrew original, what is especially puzzling is why the King James translators did not translate what *is* there. The Hebrew word in question is the very common, ordinary word *yamim* ("days" from *yom*, "day"). The LXX translators render this word with the Greek *hēmera*, the common Greek word for "day." And commentators of this psalm, many of whom note and reject the KJV rendering, uniformly take this word in its normal sense to indicate that the psalmist's "days" were ordained by God before any of them had come to pass.[15] There simply is no legitimate lexical or grammatical basis for translating *yamim* as "members."

The meaning of the verse, then, is clear. As he considers his earliest beginnings, while still in the womb of his mother, the psalmist cherishes the realization that, even then, God had planned and formed the very days of the life he would come to live. And with days lived that are ordained by God before there was even one of them, the psalmist has complete confidence that God is in control of his life, that he can fully rest his life and well-being in God's capable, ordaining hands, so that even when he faces agonizing opposition and threats to his life (139:19-20), he knows that *he will live every single day God has given to him*. To mirror the language of Romans 8:31, if God has ordained the psalmist's days, who can shorten his life? So take heart! God is so intimately aware of our lives—past, present, and future—that he knows every word that will come forth from our lips (139:4) throughout all the days of our lives (139:16). Such is life with the God who knows all that will be.

Daniel

The book of Daniel, with its series of highly specific and detailed predictive dreams, whose predictions span the breadth of many centuries and involve the rise and fall of many nations, offers enormous data in sup-

---

[15] I wish to thank Russell Fuller for his helpful discussion and insight concerning the KJV translation of this text. See, e.g., Franz Delitzsch, *Biblical Commentary on the Psalms*, trans. F. Bolton (Grand Rapids, Mich.: Eerdmans, 1952), III, 350-351, where he demonstrates that grammatically it must be the "days" and not the "unformed substance" that were written in the book before there was one of them. Cf. W. A. VanGemeren, "Psalms," in *Expositors Bible Commentary* (Grand Rapids, Mich.: Zondervan, 1991), V, 838; and A. Weiser, *The Psalms: A Commentary* (Philadelphia: Westminster, 1962), XVI, 800-806.

port of God's exhaustive knowledge of all that will take place in the future. One cannot dismiss the predictions of chapters 2, 4, 5, 7, 8, 9, 10, and 11 by saying that God controls merely *a minimal select portion* of the features of the future, sufficient to ensure that these predictions come true. A reasonable consideration of the details as well as the breadth involved renders this accounting of these data facile. Especially when one factors in the staggering number of future freewill decisions which have to line up just right for these events to come true, these chapters provide overwhelming evidence for God's comprehensive knowledge of and control over the future. In the limited space that can be devoted to Daniel's predictions, I will try to summarize what is involved predictively from just some of the detailed prophecies of *one* of these chapters.

Daniel 11 contains, by itself, an amazing array of instances in which God predicts, and hence foreknows, many future events and many future free creaturely actions. For example, Daniel, prophesying in the first year of Cyrus, king of Persia (ca. 539 B.C.), predicts three kings to come after Cyrus, followed by a fourth (11:2). This fourth king, likely a reference to the coming Alexander the Great (reigned ca. 336–323 B.C.), died young, and his sons were murdered. Daniel predicts this, along with the fact that his kingdom would be divided into four parts (11:4). Amazingly, as history unfolds, Alexander's four generals vie for control and split the kingdom into the four regions of Egypt (south), Syria (north), Asia Minor, and Greece proper. The general of the south (Egypt), Ptolemy, began the line of the Ptolemies, while Syria's king, Seleucus I, began the line of the Seleucids. Daniel 11:5-35 then describes predictively roughly 155 years of warfare between the Seleucids and Ptolemies, with special focus given to the despicable reign of Antiochus IV Epiphanes (11:21-35), an unrightful heir to the throne. All these events, the people who fulfill them, and many more details than here described, are predicted with amazing accuracy by Daniel. Furthermore, it must not be missed that most, perhaps all, of the items prophesied required for their fulfillment enormous numbers of future free human choices and actions. God knew that three kings, then a fourth, would come to power. He knew the kingdom of this fourth king would be divided and that its four parts would be ruled over by kings other than his descendants. He knew of the battles that would take place between two of these powers and of the ultimate victory of one.

He knew of the devastation that would come to Israel through this last wicked king, and he knew that this wicked king would not be the rightful heir to the throne. The fulfillment of each one of these predictions involves a multitude of future free human actions. It is no wonder that liberal scholars date this portion of Daniel very late! So many details, involving future free choices, with such precision—this is truly overwhelming evidence, in one chapter of the Bible, of the reality of God's foreknowledge.

John

John's Gospel, which presents Jesus as having the glory of his Father, portrays Jesus in a way strikingly similar to the God portrayed in Isaiah. In several places in John we find Jesus appealing to his knowledge of the future as the reason why people should believe, as Jesus puts it, that "I am He." The correlation with these themes in Isaiah is notable (remember John 12:37-41, where John identifies Jesus with the God of Isaiah's vision). Consider John 13:19: "From now on I am telling you before it comes to pass," Jesus tells his disciples, "so that when it does occur, you may believe that I am He" (cf. 14:29; 16:4). The point is the same as in Isaiah: Jesus' knowledge of the future is evidence that he is God in human flesh (John 1:14).

Beyond these explicit statements, consider a few specific examples of Jesus' foreknowledge. We find Jesus telling Peter of his three denials before the rooster crows (see John 13:38 with 18:19-27); predicting the kind of death Peter would die (John 21:18-19); and predicting that Judas would be the one who would betray him (John 6:64, 70-71; cf. Matt. 26:21-25). In all of these cases, Jesus' predictions require that other humans do precisely what Jesus predicted they would do. Yet, these are not presented as mere guesses regarding the future. Rather, Jesus *knows* what other free agents will in fact choose to do, *states* what these future actions will be, and provides his *reason* for so doing: "so that when it does occur, you may believe that I am He."

Consider more fully Christ's remarkable prediction that before the cock crowed, Peter would deny him *three*—not one, or two, or four, or forty, but *three*—times. We have seen that Boyd explained this remarkable prediction on the basis of Jesus' perfect knowledge (as revealed to him by the Father) of Peter's past conduct and character.[16] Is this a reasonable basis for explaining this account? Surely it is true that Jesus knew Peter's character, but how could he surmise *three denials* (i.e., precisely *this* future occurrence) from knowledge of Peter's character? Consider: What if Peter had become so frightened, shocked, bewildered, and confused after the first confrontation and denial that he decided to run off into the wilderness, thus making the second and third denials impossible? What if, after the first or second denial, those surrounding Peter had grabbed him and taken him before the chief counsel, where Peter then denied Christ repeatedly and incessantly to avoid the torture he otherwise would have received—thus denying Christ a multitude of times, not merely three? What if James and John had gone with Peter, and because of their presence with him, Peter found himself ashamed either to deny Christ or to affirm him, but rather remained silent and then made some excuse in order to leave as hastily as possible? In the open view, since Jesus (or the Father) does not know the future free actions of people, he could not have known whether any of these possible and reasonable scenarios (or innumerable others) might have occurred. Honestly, I am simply incredulous that the proposal would be seriously made that Jesus could accurately predict that *Peter would deny him three times,* based on God's perfect knowledge of Peter's character.

Furthermore, consider another feature of this case, that is, how many future free actions were involved in the fulfillment of this prediction. Clearly each of Peter's choices to deny Christ were his free choices. And those who questioned and confronted Peter did so freely as well. That they confronted him exactly three times was of their own free choice. That all three questions but no more occurred before the cock crowed involved their free choice, for many factors may have led either to their delaying to ask Peter the questions they did until well after sunrise, or to their asking several more questions in rapid succession, thus causing Peter to make more than three denials before the cock crowed. That no harm fell to Peter, preventing him from arriving at the fireside, involved both his and many others' free choices. That there were with Peter no other disciples who might have strengthened his resolve not to deny Christ involved many people's freedom of choice. And on and on.

---

[16] Boyd, *God of the Possible,* 35-37.

Clearly, the only full and satisfying explanation of this prediction is that Jesus knew exactly that, how often, and when Peter would deny him. To deny foreknowledge here is to deny the obvious basis for this prediction, and it is to rob Jesus of the grounding of his own claim to deity.

Finally, Luke's description of Jesus' prediction of Peter's three denials contains another element worthy of notice.[17] Luke 22:31-32 records Jesus' words to Peter just before he tells Peter of his upcoming denials. Jesus says, "Simon, Simon, behold, Satan has demanded permission to sift you like wheat; but I have prayed for you, that your faith may not fail; and you, when once you have turned again, strengthen your brothers." Remarkably, Jesus not only predicts with accuracy that Peter would deny him, and that he would do this exactly three times (see Luke 22:34), but here in verse 32 he also predicts that Peter will "turn again," that he will not utterly deny Christ but that he will return and even be used to strengthen the faith of fellow Christian believers. Given Peter's libertarian freedom, how could Christ possibly have known with such certainty that Peter would in fact return? Knowing the penalty for prophesying falsely, and staking his own claim to deity on announcing in advance what will occur, Jesus would have taken an enormous risk to make such a specific prediction unless he knew precisely what Peter would do.

No appeal to Peter's character will suffice in explaining Jesus' words. Consider Peter's mental and emotional state following his three denials. Why would it not be entirely reasonable to imagine that Peter, racked with guilt and shame, would leave the eleven and hide out in the hills of Galilee, far away from any who might know his identity or past deed? Isn't it conceivable that Peter might wish never again to show his face to Jesus or to his fellow disciples? Might Peter even crack mentally under the strain of such a horrible betrayal? So, is it reasonable to conclude that Jesus would be able to discern from Peter's character that, contrary to these highly realistic possible scenarios, it would be so *likely* that Peter would return that he could go on record predicting that this would occur? All this makes a mockery of Jesus' own prediction. The fact is *he knew.* He knew and predicted that Peter would deny him. He knew and predicted Peter's denials would be exactly three, not more or

---

[17] I am grateful to Lyle Bierma for pointing out this feature to me in a conversation on these issues.

less. And he knew that Peter would not ultimately and finally betray his Master but would return to be used by God even to strengthen others. These future realities, involving a multitude of free human choices and actions, Jesus absolutely knew. No other explanation works.

TYPES OF BIBLICAL PROPHECY

The above examples fit the pattern of much predictive prophecy throughout the Bible—a pattern not acknowledged in open theism. Openness proponents argue that all biblical prophecy fits into one of three categories,[18] none of which includes what we have repeatedly seen above, namely, *unconditional* and *exact predictions* that involve *specific future choices or actions of free creatures.* The three openness categories for biblical prophecy are: 1) prophecies relating to what God himself will do unilaterally, totally apart from any future free decision of volitional creatures; 2) prophecies that predict some outcome, whose occurrence is conditional (either explicitly or implicitly stated) and so are understood as occurring only when the necessary conditions are present; and 3) prophecies that represent what God believes (rightly or wrongly) most likely will occur as informed by his comprehensive knowledge of the past and present.[19]

Regarding these three categories, it appears that for open theists the vast majority of biblical prophecy must be fit into category two. Consider for a moment the first and third categories. How much prophecy is accounted for by *category one?* What prophecies are there whose fulfillment involves *absolutely no* future creaturely free choice or action over which, then, God would have *perfect foreknowledge* due to having *absolute regulative control?* Perhaps predictions such as God's promise to provide wandering Israel a cloud by day and pillar of fire by night would fit, yet the larger prediction that he would "lead" Israel by

---

[18] For openness discussion of biblical prophecy, see Richard Rice, *God's Foreknowledge and Man's Free Will* (Minneapolis: Bethany, 1985), 75-81; Rice, "Biblical Support," 50-53; and Sanders, *God Who Risks,* 129-137.

[19] David Basinger ("Can an Evangelical Christian Justifiably Deny God's Exhaustive Knowledge of the Future?" *Christian Scholar's Review* 25 [1995], 141) summarizes the three openness categories of prophecy as follows: "the announcement ahead of time of that which God intends to ensure will occur, conditional prophecies which leave the outcome open, or predictions based on God's exhaustive knowledge of the past and present."

these means clearly cannot fit this category, for Israel must choose to follow the cloud and fire.

Or perhaps the prediction in Isaiah 7:14 that a virgin would conceive and bear a son might be controlled and fulfilled by God unilaterally. After all, God would simply choose some future young virgin, accomplishing in her this miraculous conception totally apart from any consent or future free choice on her or anyone else's part. But I suspect open theists would frown on this idea, since it would undermine the integrity of Mary's own willful acceptance of this act *prior to* her miraculous conception, and it might even be viewed, on Sanders's criteria, as a case of "divine rape."

If not these events, then surely the second coming of Christ is *completely* in God's control, without any necessary involvement of freewill agents other than God. But even here, is Christ free when he obeys the Father and comes again to earth when the Father has ordained that he should? If so, the fulfillment of the Father's will depends on Christ's willing obedience. Also, isn't a *second* coming necessarily after the *first,* and doesn't Christ's first coming involve many freewill actions for God's predictions to have occurred (e.g., only one who is in the line of David, born in Bethlehem, born of a virgin, etc.)? But if the second coming is logically tied to the first (i.e., you can't have a second without a first), and if the first involves *many* future free actions, then the second, indirectly, can only occur in connection with these free human choices and actions. So it appears that even here, for God to fulfill his promise of Christ's second coming, many freewill choices are directly and indirectly connected.

Certainly Rice's, Sanders's, and Boyd's suggestions that Isaiah 46:9-11 illustrates this category of prophecy is misguided.[20] As was seen above, the promise of this text involves calling "the man of My purpose," and this aspect introduces unavoidably the presence of *future free human choice* for its fulfillment. Yes, God can *declare* what will occur, but when this includes a human being, on openness grounds either God gives up unilateral control or he takes away the freedom and moral responsibility of the human agent.

So, as one ponders what biblical prophecies might apply to the first of these three categories suggested by open theists, one realizes

---

[20] Rice, "Biblical Support," 51; Sanders, *God Who Risks,* 130; and Boyd, *God of the Possible,* 30.

that precious few, if any, fit. It appears, in fact, that every biblical prophecy one might consider involves, for its fulfillment, either directly or indirectly, some aspect of *creaturely free choice*. Perhaps there are some that would fit (although I haven't seen any clear, indisputable examples offered in openness literature), but even if so, they are likely extremely rare.

Category three could certainly, in principle, be applied to much biblical prophecy, but I suspect that openness advocates would be reluctant to put more prophecy than absolutely necessary into the category of what might be thought of as "God's best guess." As Sanders puts it, "God is the consummate social scientist predicting what will happen. God's ability to predict the future in this way is far more accurate than any human forecaster's, however, since God has exhaustive access to all past and present knowledge."[21] Although much more accurate than the best of human futurists, however, God too is mistaken at times. Sanders cites Exodus 3:16–4:9 and Jeremiah 3:7, 19-20 as examples where God believed and stated that one thing would happen, yet something different actually occurred.[22] It stands to reason that open theism could tolerate, at best, only a limited number of prophecies in this category, for if it turns out that God is mistaken about much of what he predicts will occur, the surety of his word becomes severely undermined, no matter what positive accounting one might attempt to give to it.

Furthermore, given the assertion of open theists that accuracy in God's prognostications is strong only in *short-range* predictions, and given that nearly all instances of biblical prophecy are of events at least somewhat (and at times significantly) *long-range* in nature, it appears that God would be foolish to put his reputation on the line with such a low probability of success. Category three may not be empty, as it appears category one is, but it will be close to bare, even on openness grounds.

This leaves *category two* to accommodate the overwhelming amount of biblical prophecy. But what shall we say of the proposal that most biblical prophecy is by its very nature conditional? First, *explicitly* conditional prophecies are not problematic for either classical or open

---

[21] Sanders, *God Who Risks*, 131.
[22] Ibid., 131-132.

theism. If God states up front that he will act in a certain way *only if* something else occurs, we are to understand that he will act one way *or* the other, depending on whether or not the condition is fulfilled.

Second, when prophecies are *implicitly* conditional, there are often clues in the contexts of these prophecies as to what the unstated, implicit condition may be. As discussed in chapter 4 in relation to Jonah's mission to Nineveh, Hezekiah's extended life, and Moses' pleading for Israel, there are good reasons for thinking that God's *stated prediction* was given to elicit some response, after which God then did what he *secretly intended to do all along.* The response fulfilled the *implicit condition* on the basis of which God "changed" from what he had stated he would do. Recall, for example, that Jonah understood from the outset that God's *stated prediction* ("forty days and Nineveh will be destroyed") contained the *implicit condition* that if Nineveh responded by repenting, God would be merciful. Only if this is so can we explain why Jonah strongly objected and resisted God's command to proclaim judgment on a people he despised. He strongly suspected that God intended to be merciful and was giving Nineveh opportunity ("forty days") to repent. The stated prediction accomplished the response God intended (i.e., Nineveh repented), and God then did what Jonah feared he would do—he showed them mercy.

Third, how often should we expect divine prophecies to contain implicit conditions? Open theists appeal to Jeremiah 18:5-10 to provide a normative basis by which to claim that virtually *any* divine prophecy may be exempt from exact fulfillment. How can this be? Since all prophecy is *potentially* set in a framework in which unstated and implicit conditions are present, in all such cases, according to open theists, God is not obligated to do just what he said. Although God has stated that he will bring about one state of affairs, he understands (and so should we) that he is not bound to do just what he prophesied—*if the conditions for its fulfillment change.*

Jeremiah 18:5-10 reads:

> [5] Then the word of the LORD came to me saying, [6] "Can I not, O house of Israel, deal with you as this potter does?" declares the LORD. "Behold, like the clay in the potter's hand, so are you in My hand, O house of Israel. [7] At one moment I might speak con-

cerning a nation or concerning a kingdom to uproot, to pull down, or to destroy it; *⁸ if* that nation against which I have spoken turns from its evil, I will relent concerning the calamity I planned to bring on it. *⁹ Or* at another moment I might speak concerning a nation or concerning a kingdom to build up or to plant it; *¹⁰ if* it does evil in My sight by not obeying My voice, then I will think better of the good with which I had promised to bless it."

Consider a few observations on this passage.²³ First, the verses immediately *preceding* this passage (Jer.18:1-4) describe God as a potter and Israel as clay. The clear emphasis of these first four verses of Jeremiah 18 is *not* that what God, the potter, will or will not do *depends on* the clay. Just the reverse is true. As Jeremiah 18:4 describes, "But the vessel that he was making of clay was spoiled in the hand of the potter; so he remade it into another vessel, *as it pleased the potter to make*" (emphasis added). The clear message here is that God does as he pleases, and the clay takes the shape that the potter decides.

Second, in the verses that *follow* this passage, God states that he knows (in advance) just what Israel will do in response to his prediction of impending calamity. Jeremiah says,

> *¹¹* "Thus says the LORD, 'Behold, I am fashioning calamity against you and devising a plan against you. Oh turn back, each of you from his evil way, and reform your ways and your deeds.' *¹²* But they will say, 'It's hopeless! For we are going to follow our own plans, and each of us will act according to the stubbornness of his evil heart'" (Jer. 18:11-12).

Oddly enough for open theists, in the very text they appeal to most regularly to support the idea that God does not know how people will act and so his prophecies must be alterable depending on what unfolds, here in fact God declares that he *knows exactly what his people will do*. Despite his warning of judgment, Israel will not turn from their stubbornness and evil ways, and God declares in advance that this will be true.

Third, what, then, can Jeremiah 18:5-10 mean, when these verses

---

²³ I express my thanks to Peter Gentry for helpful discussions regarding this passage.

are bracketed by affirmations of God's *sovereign control* (18:1-4) and *certain future knowledge* of what Israel will do (18:11-12)? The answer, I believe, is that these verses simply state what God has *always* made clear (see Lev. 26; Deut. 28–29): When people repent of their sin, God has pledged that he will forgive; when people turn against him, God has warned that he may bring upon them his swift judgment.

So, what Jeremiah 18:5-10 is presenting is *God's constancy* to act in ways that are appropriate to the moral situations that he faces. When some moral situation changes, God will change in ways that are called for and appropriate to the new situation. In *this* sense, God "changes" because he acts differently than he previously stated he would. But notice, it would violate the context of this passage to go further (as open theists do) and say that God *learned something new* and therefore literally changed his mind. When the verses that precede speak of God's *sovereign control* and the verses that follow declare God's *knowledge of what will be,* it is inappropriate to assert that God doesn't know what free creatures will do. All that is needed to account for God's change in action in 18:5-10 is that God faces and responds appropriately to a *changed situation*—not that God has learned *new information.*

Fourth, how inappropriate it would be to take Jeremiah 18:5-10 as a normative template to overlay onto biblical prophecy generally. Where the principle of this passage rightly applies is to promises of blessing or warnings of judgment, when the anticipated blessing or judgment is understood as conditioned on the peoples' moral disposition. It is glorious news that, despite previously predicted judgment, if these people in question repent, this will elicit from God his merciful forgiveness.

But if we apply this conditional framework broadly, we dilute the force of so many biblical prophecies and so rob God of the honor due him for *fulfilling them exactly as he has predicted he would.* Shall we turn God's prediction to raise up the king he named "Cyrus" into a conditional prophecy? What would this mean? Evidently this: Despite God's claim that he would be named Cyrus, the boy could have been given a different name by his parents, and this would have caused no difficulty for God! Why? Because we should understand God's prediction in Isaiah 44:28 to indicate his endeavor to have his name be

"Cyrus," but whether this happens or not is conditioned by what his parents freely decide. Introducing our implicit condition here, then, evacuates the force of the prophecy and makes a mockery of God's exclusive claim to deity based on his *accurate prediction* of this future king's name. This one example illustrates how grave would be the error to introduce the notion of implicit conditionality into the vast majority of biblical prophecy, and yet this is exactly what the openness view requires.

Amazingly, in all this discussion, the one category of biblical prophecy omitted (necessarily) by open theists is the category of unconditional predictions (i.e., God declares what *will certainly* occur even though their occurrence happens through the means of human choices and actions), which necessarily involve future free choices and actions of volitional creatures. And it is precisely here that God *most clearly manifests himself as God over history.* Even though some biblical prophecy should rightly be placed into a category of "conditional" prophecies (open theism's category two, above), in which events are predicted that may not be fulfilled if the necessary conditions (implicit or explicit) do not obtain (e.g., Jer. 18:5-10), certainly much biblical prophecy is unconditionally and uncategorically declared, while at the same time its fulfillment involves creaturely free action. In such cases, the fulfillment of these prophecies must occur precisely in the manner foretold lest God be considered a liar and unfaithful to his word.

Consider the force of Deuteronomy 18:18-22. God declares:

> "'I will raise up a prophet from among their countrymen like you, and I will put My words in his mouth, and he shall speak to them all that I command him. It shall come about that whoever will not listen to My words which he shall speak in My name, I myself will require it of him. But the prophet who speaks a word presumptuously in My name which I have not commanded him to speak, or which he speaks in the name of other gods, that prophet shall die.' You may say in your heart, *'How will we know the word which the LORD has not spoken?'* When a prophet speaks in the name of the LORD, *if the thing does not come about or come true,* that is the thing which the LORD has

not spoken. The prophet has spoken it presumptuously; you shall not be afraid of him" (emphasis added).

I cannot imagine why God would go on record as he does here and tie his claim of *deity* to the *exact fulfillment* of his predictions if nearly *all* of these predictions are in fact conditional. The problem is this: *Conditional* predictions, by their nature, give to God a "back door," as it were. If things don't go as he hoped or thought, he can always change what he had said. In all such cases, we *cannot rightly expect exact fulfillments* of these predictions, because it all depends on how things develop. Yet here in Deuteronomy 18, God calls his people to *look for and expect exact fulfillment* as authenticating evidence that *God alone* predicted what now has come about, just as God has said. If as a general rule, however, God's predictions may *not* come about just as he predicted, the force of the passage is obliterated.

And so it must be asked: If God lacked knowledge of the future, how could he predict such matters with such accuracy and certainty, and why would he tie his integrity and deity to their exact fulfillment? Besides the many examples discussed above that fit this category, several others could be given. For example, Scripture specifically predicts: Israel's 400 years in Egypt; Judah's seventy-year captivity; the destruction of Jeroboam's altar (predicted 300 years in advance), specifically indicating Josiah by name as the king to carry out this destruction (1 Kings 13:1-3); and Jesus' death by crucifixion, with the casting of lots for his clothing (Psalm 22:18), his bones not being broken (Psalm 34:20), and his being buried in the tomb of a rich man though he should have been with the two thieves (Isa. 53:9); and on and on—all events in which the fulfillment depends, in significant part, on what humans freely choose.

Concerning Christ, think specifically of Acts 2:23, "this Man, delivered over by the *predetermined plan and foreknowledge* of God, you nailed to a cross by the hands of godless men and put Him to death" (emphasis added); and Acts 4:27-28, "For truly in this city there were gathered together against Your holy servant Jesus, whom You anointed, both Herod and Pontius Pilate, along with the Gentiles and the peoples of Israel to do *whatever Your hand and Your purpose predestined to occur*" (emphasis added). As these passages illustrate, God often is said to know and predict what free human beings will carry out. The alternative here is appalling: Due to God's ignorance as he "predicts" (read: guesses in regard to)[24] the future crucifixion of Christ, it is a good thing (read: God gets lucky that)[25] the Pharisees and Roman soldiers did not repent at the preaching of Jesus, lest God's promise to offer his Son might have failed. No, such divine predictions are not dependent on unknown and unforeseen human choosing which might thwart God's purposes. God knows the future; he predicts much of what will come to be; and in many cases these predictions include the future free choices and actions of his creatures. This is not philosophical sophistry; it is the straightforward meaning of text after text of Scripture. God knows the future, and if we have understood Moses, David, Isaiah, Daniel, John, Peter, Luke, and Jesus rightly, by its denial of this truth the openness doctrine of God diminishes God's deity.

CONCLUSION

As we draw this discussion to a close, recognizing that we have sampled only a small portion of the full data in support of God's foreknowledge, we would do well to consider two questions that have been in the foreground throughout this chapter and that are at the heart of this debate. First, can the teachings of these respective passages regarding God's prediction, knowledge, and determination of the future be accounted for in open theism? And second, do any of these teachings require that we affirm specifically God's exhaustive knowledge of the future? In addressing both questions, please consider the following observations.

First, notice the specificity and exactness, as well as the breadth and variety, of God's knowledge and prediction of innumerable future items. God knows in advance our every word before we speak it, to

---

[24] This is a fair assessment of the openness position, given Sanders's view, noted earlier, that it was not until the moment of Father-Son interaction in the garden of Gethsemane that the decision was made for Christ to go to the cross (see Sanders, *God Who Risks*, 100-101).

[25] This likewise is fair, insofar as (in the openness view) God cannot know what the Pharisees and Roman soldiers in fact will choose. In Sanders's view, God "anticipated their response and so walked onto the scene with an excellent prognosis" of their future actions (*God Who Risks*, 103). But because the "implausible," "the entirely unexpected" can always happen, ultimately it is fair to say God got lucky that they did not repent—clearly an odd position for openness proponents to be in. Note also that if David Basinger (*The Case for Freewill Theism: A Philosophical Assessment* [Downers Grove, Ill.: InterVarsity, 1996], 47), quoted in a footnote in chapter 3, says the God of middle knowledge depends on "luck," how much more does presentism's God rely on luck for his success?

the full number of the days of our lives. God predicts the naming of certain individuals long before they are born, as well as their places in specific kingdoms that are yet future. He declares how many kings will come at some future time, which alliances will be made, the effect of these matters on other nations and on Israel, and how long governmental structures will last. He predicts for specific situations such things as "seven years," "fifteen years," "seventy years," "400 years," "three denials," "sixty-two and seven weeks." Regarding Christ, God predicts the birth in Bethlehem, the slaughter of the infant boys, the flight to Egypt, the nail-pierced hands, the dividing of the garments, the unbroken bones, the death with criminals, and the burial in the tomb of the rich. I could go on and on. Imagine how long the list would be were we to include *everything in the Bible,* in all its detail, specifically predicted by God. The amount of his predictive revelation is, simply put, overwhelming.

Second, notice how frequently what was foreknown, predicted, and/or determined by God involves future free choices and actions of various individuals and groups. To make this point most forcefully, just consider for a moment the overwhelming listing of specific predictions just mentioned, and ask yourself: For how much of that body of predictive material does *some involvement of future free choices* enter into the fulfillment of those predictions? As one realizes that the answer is, "for the vast majority of it to be sure, and perhaps for all of it," one begins to see just how much God knows of all the free choices, decisions, actions, and contingencies relating to the totality of the future, both near and far.

Third, the extensiveness, specificity, and accuracy of God's knowledge of these manifold future actions and events are *fully explicable* in a model that affirms *exhaustive divine foreknowledge,* whereas these examples are fully inexplicable in open theism. Why does open theism fail? It fails, in part, because the fulfillment of these predictions involves innumerable future *free choices, none of which God could know* if the openness model is assumed; it is simply impossible, within the framework of the openness model, for God to know and predict and regulate these manifold future realities. In addition, on openness grounds, *neither the scope, nor breadth, nor volume, nor specificity, nor accuracy of this massive body of predictive material can be accounted for.*

How often can one say that God gets lucky before it begins sounding a bit like special pleading? How often can one appeal to God's conjecturing as the explanation for so many of these samples that are so distant in the future? How can the specificity and accuracy be explained? The fact is, open theism excludes from God the very qualities needed to explain these features.

Fourth, in contrast, versions of the classical model which hold that God knows and regulates *all* future realities have no difficulty accounting for how he can know and regulate the immense number of specific predictive elements that make up the whole of biblical prophecy. Furthermore, *exhaustive divine foreknowledge seems to be demanded* in order to give a *full* and *complete* accounting of these elements. These predictions and all they involve are so extensive that anything less than exhaustive foreknowledge would render full and satisfying explanation impossible. One would have to invoke God's *ad hoc* intervention in literally multiple thousands of details, and God would have to constrain free choosing to the point of eliminating it in as many cases. But of course these notions are fully unacceptable even within open theism because of the disruption this causes to the normal flow of life and the mockery this would make of libertarian freedom.

Fifth, what is the purpose of God indicating over and again that he has knowledge of and control over so many specific future actions and events? Perhaps the reason is that by doing this, the impact on the reader is stronger. To stress again and again God's control over yet more specific occurrences has a cumulative effect that is greater than likely would be the case if God said once, with one simple declarative claim, that he knows and regulates all future actions and events. The repetition reminds us over and again that God is great, God is glorious, God is sovereign, God is infinitely knowledgeable, God is worthy of worship and honor; in short, that God is God.

Sixth and last, the fact is that, amid the repetition, God does make clear that these instances are part of the bigger, comprehensive sphere of his exhaustive knowledge of and ultimate control over *all* of history. As we noticed in our discussion of the Isaiah texts, we dare not miss the broader context in which the vast multitude of specific declarations and predictions of the future occur. God reigns over heaven and earth, and his claim to exclusive deity and glory depends on his "declaring the end from the beginning." Since God encourages our thinking of his fore-knowledge in the broadest possible ways, and since the multitude of specific predictive instances illustrates the whole spectrum of this vast and broad array of God's foreknowledge, without question the most reasonable and only fully satisfying conclusion to draw is that God intends for us to affirm that he knows *all of the future.* All the instances of his knowledge of what free creatures will do indicate there is nothing he cannot and does not know. That God has exhaustive foreknowledge is the most compelling conclusion from these data.

6

The God Who Risks
and the Assault on God's Wisdom

At the heart of the openness proposal are the formative ideas that 1) *the future is open,* i.e., it stands mostly unknown and undetermined, even by God; and 2) as a result, *the future is risk-filled,* i.e., unforeseen and unpredictable actions and events may occur, many in relation to the unknown future choices of free creatures, which may frustrate God's purposes to such a degree that God may or may not triumph over them. God, then, accepts genuine and enormous risks when he creates the world. Yet openness advocates reassure us that God is fully capable of overcoming most obstacles and winning in the end. As the five *Openness of God* authors tell us, "God takes risks in this give-and-take relationship, yet he is endlessly resourceful and competent in working toward his ultimate goals."[1] In his desire to accomplish his purposes, God always faces the stubborn reality that humans may successfully resist his will. They may use their freedom in ways that God disapproves of and that greatly harm themselves and others whom he loves. From the outset, then, God knows that he will never get all that he would like, and he must work hard to persuade if he hopes (which he does) to fulfill most of what he desires. God is optimistic, but the entire creation project truly faces God with massive risk.

To a great degree, the openness proponents are saying only what their Arminian colleagues have long argued. The Arminian view has long been that God's power to fulfill his perfect will may be and is

---

[1] Clark Pinnock, Richard Rice, John Sanders, William Hasker, and David Basinger, *The Openness of God: A Biblical Challenge to the Traditional Understanding of God* (Downers Grove, Ill.: InterVarsity, 1994), 7.

thwarted by human resistance (e.g., when humans hear and reject the gospel). But what is especially poignant in the openness view is the notion that God plans and works without the advantage of knowing the future. Hence, the whole venture is, quite literally, an enormous risk for God, not to mention for the entire world that he has made.

This chapter will investigate three areas relating to this central openness notion of God as risk-taker. We will begin with a sketch of open theism's vision of God in which it will be clear that God's immanence is highlighted in ways that overshadow his transcendence and allow also for human significance to be unduly elevated. God becomes more like us, such that his transcendent power, knowledge, wisdom, and sovereignty all suffer. Excessive divine immanence grounds the notion of God as risk-taker but is at odds with the notion of his great and glorious sovereignty.

The question of the second section, then, will concern the nature of God's sovereign rulership as revealed in Scripture. Here we will consider a sampling of biblical teaching that upholds a very high, lofty, reverent, majestic, and glorious view of God's absolute rulership of all that is. This view does not entail adopting an excessive view of the divine transcendence, however, because it is precisely this incomparable and glorious King who is none other than our Father, the Lover of our souls, and our dearest Friend.

Finally, we will consider the cost of open theism's diminished view of God as it pertains particularly to the divine wisdom. Can God be trusted? Can we rightly follow his leading? Can we be confident that God will have the ultimate victory? And even if he is victorious in some qualified sense, how much will he lose along the way? We will see that the diminished view of God in open theism cannot avoid directing a frontal assault on God's matchless wisdom while it calls into question the basis for our hope.

AN UNBALANCED AND EXCESSIVE VIEW OF GOD'S IMMANENCE

The transcendence/immanence balance in the doctrine of God is extremely difficult to establish and maintain. Open theism proposes to chart a middle position between classical and process theism, and in certain respects it accomplishes just this. According to open theism, God is ontologically independent of the world (as with classical theism)[2] while he enters freely into real and interactive relationship with his creatures (as stressed in process theism, but held in both). Yet in the openness view, the actual outworking of God's providence and relationality with the world extends God's immanence beyond proper biblical parameters. There is a tendency to see God's relationship with his human creatures according to an incarnational model. Citing John 1:14, Richard Rice explains:

> The fundamental claim here is not simply that God revealed himself in Jesus, but that God revealed himself in Jesus *as nowhere else*. . . . Accordingly, from a Christian standpoint it is appropriate to say not only that *Jesus is God*, but that *God is Jesus*. For Christians, Jesus defines the reality of God.[3]

If Jesus defines God's reality, as Rice has stated, it is easy to see that we end up not only with an incarnational Christology but with an incarnational theology proper. And what's wrong with this? Only that the incarnation marks a historical time when Jesus, the eternal Son of God, veiled his glory (see John 17:5) along with many privileges and prerogatives of deity (see Phil. 2:5-8) in order to take on the finitude, weaknesses, and limitations of human servanthood. Incarnation marks, in one sense, a limitation of full divine expression (John 17:5, Phil. 2:5-8) while it also expresses, in another sense, God's nature gloriously manifest (John 1:14, 18). Therefore, our theology proper dare not be incarnational lest we conceive of God wrongly as being subject to experiencing those aspects of human weakness and limitations which Jesus underwent for the purpose of his mission.

Yes, God is immanent. He is intimately involved in the affairs of his people and in governing and overseeing the whole sweep of human history. But *his immanence is from the standpoint of undiminished and fully glorious transcendence.* Consider the balanced portrayal of God in

---

[2] To their credit, open theists hold strictly to the classical doctrines of God's aseity (self-existence) and self-sufficiency. See, e.g., Pinnock, "Systematic Theology," in Pinnock, et. al., *Openness of God,* 108: "The triune God (unlike God in process theism) does not need the world to make up for a love and mutuality lacking in his nature. The Trinity allows the church to confess that God is both self-sufficient and loving at the same time."

[3] Richard Rice, "Biblical Support for a New Perspective," in Pinnock, et. al., *Openness of God,* 39.

the Bible, in which clearly God is both transcendent and immanent yet his immanence is the gracious and undeserved expression of his mercy toward his creatures without any compromise of or limitation to his transcendent excellencies. Isaiah 57:15 and 66:1-2 are both wonderful examples in which priority is clearly given to God's eternal and glorious transcendence, on the basis of which we then marvel that *this God*, this *fully majestic and self-sufficient God*, should deem it good and right to show such kindness to us. These glorious passages read:

> For thus says the high and exalted One
> Who lives forever, whose name is Holy,
> "I dwell on a high and holy place,
> And also with the contrite and lowly of spirit
> In order to revive the spirit of the lowly
> And to revive the heart of the contrite" (Isa. 57:15).

> Thus says the LORD,
> "Heaven is My throne and the earth is My footstool.
> Where then is a house you could build for Me?
> And where is a place that I may rest?
> For My hand made all these things,
> Thus all these things came into being," declares the LORD.
> "But to this one I will look,
> To him who is humble and contrite of spirit,
>   and who trembles at My word" (Isa. 66:1-2).

The true and living God is the eternally transcendent God who cares intimately for us while retaining all the power, wisdom, knowledge, and glory that is eternally his.

It is clear that the God of open theism is a limited God. Compared to the exalted fullness of God revealed in Scripture and affirmed in the classical tradition, the openness God has limited knowledge, limited power, limited wisdom, limited control, limited sovereignty, and hence, limited glory. While open theists admit in very qualified ways their views concerning God's limited power, control, and sovereignty, they are quite resistant to the charge that in their view God suffers from either limited knowledge or wisdom. In the sections that follow, I shall seek to demonstrate that the God of the Bible is inexhaustibly powerful, sovereign, and wise, and that the open view tragically portrays God in ways that conflict fundamentally with this biblical teaching. But here, I wish to address briefly the issue of God's *limited knowledge* in open theism. Is it right to charge that open theists reject the divine omniscience and so believe that God's knowledge is limited? Concerning the divine omniscience, Boyd writes:

> Though open theists are often accused of denying God's omniscience because they deny the classical view of foreknowledge, this criticism is unfounded. Open theists affirm God's omniscience as emphatically as anybody does. The issue is not whether God's knowledge is perfect. It is. The issue is about the nature of the reality that God perfectly knows.[4]

Despite Boyd's insistent affirmation of the term "omniscience," it is indisputable that he denies the *classical definition* of omniscience, which of necessity includes exhaustive divine foreknowledge. As I noted earlier,[5] this is very much like a time in the early 1980s when I heard that John Hick was asked directly whether he denied the deity of Christ. Of course, the background for this question was the publication just a few years earlier of his book, *The Myth of God Incarnate*, in which he and all its contributors denied the reality of the incarnation and that Christ was God. Hick's response, as reported to me by one present at this meeting, went something like this: "I absolutely do not deny Christ's deity. I would no more deny the deity of Christ than I would deny the deity of any of us!"

The point of this is that terms are shells. The definitions that fill them are what matter. Boyd can complain if he chooses that others charge open theism with denying omniscience, but the fact remains that the definition of omniscience that he invokes is fundamentally contrary to the definition of omniscience in classical theism. If, in the classical view, God's *comprehensive knowledge of the future* is a *necessary condition for the divine omniscience*, then a denial of the divine exhaus-

---

[4] Gregory A. Boyd, *God of the Possible: A Biblical Introduction to the Open View of God* (Grand Rapids, Mich.: Baker, 2000), 15-16.

[5] In a comment to George Brushaber, president of Bethel College and Seminary, in my October 15, 1999, letter to him, quoted in note 6 in chapter 1.

tive foreknowledge is unavoidably a denial of the classical doctrine of omniscience. So, open and classical theists can both use and affirm the same term, just as Hick can continue affirming the "deity" of Christ along with orthodox defenders of Christ's deity, but the *doctrine* affirmed in open theism is a denial of the doctrine classically held throughout the history of the church. All protestations aside, this is what matters.

Along with open theism's view of God's limitations comes a corresponding exaltation of human beings. God is lowered while man is elevated. Herein lies both the appeal (sadly) and the danger of open theism. The culture in which we live, including much of the Christian subculture, has drunk deeply at the well of self-esteem. Where the Bible enjoins unfettered but deeply humble "God-esteem," we have been conditioned to think that we should have some of that esteem for ourselves. So, when a theology comes along that says, "God often doesn't make up his mind what to do until *he hears first from you*," or, "God and *you together* chart out your course for the future as *both of you learn together* what unfolds," or, "Sometimes *God makes mistakes* but we need to realize that he was doing his best," such a view plays well with many in our culture. We feel like we are almost peers with God, in a relationship in which we are encouraged to have an elevated view of what we think and feel, struggling along together with God while we are both subject to many of the same limitations—and all of this feels so right.

In fact, it is so very, very wrong. It is so demeaning to God as it is so unrightfully exalting of us. The diminished God of open theism, then, is a God whose immanence has outstripped his transcendence. Does the God of the Bible take risks as open theism would have us believe? What are the implications of the openness view for the question, in particular, of God's wisdom? We turn now to examine and assess these two areas in regard to the open view's portrayal of God.

RISK-TAKING AND THE GOD OF THE BIBLE

Since the question of God's exhaustive foreknowledge has been considered in chapters 4 and 5, here I wish to focus attention on a clear and consistent stream of biblical teaching emphasizing God's control of all things. Consider first the amazing account of what an arrogant pagan king learned about God. In Daniel 4, Nebuchadnezzar had boasted about his great city Babylon and had taken credit for his power, his wealth, and his greatness to accomplish the building of such a magnificent city (Dan. 4:29-30). Immediately upon Nebuchadnezzar's boasting of his own greatness, God humbled this mighty king, put him out to pasture (literally!), and brought him to his right reason only after he had learned the true nature of his own finitude in contrast to the infinite greatness of the one and true sovereign God. Following the period of his humiliation, we read these words from Nebuchadnezzar in Daniel 4:34-35:

> But at the end of that period, I, Nebuchadnezzar, raised my eyes toward heaven, and my reason returned to me, and I blessed the Most High and praised and honored Him who lives forever;
>
> > For His dominion is an everlasting dominion,
> > And His kingdom endures from generation to generation.
> > All the inhabitants of the earth are accounted as nothing,
> > But He does according to His will in the host of heaven
> > And among the inhabitants of earth;
> > And no one can ward off His hand
> > Or say to Him, "What have You done?"

The point clearly is that God raises and puts down, he rules over all, and people (even great kings) are unable to thwart God's will and ways. Notice particularly the phrase, "All the inhabitants of the earth are accounted as nothing, but He does according to His will . . ." The contrast is extremely important to understand if we are to interpret the statement correctly. Certainly we would err if we took "all the inhabitants of the earth are accounted as nothing" to mean that God did not value or care in the slightest for the entirety of his human creation. To avoid this misinterpretation, one must see this statement in the light of what follows: "but He does according to His will." Now the point becomes clear. All the inhabitants of the earth are accounted as nothing *in respect to their ability to thwart or frustrate God's will.* Even more, what is true on earth is true also in the heavenly, spiritual realm, for God fully and unfailingly accomplishes his will "in the host of heaven" as well as among his earthly creatures.[6] Hence the ending statement: No one (human, angelic, or demonic) can cause God's hand to turn contrary to what he intends and no one can justifiably challenge or question him as he perfectly and comprehensively performs his will.

Clearly one implication of this text is that the very notion of God being a risk-taker in relation to creation is denied altogether. The very heart of this passage and its explicit affirmation expresses just the opposite of what the divine risk-taking idea proposes. None of God's creation, heavenly or earthly, can challenge, disrupt, thwart, or frustrate his comprehensive will. We his creatures are, in this sense, "accounted as nothing," and we had best bring to an end the arrogance and presumption of thinking otherwise.[7] God is glorious, in part, because he reigns over all. What folly to imagine that we may clothe ourselves with the robe of God's glory by thinking that it is we, not him, whose will stands inviolable.

Consider also Deuteronomy 32:39: "See now that I, I am He, and there is no god besides Me; it is I who put to death and give life. I have wounded and it is I who heal, and there is no one who can deliver from My hand." Notice three features of this verse. First, the point of mentioning life and death, wounding and healing, is to establish the extremes of life over which God has complete control. One could call this text (and others like it[8]) a "spectrum text," since it affirms that both ends of the spectrum, as it were, and everything in between are accomplished by God. Open theism strongly resists this teaching. This passage does not say that God merely attempts as best he can to *use* the death and wound-

---

[6] Gregory A. Boyd, *God at War: The Bible and Spiritual Conflict* (Downers Grove, Ill.: InterVarsity, 1997), 58, writes: "The warfare worldview thus presupposes the reality of relatively autonomous free creatures, human and angelic, who can and do act genuinely on their own, and who can and do sometimes go against God's will. It thus presupposes the reality of radical contingency and of genuine risk. It further presupposes that this risk has sometimes gone bad, even on a cosmic scale, and that this has turned the earth into a veritable war zone." If the presuppositions of Boyd's entire book-length (in fact, three volumes when completed, we are told) argument are that heavenly forces can withstand God's will in the risky battle for the cosmos, and if these presuppositions are exactly contrary to Scripture's teaching that "[God] does according to His will in the host of heaven and among the inhabitants of earth; and no one can ward off His hand or say to Him, 'What have You done?'" then it is clear that Boyd's entire project, from its very inception, proves sadly to be misguided and fundamentally wrong.

[7] Notice Nebuchadnezzar's humble, repentant response following his confession of the absolute will and reign of God: "Now I, Nebuchadnezzar, praise, exalt and honor the King of heaven, for all His works are true and His ways just, and He is able to humble those who walk in pride" (Dan. 4:37).

[8] Other "spectrum texts" include Exodus 4:11; 1 Samuel 2:6-7; 2 Kings 5:7; Psalm 75:6-7; Isaiah 45:5-7; and Lamentations 3:37-38. See chapter 9 for further discussion of these "spectrum" texts in relation to the issue of divine sovereignty and human suffering.

ing brought about by others (which things he cannot, without destroying freedom, stop free creatures from doing) while he himself *brings about* life and healing. The parallelism simply will not permit this distortion. Scripture affirms that God accomplishes, in some sense, *all* that takes place. Just how this is best understood and articulated is explored more fully elsewhere,[9] but here we must see and embrace the truth of this passage that God controls and in some sense accomplishes the full spectrum of the features of human existence.

Second, God's very claim to uniqueness ("I am He, and there is no god besides Me") rests on this assertion. If God himself states that his uniqueness as the only true and living God is founded on some particular truth, it is incumbent upon us who believe in God to affirm and embrace that truth. Who are we to challenge God's right to establish his unique deity on the grounds he chooses? Here, those grounds are clear. Controlling everything that occurs is God's self-chosen basis for upholding his deity. So, contrary to openness proponents, God takes no risks. His claim to deity asserts instead his absolute and final control over all.

Third, as with Daniel 4:34-35, the point is made that people are incapable to thwart God from carrying out his will. Although implied by the previous assertion that God controls the entire spectrum of human life, what was implicit becomes explicit with the closing phrase. We hear again the humbling words, "there is no one who can deliver from My hand." We who are prone to exalt ourselves and bring God down are ourselves put in our rightful place; it is his will, not ours, that prevails.

Or consider the simple assertion of Psalm 135:5-6: "For I know that the LORD is great, and that our Lord is above all gods. Whatever the LORD pleases, He does, in heaven and in earth, in the seas and in all deeps." Three features stand out here as well. First, the major claim of the text asserts God's *comprehensive control*, i.e., "whatever" the Lord pleases he does. There is no qualification that limits what God can accomplish due to obstinate or stubborn people. As Proverbs 21:1 reminds us, God can turn the heart of people as he does channels of water. Second, the major claim of the text asserts also God's *compre-*

[9] See D. A. Carson, *Divine Sovereignty and Human Responsibility: Biblical Perspectives in Tension,* 2d. ed. (Grand Rapids, Mich.: Baker, 1994); John Feinberg, *The Many Faces of Evil: Theological Systems and the Problem of Evil* (Grand Rapids, Mich.: Zondervan, 1979, 1994); and Paul Helm, *The Providence of God* (Downers Grove, Ill.: InterVarsity, 1994).

hensive sphere of control, i.e., he accomplishes all that he pleases *throughout creation.* Complete control over all that is, and nothing less, is what we are called to affirm. Third, as we find elsewhere in Scripture, God's very uniqueness as the God of gods, the Lord "above all gods," is based precisely on this feature of his nature. He is *God* because he exercises his sovereign control and meticulous providence throughout the entire created order.

It is on the basis of the truth of God's comprehensive sovereignty or meticulous providence that Paul is led to raise the question, "Why does he still find fault? For who resists His will?" (Rom. 9:19). Precisely *because* it is true that God does all that he pleases, the question arises regarding the basis for human culpability and moral responsibility. If no one can resist God's will, on what basis does God hold people accountable? To be sure, Paul does not suggest a full answer to the question he himself poses, but neither does he deny the legitimacy of the problem or deny the reality of God's meticulous providence out of which the problem arises. That is, Paul does *not* respond to his own question, "for who resists His will?" by reassuring his readers that in fact they *do* have the capability to thwart God's will. Rather, Paul's view here stands in sheer contrast to the risk-taking notion of open theism. Were Paul to have taken the open theism position on this issue, the moral difficulty he raised would vanish. It is only and precisely *because* God does in fact control all things that the moral question of Romans 9:19 arises and looms large. Furthermore, the glory of God is shown to be at stake in God's control of all that is. In the verses that follow, Paul writes:

> What if God, although willing to demonstrate His wrath and to make His power known, endured with much patience vessels of wrath prepared for destruction? And He did so to make known *the riches of His glory* upon vessels of mercy, which He prepared beforehand for glory (Rom. 9:22-23, emphasis added).

For purposes only briefly sketched in this passage, Paul indicates that God's control of all things (see Rom. 9:18, which elicited this discussion) requires that both hardening and showing mercy (9:18), both vessels of wrath and vessels of mercy (9:22-23), are the result of God's determinate choice (cf. 9:11). And the reason provided that undergirds this divine choice is that, through this, the riches of God's glory may be made known. If God's glory rests, ultimately, in his control of all that is, then it stands to reason that when God's control is diminished and human control elevated, so too is his glory diminished—while human pretense to assume that glory is encouraged.

Probably no single passage is more often referred to in support of God's comprehensive sovereignty than Ephesians 1:11 with its assertion that God "works all things after the counsel of His will." Here as elsewhere, we see the comprehensive nature of God's providential control with this claim in verse 11 following directly upon verse 10 where "all things" are summed up in Christ, "things in the heavens and things on the earth." Clearly, Paul is not thinking of some restricted "all things" in verse 10, and so it seems highly unlikely that the "all things" of verse 11 would shift to a different concept. Paul's point in verse 11, therefore, is that believers may be confident of their inheritance (v. 11a) because it reflects one aspect of the larger purpose of God, in which he "works all things after the counsel of His will." Because all, comprehensively, is done as God wills, surely our inheritance (i.e., part of the "all things") will be granted as God has promised. Furthermore, here again we see that the very accomplishment of God's will redounds to his glory. Verse 12 expresses the goal of the fulfillment of God's will in which all things are summed up in Christ, namely, that believers would marvel at the accomplishment of God's sovereign plan and bring praise and glory to him.

The feature of divine risk-taking is at one level true of every Arminian version of divine providence in which the creature's libertarian freedom can be asserted in ways that ultimately frustrate God's deepest longings and purposes. Yet the openness model of providence presents us with a more radical and thoroughgoing understanding of the risk God undertakes when he creates the world. Here, due to God's complete lack of knowledge regarding any and every future free creaturely decision and action, God can only guess what will transpire—especially as one projects into the distant future. But as we have seen above, *God's claim to deity and the expression of his glory correspond to the extent to which he rules unthwarted over heaven and earth.* This being the case, it follows that the openness model may be charged with a gravely serious assault against the very deity and glory of God. Since the higher the risk, the lower the control, and since the lower the control, the lower is the basis by which God's deity and glory are established, open theism's minimizing of God's control while elevating human freedom and divine risk produce a conception of a God with a lesser claim to deity and a lesser right to glory.[10] Such is the cost of maintaining creaturely libertarian freedom and an open future against comprehensive divine foreknowledge and meticulous providence.

ASSAULTS ON GOD'S WISDOM AND THE FULFILLMENT OF HIS PURPOSES

In the openness proposal, not only is the biblical vision of God's transcendence diminished and his sovereign rulership undermined; there are also grounds for challenging the traditional belief that God is omnisapient (all-wise). Consider for a moment Sanders's suggestion, discussed in chapter 3, that God was taken by surprise when the first human pair sinned. Recall that Sanders described that sin as "implausible" and "totally unexpected."[11] Presumably this interpretation is meant to fit with Sanders's overall proposal that the creation project faced God with many genuine and significant risks. For after all, no matter how much God provided the man and woman, and no matter how much they experienced his fellowship, love, and care, the granting to them of libertarian freedom rendered sin and all its horror possible even when simultaneously implausible.

An important question here is this: Once the totally unexpected has occurred in a perfect environment and the man and woman have sinned, how likely is it now that these embattled humans, pulled down by sin's domineering presence and afflicted by Satan's power, will resist the urges of the flesh and the enticements of temptation in order to obey? *If sin was unexpected in a perfect, loving, and sinless environment, should obedience be thought likely now?*

---

[10] Open theists, of course, deny that their view diminishes God's glory; in fact they claim, to the contrary, that their view elevates God's glory. Clark Pinnock ("God's Sovereignty in Today's World," *Theology Today* 53 [April 1996], 21) writes: "Sovereignty does not mean that God controls everything, since God gives power to other agents. It means that God is omnicompetent in relation to any circumstance that arises and is unable to be defeated in any ultimate sense. God delights in an open creation precisely because God does not completely control it. The open model of sovereignty does not diminish but augments the glory of God's rule." Notice that the key concept in this claim is that, even though God gives up power, he nonetheless "is unable to be defeated in any ultimate sense." Just whether open theists have valid grounding for such assurances will be taken up below.

[11] John Sanders, *The God Who Risks: A Theology of Providence* (Downers Grove, Ill.: InterVarsity, 1998), 46.

Perhaps appeal could be made here to the doctrine of prevenient grace as the means God will use to assist sin-infested humans in their choice of whether or not to obey. But just a moment's reflection shows that prevenient grace cannot carry the weight needed to rescue the openness model on this point from potential collapse. No matter what grace God gives to encourage or even enable sinners to obey him, they still live in a sin-saturated world and they endure constant temptations from the evil one and their own sinful flesh. No amount of prevenient grace could come close to bringing them to the condition the first pair of humans experienced prior to sin (in spite of which, contrary to all God's expectations, they sinned). Surely, would not God realize that, if disobedience occurred in a perfect environment, obedience now would be even more unlikely? Far more implausible it would seem is the *future obedience* of his sinful creatures than was the so-called implausibility of their *first sin.* For now God knows something he did not know before, namely, that even when perfect, his human creatures choose to sin. Now, as imperfect, will they choose to obey? Should one not expect, instead, pervasive, even runaway sin?

The openness model appears to be on the horns of a dilemma. On the one hand, one may question the wisdom of a God who viewed sin in the garden as "totally unexpected." Given the reality of libertarian freedom, would it not be a more reasonable expectation that at some point, in some situation, they *would* sin?[12] And after all, we have the advantage of hindsight. They *did* sin. Do we not often call into question the judgment of people in positions of responsibility for failing to anticipate realistic possible catastrophes, once those catastrophes have occurred? On the other hand, once sin has occurred one might wonder what possible basis God might have for thinking that he could succeed nonetheless in accomplishing his purposes. One might have hoped that the optimism God had in the garden would have given way to sober-minded realism about whether obedience would likely, plausibly be rendered. Might it not have been the better course of wisdom simply to end

---

[12] A version of this question, germane to all theological positions upholding the necessity of libertarian freedom for human moral accountability and genuine human love and worship, is how believers will live sinlessly for eternity (i.e., in heaven) when retaining libertarian freedom. Either they can and may sin, in which case eternal life cannot be promised with certainty, or they do not have libertarian freedom and so cannot sin, but neither, then, presumably, can they love and worship God.

this experiment with free human beings? Surely to allow Adam and Eve to live out their lives childless would be a painless but effective way to remedy the mistake as well as could be done under the circumstances. But God did not follow that path. He chose instead to perpetuate the human experiment, as it were, with the hopes that he would reclaim what was lost and win in the end. Openness proponents reassure us that, due to God's resourcefulness, we may be confident that God *will* fulfill his purposes.[13] As Sanders says, "We have confidence that God will bring his project to the fruition he desires because God has proven himself faithful time and again."[14] I must admit that these assurances ring hollow. Given the nature of libertarian freedom and the fact that the first humans sinned while in a perfect environment, I see no ground for optimism that God's project will succeed.

The central openness response at this point is to look at redemptive history and see how God has succeeded in bringing good out of evil and gaining victories through great struggle. Yet I question how the openness model itself can rightly be used to make sense of this history. Yes, the triumph of God *is* reflected throughout the entire Bible. God *will win* the victory, to be sure. But just how does the openness model account for this? *Was God not resourceful when devising his plans for the first human pair, and how successful was he then?* It appears that openness proponents use capital borrowed from classical theism's doctrine of providence to undergird hope when the basis for such optimism is lacking in their own theological system.

Pressing this issue one more step, it raises the question of ultimate or eschatological hope in open theism. Since it is true that God's *present* purposes may be frustrated by the unforeseen and unanticipated free actions of his creatures, what basis is there for believing that God's *ultimate* purposes and promises will be fulfilled in the eschaton?

Openness thinkers are caught here between a rock and a hard place. They affirm that this world is a very risky place, even for God, and yet they affirm that God will accomplish his purposes with the world. That

---

[13] See, for example, Sanders, *God Who Risks,* 42 and 129, quoted in note 20 in chapter 3, as well as pp. 127-128, 133, 138-139, 168, 171-172, 181-182, 187, 264-265; and Boyd, *God of the Possible,* 51 and 150.

[14] Sanders, *God Who Risks,* 129. But see the honest admission by David Basinger ("Human Freedom and Divine Providence: Some New Thoughts on an Old Problem," *Religious Studies* 15 [1979], 491), that "the Christian God can only ensure that his ends will be accomplished in a very general sense."

is, they wish on the one hand to uphold, even celebrate,[15] the genuineness and extensiveness of the risks God takes in creating a world of free creatures. For reasons discussed earlier, to the extent that human freedom is genuine and upheld and expressed, and to the extent that God is incapable of knowing future free choices and actions, to that extent he does, by the openness view, face genuine risk in regard to the future. And just how large is this extent? Simply put, *all* morally significant human choices and actions are free and hence uncontrolled by God, and *none* of those free choices and actions may be known in advance by God. It appears, then, that the level of risk is very, very high. On the other hand, a regular refrain in openness literature tells us not to worry, because God is omnicompetent and supremely resourceful and "will bring his project to the fruition he desires."[16]

One wonders, though, how it can be both ways. To emphasize the significance of risk is to diminish the confidence we may rightly have that God will get what he desires. Yet to emphasize the certainty of God's victory is to diminish the notion that God has really taken any significant risk at all. High risk and high confidence seem impossible together. Openness thinkers need to come clean on this point, end the double-talk, and declare clearly which it will be. It appears from an analysis of the model that openness proponents account well for risk while they merely declare, without foundation, confidence in God's victory. What will people say of God's "creation project" if, despite his having taken a big risk, it turns out that very few choose to obey God and enter his kingdom? Is there truly a basis for genuine and certain hope in open theism? Or is it just possible that indeed the risk for God has been unimaginably enormous—and that he will lose?[17]

Another very different kind of response to this problem is possible

---

[15] That Sanders' book would be titled "The God Who Risks" would seem to indicate some celebration of this concept central to the openness proposal.

[16] Sanders, *God Who Risks*, 129.

[17] Many open theists are also inclusivists on the issue of whether people must hear the gospel of Jesus Christ to be saved. I detect a theological connection between these two aspects of their overall theology. Given that risk is upheld, one would expect attempts theologically that would ensure the possibility of greater positive responses to God. They want to uphold *risk* but also to declare that God's project will *succeed*. So, the more people who have opportunity to be saved (hence the move to inclusivism and perhaps also to post-mortem evangelism), the less likely it is that someone would conclude that God has risked much and has lost. The drive toward inclusivism is strong in order to salvage the creation project within a paradigm of significant divine risk in a creation gone awry.

within open theism, yet it too has difficulties. David Basinger makes an honest admission that works against the optimism often portrayed by open theists. He suggests that without middle knowledge God cannot know what good acts might be done and whether good, on balance, will outweigh evil. So in creating creatures with libertarian freedom, God must decide "that the good inherent in significant freedom itself outweighs any amount of evil that the use of this freedom might generate in our world."[18] This appears an altogether reasonable proposal. Since God grants libertarian freedom, and since he cannot by definition control its use and cannot know what free creatures will actually do with it, the only value he can rightly uphold with full assurance is the value of libertarian freedom itself.

Will this work to salvage God's wisdom and secure the fulfillment of his purposes? The answer is yes if one means that this very narrow purpose alone can be accomplished. After all, since his purpose is *only* that free creatures exercise their libertarian freedom (irrespective of how they use it), he "wins" whether they obey or not. However, the answer is no if one inquires whether this narrow goal of granting libertarian freedom is itself a sufficient "good" to warrant making a world in which evil may vastly outweigh good. Would not a wise God choose to create only if he were confident that substantive moral goods (and not merely the instrumental good of exercising libertarian freedom indiscriminately) would be secured? So here again we face a dilemma. If God creates free creatures solely for "the good inherent in the significant freedom itself," we have grounds for questioning his wisdom. At least it would seem to many that the value attached to good or evil done with free will exceeds the value of that freedom in and of itself. But if on the other hand God creates free creatures whose future free actions he neither knows nor controls, we have grounds for questioning God's wisdom in creating a world in which it is entirely possible that evil will prevail over good. And furthermore, in such a world, not even God can guarantee or work in such a way to make it certain that his good purposes will triumph.

Another openness interpretation in relation to the question of God's wisdom is instructive here. I have in mind particularly Sanders's

---

[18] David Basinger, *The Case for Freewill Theism: A Philosophical Assessment* (Downers Grove, Ill.: InterVarsity, 1996), 92.

suggestion that God reassessed his decision to bring a flood upon the whole world, sensing the pain from that destruction to have been greater than the pain from the sin itself.[19] I see no other way to take this than as a suggestion that God in hindsight judged that he had made an enormous mistake. Granted, Sanders makes clear he believes that God was righteous in this judgment. Fine, but was he wise? Consider the magnitude of this mistake, if in fact God thought it so to be. The *whole world,* save a few people and animals, was deliberately killed by God in this action. Issues in human affairs could hardly get weightier than this. To think that God looked back and thought to himself, *This was too severe and I am not entirely sure I should have done it; in fact, I'll never do it again,* is nothing short of staggering! What confidence can we have in a God who must second-guess his own actions? What does this tell us about the wisdom of God's own plans? If God is not sure that what he does is best, can we be sure that he really knows what he is doing? The simple fact is that a God who can only speculate regarding what much of the future holds, at times second-guesses his own plans, can get things wrong, can falsely anticipate what may happen next, and may even repent of his own past conduct is a God unworthy of devotion, trust, and praise. What open theists have "gained" by their insistence on God as a risk-taker has been won at the expense of God's full wisdom, knowledge, trustworthiness, majesty, sovereignty, and glory; and it leads inevitably to doubt, worry, and fear regarding the fulfillment of God's plans. This surely is a case of trading in the family inheritance for plans to build a new home on attractively advertised but worthless swampland.

CONCLUSION

Both classical Arminian and Reformed theologies have affirmed with the orthodox heritage generally that there are no surprises awaiting God in the future. God does not gain knowledge through the passing of time, he does not second-guess his actions, he never wonders what may or may not occur, and he is never, never troubled by the question of the ulti-

---

[19] Sanders, *God Who Risks,* 50.

mate success of his purposes. He knows the end from the beginning, and he has told us in no uncertain terms what that future will be.

While various theological traditions within orthodoxy ground God's assurances of victory differently, all of these traditions affirm, without qualification, that the biblical revelation describing God's final triumph and picturing Satan as a condemned foe and the redeemed from every tribe, tongue, and nation before the throne is fixed, absolute, and certain. These are not guesses, projections, probabilities, or speculations. No, they are God's inviolable and certain word. Upon this we can fix our sure and certain hope. We must see this clearly: *Open theism stands against all theological traditions within orthodoxy in its proposal that the future is open.* And, with its open future comes, of necessity, doubt, worry, mistrust, fear, and ultimately, loss of faith.

The options are clear: classical theism's various theological models with their uniform conviction that the future, as revealed, is certain and secure; or open theism's celebration of that future's near and ultimate uncertainty. There is indeed much at stake. The two visions of God and of Christian hope are vastly different. May God be merciful. May he humble all of us. May we return afresh to his inerrant and inscripturated self-revelation, and may we behold, as never so clearly before, the matchless supremacy of his infinite knowledge, impeccable wisdom, and inviolable sovereignty—to the glory of God alone.

PART THREE

What Difference Does It Make in Daily Life?

Expressing God's Lesser Glory

7

Harm to the Christian's
Life of Prayer

Having considered some of the most important doctrinal areas central to and definitive of the open view of God and his relation to the world, we turn now to consider three main areas of practical application to the Christian life. The nature and practice of prayer, the importance of God's guidance and direction, and the Christian's response to suffering and pain are vitally important areas Christians struggle with, and they also are areas which define, in many ways, the nature of our relationship with God.

How and why we *pray* is a crucial question. Do we believe that prayer is effective? Do we believe that our prayers make a difference? How does God provide *guidance* for his people? Can we trust his leading and be confident that his direction is best? And how shall we interpret and make sense of terrible *suffering* in our and in others' lives? Is God at work to bring about good through all our suffering, or is suffering or pain sometimes simply an unavoidable and pointless by-product of this sinful and evil world?

Our purpose here is to assess open theism's proposal as it relates to these three test-case areas of practical Christian experience. Our assessment of the central doctrinal proposals of open theism has revealed serious deficiencies. Shall the same be true in the realm of Christian living as well? We begin by an examination in this chapter of the openness proposal in relation to prayer.[1] Chapters 8 and 9 follow with assessments

---

[1] A recent work, just released, offers sustained discussion of the open view of prayer along with several other leading models of divine providence in relation to prayer. See Terrance Tiessen, *Providence and Prayer: How Does God Work in the World?* (Downers Grove, Ill.: InterVarsity, 2000). The openness model is dealt with in chapters 4 and 5 of Tiessen's work.

of open theism's understanding of divine guidance and of the Christian's response to suffering.

THE ROLE OF PRAYER IN PROMOTING REAL RELATIONSHIP WITH GOD

Open theists are certainly right to seek to ground and embrace the *real relationship* between God and his human creatures, particularly his own people. Classical theism is vulnerable at this point and is in need of some correctives. However, the classical model *can* be modified and *can* sustain the real, vibrant, and reciprocal relationship between God and others.[2] What simply is wrong is the notion that, to uphold the real relatedness of God with others, one must adopt some newer version of freewill theism.

The openness model is itself vulnerable and fundamentally flawed in areas viewed by its supporters as displaying some of its strengths. Practical areas such as the role of prayer in the Christian life (and the same could be said for the nature of divine guidance and the Christian's response to suffering)—areas which openness advocates claim vindicate just how practically useful and spiritually beneficial their model is—are, in fact, problematic.

Every committed Christian wants to believe that prayer makes a difference. What is the point in praying if prayer itself turns out to be superfluous and ineffectual? Openness thinkers believe they have good news here for the Christian community. "Prayer matters!" is the message in brief.[3] How do we know? Because the future is not exhaustively foreknown by God and settled (i.e., there is no divine blueprint), and because God seeks to know our thoughts, concerns, longings, feelings, and requests, it follows that *all that we bring to God in prayer can truly make a difference to what happens in the future.* God often takes into account our prayers before he decides what to do. As initially appealing

---

[2] My own work on reformulating the doctrine of divine immutability (Bruce A. Ware, "An Evangelical Reformulation of the Doctrine of the Immutability of God," *Journal of the Evangelical Theological Society* 29, no. 4 [1986], 431-446) is a case in point in which I describe senses in which God is rightly thought to be immutable, and also senses in which he is rightly thought of as mutable. Obviously some reformulation of classical theism is involved here, but the end product is really only a variation and refinement of the classical model.

[3] See, e.g., John Sanders, *The God Who Risks: A Theology of Providence* (Downers Grove, Ill.: InterVarsity, 1998), 271, where he claims that "our prayers make a difference to God because of the personal relationship God enters into with us."

as this approach may sound, consider some difficulties attending to the nature of prayer as construed in open theism.

The Problem of Divine Omniscience

Oddly, even the truncated definition of divine omniscience defended in open theism is not trimmed quite enough when it comes to the question of the efficacy of prayer. As discussed earlier, openness thinkers propose that God has exhaustive knowledge of the past and present but not of the future. Since future free choices and actions cannot in principle be known, God cannot know them. Yet, he knows *all else*. And herein lies a problem. *It is strictly speaking impossible for human beings to inform God of their thoughts, concerns, longings, feelings, and requests.*

Concerning God's intimate knowledge of our inner thoughts and lives, Boyd writes, "Our omniscient Creator knows us perfectly, far better than we even know ourselves."[4] And even more forcefully, Boyd declares that God "knows the thoughts and intentions of all individuals perfectly and can play them out in his mind like an infinitely wise chess master anticipating every possible combination of moves his opponent could ever make."[5] And furthermore, because God knows *everything* past and present,[6] he already knows *anything and everything* his children would tell him in prayer.[7] Therefore, it becomes difficult to see how their prayers can influence God's decision-making process. Perhaps when people plead with God repeatedly, we might conclude that at least he learns more fully the seriousness of their longings over time. Although even here, since *God knows fully their thoughts and attitudes of heart* all the time prior to the times they come to him in prayer and, as we were just reminded, since *God anticipates fully every possible state of heart or mind we might have*, it seems that the openness proponent cannot rightly believe that he or she actually tells God anything in prayer that

---

[4] Gregory A. Boyd, *God of the Possible: A Biblical Introduction to the Open View of God* (Grand Rapids, Mich.: Baker, 2000), 35.

[5] Ibid., 152.

[6] Boyd (ibid.) affirms, "In the open view, God knows all possibilities and all probabilities (as well as all settled realities) perfectly."

[7] David Basinger ("Practical Implications," in Clark Pinnock, Richard Rice, John Sanders, William Hasker, and David Basinger, *The Openness of God: A Biblical Challenge to the Traditional Understanding of God* [Downers Grove, Ill.: InterVarsity, 1994], 165) writes concerning God that, "only he is aware of all the relevant factors, and only he is in a position to determine the best course(s) of action given these factors."

he does not already know and has not already fully anticipated. So the problem stands: God can gain no knowledge through prayer.

Some of the luster and appeal of the openness proposal is removed when one thinks carefully and deeply about the believer's relationship with God through prayer as portrayed in this model. The open view makes much of the dynamic nature of this relationship,[8] and yet if the truth were told, for every single prayer a believer would bring to the Lord, God could respond *every time* with, "I know . . . Yes, I know . . . Yes, I know . . . Yes, I know . . ."! But, of course, this is not at all how prayer is described in openness discussions. We rather are led to believe that God waits to hear what we think, that he learns what our thoughts are when we come to him, that he adjusts his plans only after learning from us what our longings are, and so on. The truth is, however, this is not how it works at all! God never learns what we think when we tell him in prayer. Because he knows us perfectly, he knows every thought we ever have had, he knows all our feelings and desires, and he can anticipate fully what we will be bringing to him in prayer.

If all this is true, what function does prayer really have? The answer to this question is crucial. Notice that, in open theism, prayer *can* function to foster a deeper relationship with God, it can bind us closer to God, and it can even reinforce the urgency or importance we attach to the requests we bring to him in prayer. But what prayer *cannot* do is instruct or inform God; it cannot literally bring to God new information in the dynamic interaction of our relationship with him, and hence our *prayers,* quite literally, can never be a basis by which God would learn something new from us and so change his mind. I am sure this is a disappointing realization to any inclined to open theism for the sake of its advertised dynamism of relationship with God, but on analysis it appears that open theism on this point either fails to recognize or purposely distorts the actual workings of the nature of our relationship with God in prayer.

To make this point clearer, it may help to consider our conversational relationships with one another and compare this with our prayers to God. As we speak with one another, we often (perhaps most often) do not know what the other people are thinking and so do not know

---

[8] See, e.g., Basinger, "Practical Implications," 160, where he commends the open view of God as being able "to maintain justifiably that divine activity is at times dependent on our freely offered petitions."

what they will say next. We do not have perfect knowledge of their inner psyches, emotions, desires, longings, thoughts, and aspirations. So, our relationship with one another is in fact quite dynamic. Both sides in such a relationship learn new information constantly as we speak to each other and reveal what is on our minds and hearts. But this is exactly what is lacking in our prayer relationship with God. Since God knows all and anticipates everything on the basis of his exhaustive knowledge of the past and present, we do not and cannot have the effect on him that we have on one another through our conversational relationships.

So, one might wonder, what would it take to make our prayer relationship with God match more closely the type of true, dynamic, mutually learning relationship we have with each other that is upheld in open theism? It is simple. We would only have to deny of God not only his exhaustive knowledge of the future but also of the past and present. If God did not already know everything about us and anticipate what we would say or do next, then we really and literally could tell him things he did not already know, and then our relationship with him would have that true quality of give and take, instructing and learning, that we experience at the human level.

If people really want to ground the type of dynamic and mutually learning, interactive relationship with God in prayer that openness advocates often commend, this will require an even further departure from orthodoxy, as exhaustive divine present and past knowledge is denied. It will result in both an even loftier elevation of human significance and an even greater diminishing of the richness, fullness, grandeur, and glory that is God's alone. For the sake of commending what amounts to a largely *human model of personal relationship,* the openness approach, if consistent, leads toward a view in which God is brought down increasingly to our level. In response, we must say, let God be God, and may our relationship with him, including our relationship in prayer, be the *distinctive God-human relationship* he so designed.

The Problem of Divine Wisdom

Two quite different problems arise for open theism when considering the common Christian conviction that God is supremely wise. First, closely tied to the above problem is the fact that God, being God, is in a much better position than are his finite creatures to know what is likely best in any given situation. Openness advocates make it sound so commendable that God will listen to us and make his decisions based in part on what he hears from us in prayer. However, when one considers that *only God* (and not us) knows all that can be known, and *only God* (and not us) has unsurpassable wisdom to discern what is best in any situation, and *only God* (and not us) has purity of motives and freedom from the distortion of sinful perspectives and urgings, and *only God* (and not us) is in the optimal situation to judge the probable effects of a decision on other people, situations, future developments, and kingdom purposes, it begins to make one wonder why it is so wonderful that "divine activity is at times dependent on our freely offered petitions."[9]

Given the supremacy of God in all these relevant ways, and given the deeply sinful and vastly limited perspectives we bring to the table, do we really want God to do what *we* think he should do? Again, the truth of the matter simply is that, because God's knowledge and wisdom is vastly superior to ours, we would be utter and absolute fools to want God to wait to "hear from us first" before he decides what is best to do. If we truly want what is best, we will yield to his judgment every time. We will humbly disabuse ourselves of this silly (at best) and deeply pretentious and offensively arrogant (at worst) notion that somehow we possess some special insight or perspective or desire or plan that we must inform God about before he decides what is best to do. What fools we can be! By analogy (and a very weak one, at that), what folly we would ascribe to the financial novice who continually offered urgent investment directives that were contrary to the best judgment of his highly successful and experienced investment advisor.

Or, consider the reverse side of the same problem. Would it not be an indictment of God's wisdom were he to follow advice (i.e., in prayer) that he believed was wrong or at least misguided? That is, would not God be a fool to listen to his people and follow their longings, thoughts, and prayers when he knew that another course of action would be better? Consider that, since God is supremely wise (even in the deficient form of this concept found in open theism), he will know one of two things when we bring to him our petitions: 1) he will know that what we are asking is

---

[9] Basinger, "Practical Implications," 160.

in some way *inferior to* the plan and purpose he already knows is best; or 2) he will know that what we are asking *matches* the plan and purpose that he already knew to be best. In a given case, then, if God does what we ask him to do, he will either do what he knew already is best, in which case our prayer did not inform or direct him, or he will follow our desires and do what he knows is less than the best. In such a case, since God knows better, *he would act as a fool were he to carry out our wishes.*

In this whole discussion, one prevailing, all-important truth must be honored. *Scripture makes clear that we simply cannot counsel God.* That is, regardless of whether we act as fools in wanting God to hear first from us or whether God would be a fool to listen to our misguided prayers and act accordingly, in one sense this is a moot point. The Bible declares that part of what it means for God to be God is precisely this: *No one has ever been his counselor or has ever informed him!* The words of Isaiah 40:13-14 are so apt at this point:

> Who has directed the Spirit of the LORD,
> Or as His counselor has informed Him?
> With whom did He consult
>   and who gave Him understanding?
> And who taught Him in the path of justice
>   and taught Him knowledge?
> And informed Him of the way of understanding?

Clearly, each of these rhetorical questions requires "no one" as its answer. Just how completely absurd it is to imagine giving knowledge or insight to God is stressed in the verses that follow. Verse 15 begins, "Behold, the nations are like a drop from a bucket, and are regarded as a speck of dust on the scales." Imagine this! The nations as a whole with all of their collective knowledge, wisdom, and insight, all taken together, constitute before God "a drop from a bucket" or "a speck of dust on the scales." How lofty we consider our great learning and wisdom, but how utterly insignificant it is before God. In contrast to the openness view of God taking into consideration what we think before he decides, the humbling truth is this: What we can contribute to God's store of knowledge or wisdom is, in a word, nothing.

Surely it is precisely *because* of God's infinite knowledge, wisdom, and purity of character that Jesus instructs his disciples to pray, "Your kingdom come, *Your will be done,* on earth as it is in heaven" (Matt. 6:10, emphasis added). Jesus' mindset is exactly the opposite of that indicated by openness thinkers. Prayer is not a means by which the will of God is shaped in the historical moment, as if God hears and takes into account what we bring to him and only then, at that moment, forms his will. To the contrary, we should view the will of God as a *previously existing reality,* already formed and perfectly wise. We pray not to contribute to the shaping of an evolving divine will but to align ourselves with the purposes and directives of a will so perfect and wise and fully informed that we would be fools to attempt to alter it, were that even possible. The presupposition of all healthy, humble, God-honoring petitionary prayer is not "Your will be *formed,*" but, "Your will be *done.*"

To summarize, God already knows all that can be known, and he alone has unsurpassable discernment regarding what is best to do. We, on the other hand, have extremely limited knowledge, warped perceptions, and sinful inclinations. Since all of these tenets are affirmed in open theism, much of the glitter seems to have fallen off the banner announcing the divine dependency on our freely offered petitions.

Second, an opposite kind of problem attaches to the relation of prayer and the divine wisdom. While openness thinkers hold that God's wisdom is unsurpassable, they also hold that God is capable of getting things wrong. In fact, since God does not know any aspect of the future that relates in the slightest to free creaturely choices and actions,[10] every belief of his about that future is potentially wrong. That is, whatever belief God may have about some future free creaturely decision may prove to have been mistaken once the actual free decision is made.

As noted elsewhere in this book, openness proponents point to Jeremiah 3:7 and 32:35 for biblical support for the notion that God can have mistaken beliefs. They also cite God's disappointing choice of Saul as evidence that God can truly regret decisions he makes (1 Sam. 15:11, 35). Added to this is the fact that God may, as Sanders suggests happened in regard to the flood,[11] also reassess what he himself has done and judge

---

[10] Basinger, ibid., 163, writes (presumably for the five authors of *The Openness of God* volume) that, "since we believe that God can know only what can be known and that what humans will freely do in the future cannot be known beforehand, we believe that God can never know with certainty what will happen in any context involving freedom of choice."

[11] Sanders, *God Who Risks,* 50. See the discussion on this interpretation in chapter 6.

that it was not the best thing to do. All this results in a view of God in which we have reason to doubt whether God's perspective is best and whether his will should be followed. After all, what if God is wrong about things that matter to our own future? No doubt he means well and no doubt he wants what is best, but the lingering doubt is raised: *What if God is wrong?* Lest the reader think that this is unfair to the openness position, consider the strikingly honest words of David Basinger:

> [S]ince God does not necessarily know exactly what will happen in the future, it is always possible that even that which God in his unparalleled wisdom believes to be the best course of action at any given time may not produce the anticipated results in the long run.[12]

Prayers, then, that are founded on the presupposition, "Your will be done," begin to falter. Perhaps when things work out badly, we might wonder if God got it wrong again here as he did in other cases. And perhaps in the midst of agonizing disappointment, given this paradigm of the relation between prayer and God's fallibility with respect to the future, an earnest but troubled believer might even contemplate praying, "Father, I forgive You for You know not what You do."[13] Is this too harsh an assessment of where the openness position leads? No, rather it exposes just how contrary to fundamental biblical truths and how demeaning to God's infinite wisdom and glory this proposal is.

In summary, although the above two problems are very different kinds of problems, both result from an honest application of the openness proposal. Oddly enough, the openness view understands God as *sufficiently* wise (i.e., always more knowledgeable and wiser than we are) to make its claim of his dependence on our freely offered petitions a shallow one; yet it does not understand him as *perfectly* wise, thus robbing us of complete and unquestioning confidence in him. Or put more simply, God is *too wise* to need or benefit from our help, but *not wise enough* to remove all doubt or lack of confidence in him. Prayer, then,

---

[12] Basinger, "Practical Implications," 165.

[13] This telling rephrasing of Jesus' prayer was suggested to me by a seminary student critical of this implication of the openness view.

suffers from opposite kinds of problems because the God-concept of open theism suffers from such unfortunate distortion.

The Problem of Divine Love

Another striking difficulty with the openness conception of prayer relates particularly to petitionary prayer. This problem can be seen when two deeply held tenets of the openness view are placed side by side. First, open theists hold, along with other Arminians, that God's love for people is impartial, equal, universal, and perfect. God plays no favorites and loves everyone with a pure and selfless longing for their best.[14] Second, human prayers make a difference in whether God acts and in what God decides to do. Our prayers may be a basis of bringing about good that would not have occurred had we not prayed; correspondingly, our failure to pray may result in God withholding some good which he wanted to give and knew would be best to give.

Once again, it appears that the openness position rests on the horns of a dilemma. If it is true that God's love is impartial and perfect, does it stand to reason that God might choose to give or withhold some good gift to people on the basis of whether or not they pray? The problem here is less severe when it is a matter of God helping one of his children learn the lesson that he or she will only receive certain gifts when prayer has first been offered. Just as a loving parent may withhold some good thing from a child until the child's attitude is right, so too God may want one of his children to learn to pray humbly as the basis for receiving his gifts. Nevertheless, one still wonders, even in this case, how loving it would be for God to *continue* withholding, due to our negligence in prayer, what he knows we desperately need.

The problem seems especially severe, however, in relation to petitionary prayer on behalf of others. Are we to imagine that God will withhold some good gift from another person because of *our* failure to pray? How far can this be extended? How long may God withhold the good he knows one person needs just because another person is negligent or disobedient in praying? Yet, as David Basinger indicates, some propo-

---

[14] David Basinger ("In What Sense Must God Be Omnibenevolent?" *International Journal for Philosophy of Religion* 14 [1983], 3) argues that it is important to maintain "that an omnibenevolent God is obligated to maximize the quality of life for those beings he chooses to create."

nents of the openness model "see no necessary incompatibility in affirming both that God always seeks what is best for each of us and that God may at times wait to exert all the noncoercive influence that he can justifiably exert on a given person until requested to do so by another person."[15] I wonder how it will stand with some people one day when they realize that God withheld from them gifts he knew would be for their best and longed for them to have, and he did so because "friends" of theirs failed to pray as they ought to have. One would think that, if God truly loves all equally and impartially, he would not diminish the good he knows is best for someone because of another's negligence or disobedience in prayer.

Other openness proponents (including Basinger) argue, rather, that "God would never refrain from intervening beneficially in one person's life simply because someone else has failed to request that he do so."[16] Clearly, this position is consistent with the view of God's impartial and perfect love so elevated by open theists. But now it appears that the efficacy of petitionary prayer is jeopardized. Certainly petitionary prayer can still function to encourage the one who prays for another as God grants that for which one prayed. But in such a case what was granted was simply the good he would have given anyway, even if no prayer had been offered. One can no longer say, then, that there is a causal relation between our prayers for others and what God does on their behalf. Petitionary prayer cannot be efficacious, strictly speaking. So, the dilemma faced is clear. Either God's impartial and perfect love is maintained without compromise at the cost of the efficacy of prayer (for God will do what is best regardless of whether or not people pray); or it really does matter whether or not we pray for others (i.e., petitionary prayer is efficacious), but only at the expense of compromising the impartial and perfect love of God for all.

The Problem of Divine Power

What is it that one asks God to *do,* in an openness perspective? Since, according to this perspective, the power God has in relation to his free

---

[15] Basinger, "Practical Implications," 161. Basinger indicates that Hasker and Sanders hold this position.

[16] Basinger, ibid. Cf. David Basinger, "Petitionary Prayer: A Response to Murray and Meyers," *Religious Studies* 31 (1979), 475-484.

creatures is fundamentally his power of persuasion, one's prayers on another's behalf must be for God to work in a persuasive way to accomplish what one believes is best. But, since God's power of persuasion cannot necessarily succeed in guaranteeing the desired outcome, one must realize how very much God's power is limited and stifled by human freedom. As in the three areas already discussed, the openness theology of prayer faces the horns of a dilemma in relation to God's power.

First, if we truly believe when we pray on another's behalf that God *can* work decisively in that person's heart so that God can *guarantee* that the person will choose what God wants, then this view of prayer calls into question the reality of *libertarian freedom* so cherished in open theism. As discussed earlier, libertarian freedom is the notion that we are free if and only if, for any choice we make, and given the identical set of conditions in which we made that choice, we could have chosen differently. If libertarian freedom is the kind of freedom we have, then it simply is not the case that God can work in such a way that he can guarantee that we will freely do what he wants us to do. If we are free, then even if we did follow God's prompting, we could have chosen differently. And if we could have chosen differently, then God cannot guarantee the result. But if God works in a way that assures success, at least one can affirm the efficacy of prayer! We can know that when our prayers accord with the will of God to accomplish something he guarantees will occur, our prayers will be answered.

But second, if we truly believe that when we pray on another's behalf, God cannot work *decisively* in another's heart and so cannot *guarantee* that the person will choose what both we and God would want, then this view of prayer calls into question the effectiveness of prayer so cherished in open theism. If we know God cannot penetrate the stubborn heart of an individual, if we know God cannot soften and move decisively the free will of another person, then are we not asking God to do something he simply cannot do? Or if we believe, as discussed above, that God loves all perfectly and so would already be working in every way he could for their good, then would we not wonder what is the point of prayer? What are we asking God for that he is not already doing? Do I care about this person more than God does? Of course the answer is no. So, is not God already working in ways far better than anything I can imagine in order to accomplish his purposes? And yet, if God ultimately cannot break through the stubbornness, apathy, and misconceptions of free moral creatures, then all this calls for the question, What really, then, is the point of prayer?

The open theists' view of God's limited power, as with his limited knowledge, limited wisdom, and hence limited glory, all portrays a god very different from the God of the Bible. Recall the words of Nebuchadnezzar: "[God] does according to His will in the host of heaven and among the inhabitants of earth; and no one can ward off His hand or say to Him, 'What have You done?'" (Dan. 4:35). Sadly, open theism has once again adjusted its view of God to be culturally appealing at the expense of biblical fidelity. But in the end, even this attempt will not succeed. The inner conflicts are of such a magnitude that the model is in peril. May God in his mercy help us all to come humbly back to him.

CONCLUSION

It is evident, then, that one of open theism's most highly touted elements—its understanding and practice of prayer—is in fact embroiled in major conceptual and practical difficulties. Dilemmas are faced on several fronts. Either God's knowledge of the past and present is truly exhaustive, in which case we literally cannot in prayer instruct God of anything that he does not already know; or we honor the notion of true give-and-take relationship seriously and deny of God even more than has already been denied of him, as we risk proposing his limited knowledge of the past and present as well as of the future. Either God's wisdom is so much more vast than ours that it is silly and foolish for us to want seriously for God to wait to hear from us before he decides; or we take seriously the notion of God waiting to hear from us, in which case God is faced with the options of disregarding what we think or of going against his best judgment in order to honor our wishes. Either God is truly wise, in which case his decisions and actions are always right and good, and he makes no mistakes and so never has to "repent" of his past actions; or God repents (literally), showing that his wisdom is fallible, his judgment impaired, and his decisions sometimes untrustworthy. Either God loves us perfectly and as such will always seek to do what is best for his creatures, in which case the efficacy of prayer is called into question; or God waits until we pray before he bestows his favors on us and others,

in which case we wonder how God could truly love us and others unconditionally and yet withhold from them good gifts just because of our own
failure or negligence in prayer. Either God's power is such that he really
can act in ways that accomplish his purposes in the lives of others, in
which case their supposed libertarian freedom is called into question; or
God's power is limited so that he cannot accomplish what he and others
would like him to, in which case the efficacy of prayer seems fully
thwarted.

When one considers these weighty problems, it is apparent that
open theism's theology of prayer is practically and existentially unwork-
able. Either way one goes on so many important matters, serious problems result for the openness model. When one couples the theological
problems we have observed in the previous chapters with these serious
practical concerns, one has strong reason to question the viability of the
openness model. As we consider next open theism's handling of the
question of divine guidance, and then of how suffering is accounted for,
we shall see a continuing pattern of deeply troubling practical implications that flow out of a deeply flawed understanding of God and his relationship to the world.

8

Weakening of Our Confidence in God's Guidance

Every committed Christian wants to believe that God's will is best. If we cannot have confidence in God's will, where can we turn? If we cannot entrust our lives, the lives of our families, and our very futures to God's perfect oversight and direction, how shall we avoid chronic anxiety and fear over what lies ahead? If we wonder whether God knows for sure what he is doing, and if we doubt that his will and ways are always best, why should we trust him instead of simply following our own instincts, thoughts, and desires in charting out our futures? And yet it should be apparent from our discussion in the preceding chapters that, in the open view, believers do have serious reason to wonder whether God is right in his leading and whether his will ought to be followed.

Central Openness Tenets Relating to Divine Guidance

I will review six summary statements of central openness tenets that relate in a particular way to divine guidance. The first three are principles that have caused many to wonder if open theism has any room for a genuine and vibrant concept of divine guidance; the latter three provide openness commitments that are meant to reassure us that the problem is not as great as might first be thought.

First, topping the list of course, is the openness denial of exhaustive divine foreknowledge. Since God cannot know any future free actions of his moral creatures, he is seriously limited in his ability to make plans and give direction for the future. So much of the future is entirely unknown to God, and so much of that future is contingent and unpredictable. Obviously, then, divine guidance must be considered largely in the realm of possibilities and, at best, probabilities; but it offers to believers little of real certainty.

Second, and related, open theists hold that God cannot control the free actions of his moral creatures. An uncompromising commitment to libertarian freedom renders it impossible, in their model, for God to guarantee or ensure that some wise purpose of his will indubitably be accomplished, so long as any aspect of its accomplishment involves a future free creaturely choice or action. Again, it is apparent that God's guidance is severely limited because so very much of the future is affected by future free choices and actions over which God has no regulative control.[1]

Third, God constantly reassesses his own beliefs and prior actions as he learns new things from what transpires as the future unfolds moment by moment. As God learns, there may be many times when he reevaluates his decisions, reassesses the choices he has made, corrects mistaken beliefs he held in the past, and recognizes that what he thought was wise and best now appears to be flawed. As this relates to divine guidance, it should be clear that the believer must always recognize that, in following God's leading, it may in fact turn out that God's direction misfired, as it were. Just as we often realize, in the light of new information, that the decisions we made were not best, so God faces this same stubborn reality, and so our following his leading enters into this same unavoidable uncertainty.

Fourth, topping the list of open theism's tenets meant to reassure us on the issue of divine guidance is its commitment to the unconditional and uncompromising love of God for his creatures. We can always be assured that God wants our best and that his motive in providing guidance is one of genuine and deep love. Unlike versions of classical theism in which God controls the future and so intentionally leads us into suffering or tragedy,[2] believers in the God of open theism can know that

---

[1] Some open theists allow for times that God may unilaterally control some otherwise free action in order to ensure the outcome he desires. But, on openness criteria of human freedom, whenever and wherever this occurs, the freedom of the individual has been precluded by the unilateral control of God. Openness advocates are reluctant to appeal to this type of situation very often for the obvious reasons that God would then trivialize his bestowing of freedom on his creatures, the operation of the world becomes less natural and normal, and the extent of divine determination of actions and events is increased.

[2] See chapter 9, where this issue is taken up.

God in his love always and only wants to enhance their well-being and to keep them from such suffering and pain.

Fifth, even though God does not know much of the future, he does know the past and present *exhaustively.* He possesses a far greater grasp of the relevant facts than we do, and so we can be confident that God's leading will be based on the best and only complete set of relevant information available.

Sixth and finally, even though God cannot control the future free choices and actions of his moral creatures, he nonetheless is eminently resourceful and extremely capable. God, we are told, is able to devise many creative avenues to see to it that his purposes are fulfilled. No divine blueprint is necessary for assurances that God's will is largely upheld. Divine guidance may generally be taken as reliable because God is unsurpassed in his ability to work out his purpose and direction for our lives.

CONCEIVING CORRECTLY THE NATURE OF DIVINE GUIDANCE

How shall we assess the question of whether we can rightly place full confidence in God's guidance, in light of these seemingly conflicting sets of beliefs in open theism? Openness advocates suggest that part of our problem here is that, through much of the tradition of the church, we have thought wrongly about "knowing the will of God." We should not, they say, think of God's will as some single purpose in each and every situation such that if we miss that purpose we are outside of his will.[3] Rather, we need to understand that God's will is evolving, not fixed. As God learns more about what occurs through time, his will becomes more informed than it was previously. And as a result, we must be open to changes in God's will—mid-course corrections, you might say. The hope that God actually knows *now* what is best for us, in light of what will occur *far ahead in the future,* is unfounded and hence unfair for us to expect of him. The most we can hope for is that God's will offers us the best plan, as God fallibly foresees it, for the *present.* David Basinger writes:

> [W]e must acknowledge that divine guidance, from our perspective, cannot be considered a means of discovering exactly what

---

[3] John Sanders, *The God Who Risks: A Theology of Providence* (Downers Grove, Ill.: InterVarsity, 1998), 275.

will be best in the long run—as a means of discovering the very best long-term option. Divine guidance, rather, must be viewed primarily as a means of determining what is best for us now.[4]

In open theism, then, divine guidance must be understood as *evolving*, not fixed; and as *relative* in its level of accuracy, not uniform. Increased knowledge results in the need to make changes in direction, thus accounting for the evolving nature of God's guidance. And, because the distant future has so many more unknown and unpredictable variables and contingencies than does the immediate future, the probabilities of God's guidance being on target, as it were, are far greater in the near than in the distant future. Consideration should be given to each of these features, to see their effect on our question of confidence in God's guidance.

First, if God's guidance evolves, then at any point when one receives guidance from God *one may question from the very outset whether his direction is in fact best.* We all have experienced many times the problem of making decisions which turned out to be harmful to us or others because we did not know future developments which, had we known them, would have led us to decide differently. Now, according to open theism, we realize that God is in this same position. Every bit of counsel he gives, to every person, in every situation, of necessity lacks vital information that he has no access to because that information is located in an unknown future. There simply is no way to dodge this. Yes, it is comforting to know that God loves us and wants our best. And yes, it helps to know that God knows the past and present exhaustively and is resourceful in accomplishing his purposes. But the fact remains that an evolving kind of divine guidance *is* evolving *precisely because it must compensate and adjust for new information.* To the extent that this new information is relevant to the counsel given in the past, yet that new information could not have been known when the past counsel was offered, it follows that one simply cannot trust God's counsel and guidance with anything like unqualified confidence. The belief that God sim-

---

[4] David Basinger, "Practical Implications," in Clark Pinnock, Richard Rice, John Sanders, William Hasker, and David Basinger, *The Openness of God: A Biblical Challenge to the Traditional Understanding of God* (Downers Grove, Ill.: InterVarsity, 1994), 163.

ply might be wrong, despite his longing to provide guidance that is right, cannot help but create some measure of distrust of God's counsel. Furthermore, if divine guidance is an evolving reality, it would seem that one would need regularly to *keep seeking* God's leading on each specific question or burden, even if one had sensed strongly just what the Lord's leading was on that matter. One might receive confidence from the Lord that he was leading in a particular direction, but due to the evolving nature of God's guidance, one would never be able to settle in, simply accept this course of action as God's direction, and live with peace and confidence that one was within God's will. A lingering question that any conscientious Christian would regularly raise is, "Has God's will in this matter changed? Can I be sure I should still be going in this direction?" Even if one had initial assurance, because the unfolding future brings new information to God, who knows but that God may now think this is not the best way to go after all? The effect of all this is to undermine confidence in God's leading *even when that leading was initially received with strong assurance.*

Related to the above problem is this: How should you interpret the difficulties that may come into your life or ministry after following what you believed was God's will? We've all heard advice such as, "When trials mount, the only thing that gets you out of bed some mornings is knowing God called and led you to be there." But since God's guidance is an evolving matter, perhaps God was unaware of the trials you are now experiencing, and had he known about them he would not have led you to be where you are. How can you tell whether to persevere in difficulty? How can you be confident that it is God's will for you to stay? The fact that God led you to this specific place may not at all indicate that he intended for you to endure the hardship here, if he did not know this was part of the leading he was giving you. The only way one could be confident of God's leading in the midst of hardship is if *he knew* that *God knew* that these trials were part and parcel of the place God had called him to serve. Once God's advance knowledge of the hardships is removed, so too is confidence in God's leading undermined.

It is evident that the evolving nature of God's guidance, a necessary feature of the openness model, cannot sustain vibrant, consistent, enduring, unqualified, and fully confident trust in that guidance. Should not this feature, in and of itself, tell us that something is fundamentally wrong with the openness model? And we have yet to consider the other feature Basinger discusses. What are the implications for confidence in God's guidance from the notion that God is relatively more accurate with short-range than with long-range guidance? Consider a few observations.

First, is it not the case that many, if not most, of the weightiest decisions we have to make in life have long-range implications? The agonizing questions nearly all Christian people struggle with are predominantly long-range questions. What career would be best for me and for my service in the kingdom? What college should I attend? Should I marry; and if so, whom? Shall I get involved in this ministry instead of another, and would this be the best use of my gifts? Should I consider a short-term missions trip to explore whether God would have me serve him overseas? Should we have children now or wait, and how many children should we have? And on and on and on. All of these questions have in common the sobering reality that whatever path is taken, in whatever direction, the decision will have a major impact on much of one's future life.

Amazingly, if we follow openness counsel here, we are told that we should not expect reliable and accurate guidance from God on any of these long-range matters. At least in terms of the specific question, "What is the best path to follow *now* in light of my long-range *future* ministry, contribution, and service?" open theism tells us that God cannot really help much. To say that God is pretty good at short-range guidance but can't really handle long-range direction is to say that, concerning the *weightiest decisions we make* in our lives, God has little if any solid help to give. Surely this only discourages greatly what the Bible commends throughout: trusting God implicitly with all of our lives.

Second, Basinger claims that God is much better with guidance for the present. God's accuracy, he states, is significantly higher in "determining what is best for us now." On analysis, however, one wonders just how significant this is. Matters that affect *just the present moment* but do not have long-range implications are usually fairly trivial. Shall I drive this way to work or another way? Shall I have a bowl of soup for lunch or eat a bagel? Shall I wear my oxford blue shirt or the pinstriped one? If your response is, these are not really things on which we would seek God's guidance anyway, then you are getting the point. Nearly[5] any immediate concern that is *significant and important* will be so because of its impact on the *future*. But in these matters, according to open theism, God cannot give the kind of help we need most. In contrast, those matters in life which relate *merely to the present* and have no significant impact on the future are usually fairly *inconsequential*. But in these matters, says open theism, God can help quite well! (Our response might well be, "Thanks, but no thanks.") Yet, on those weighty matters on which much depends for many years to come, God is not able to offer reliable counsel. If God's direction is reliable for short-range and inconsequential decisions while increasingly unreliable for longer-range and weightier ones, what genuine confidence can we rightly place in God? This truly is the God of lesser glory, because of his lesser knowledge, lesser wisdom, lesser discernment, lesser ability, lesser reliability, and lesser guidance. And how can the God of lesser glory but fail to elicit from his people lesser confidence? No, this is not the God of the Bible. This is not the God who inspired the confidence and faith of Noah, Abraham, Isaac, Jacob, Joseph, Moses, Joshua, David, Hezekiah, Ezekiel, Daniel, Isaiah, Jesus, Paul, Peter, and John, the same God who also longs to inspire in us uncompromising allegiance, unfailing hope, and undiminished confidence and trust. The God of the Bible is the God of greater glory, the One upon whom we trust every moment of every day, knowing that his ways are absolutely perfect.

Partnering with God in Planning Our Lives

If God cannot be trusted for guidance "in the long run," and if his guidance evolves to make needed corrections, what commends this model of divine guidance to thoughtful, prayerful Christians? Essentially, the

---

[5] There are, of course, some immediate concerns of great magnitude which *may not* have long-range implications. For example, some morally significant decisions (e.g., truth telling, promise keeping, resisting temptation, etc.) may be weighty in respect to their importance in God's sight regardless of whether or not any future consequence stems from the decision made. But even here, it is impossible to know that such weighty immediate decisions in fact do *not* have long-range implications and consequences. Therefore, even though in principle there may be highly significant immediate concerns for which there is no significant future impact, one can never know that this is the case, and so one must consider whether even these concerns may, in unforeseen ways, affect one's future.

attraction of this model is its emphasis on God as lover, counselor, and friend. The openness God works *with* us in forming his will *for* us. This model is repelled by the notion of divine authoritarianism. Since the will of God is shaped and reshaped moment by moment by a God who values our thoughts and desires, we can be confident that our input is given full attention. Regarding the partnering nature of divine guidance, Sanders writes:

> It is God's desire that we enter into a give-and-take relationship of love, and this is not accomplished by God's forcing his blueprint on us. Rather, God wants us to go through life together with him, making decisions together. Together we decide the actual course of my life. God's will for my life does not reside in a list of specific activities but in a personal relationship. As lover and friend, God works with us wherever we go and whatever we do. To a large extent our future is open and we are to determine what it will be in dialogue with God.[6]

The response I propose here to this conception of our life with God is made with genuine love for my openness friends. This is my heart, and I wish you to know it. Yet, for the sake of the honor of God, to whom I owe my only absolute love and loyalty, I must endeavor to express to the best of my ability how deeply and fundamentally abhorrent this perspective of our life with God is. Perhaps the best place to begin in showing this is with the example of Jesus and the mindset with which he lived his life in relationship to his Father. Would it be correct to characterize Jesus' perception of his life as open, so that he determined what the course of his life would be in dialogue with God his Father?

Consider one passage as illustrative of the prevailing tone of Jesus' self-understanding. In John 8 Jesus says, "He who has sent Me is true; and the things which I heard from Him, these I speak to the world" (8:26); "I do nothing on My own initiative, but I speak these things as the Father taught Me" (8:28); and, "I always do the things that are pleasing to Him" (8:29). In striking contrast with the openness model

---

[6] Sanders, *God Who Risks,* 277.

of life lived with God, Jesus does not depict some sort of mutual dialogue with his Father by which the two, together, come to common agreement on the actual course of his life. Rather, Jesus says here what he says so many times and in so many ways: He came precisely and only *to do the will of his Father.* Life lived with God, for Jesus, was not one of joint agreement and mutual determination. No! The Father sent, Jesus came; the Father led, Jesus followed; the Father spoke, Jesus listened; the Father directed, Jesus obeyed; the Father decreed, Jesus died.

Even in that agonizing last night in the garden, the night when Sanders has said that the Father and the Son determined together that Jesus would go to the cross,[7] Jesus ended his prayers by saying, "not My will, but Yours be done" (Luke 22:42). Clearly, his deepest desire was to do the will of his Father, even while he had a lesser yet fully understandable desire to avoid the cross if that were at all possible (hence, the earlier part of the prayer, "If You are willing, remove this cup from Me"). But being reassured in prayer that this was indeed God's will, he submitted fully and did so with joy (Heb. 12:2)! There is no hint of mutual determination here. Jesus *obeyed* the Father when he chose to submit to the Father's will and give himself over to those who would crucify him. He was, as Paul would put it, "obedient to the point of death, even death on a cross" (Phil. 2:8). From the beginning to the very end, Jesus always and only sought one thing. In every word, thought, attitude, and deed he sought to fulfill one goal. In everything, throughout his entire life, he sought this alone: that he would *do the will of his Father.* His prayer to his Father, nearing the end of his life, reveals the wonder of this accomplishment. Jesus humbly says, "I glorified You on the earth, having accomplished the work which You have given Me to do" (John 17:3).

Observe one other remarkable feature in John 8. Directly following Jesus' statements of utter *dependence upon* and absolute *obedience to* God (e.g., "I do nothing on My own initiative"), he then proceeds to instruct his listeners on living the life of true *freedom.* His words here are well-known: "If you continue in My word, then you are truly disciples of Mine; and you will know the truth, and the truth will make you free" (8:31-32). One might question, "What right does this man have

[7] Ibid., 100-101.

to instruct anyone about living in *freedom?*" After all, he has just said that he never does anything on his own initiative but only speaks the words that he has been taught; and that he seeks not to please himself but he always and only seeks to please another. This is not freedom, some would reason; this is absolute bondage!

And so we learn our lesson. Freedom in Scripture is a full world-view away from our culture's conception of freedom. True freedom, according to Jesus, is living life *his* way. This is not a life of mutually deciding with God what is best; rather, it is a life of listening to God and learning from him what is best. Freedom is not our choosing, in relationship with God, what we together agree upon; rather, it is submitting humbly to the absolute and undisputed authority of God over our lives in order to discern his will for us. Freedom, in other words, is our bondage to the will and ways of God as the only course of life that is good and right and satisfying (cf. Rom. 6:15-23).

Herein lies one of the deepest and most distressing implications of the open view of God. In an attempt to heighten the relationality of God with us, open theists have elevated our human importance and demoted God. God is *one with us,* a *companion* on life's journey. He is a listener and a learner as much as he is a consultant and advisor. We are fellow travelers with God, offering *our* input and enjoying the realization that *our* ideas, feelings, and desires are significant in charting the course of our lives, jointly decided in conjunction *with* God and not *by* him alone. In all of this, a terrible distortion of enormous proportion has taken place.

The words of Isaiah 40:13-17 that we considered earlier again ring out an indictment against the human pretense and arrogance, and corresponding demoting and belittling of the divine, that is spawned by the openness proposal. Who can inform the Lord? asks the prophet. Who can be his counselor? With whom does God consult and who contributes knowledge to him? And the answers to these questions graphically indicate that neither we nor the total collection of humanity taken as a whole can make any contribution whatsoever to the fullness and majestic glory of the infinite power, knowledge, and wisdom that is God's alone.

What possesses open theists to revel in the notion and think it good that God waits to make up his mind until he hears from us? Why would one ever think that it is a *benefit* to us that God takes into account what we think as he decides what is best? How can it be *better* that God and I decide my future *together*, rather than leaving this altogether in God's infinitely wise and perfect hands? *Who do we think we are?* Why have we come to think that we have something—anything—that could make a difference to God's wise purposes for our lives? What fools we are to take to ourselves what is God's alone. How impoverished is the resultant relationship we have with him, and how detrimental this is to our life of faith.

Open theism robs God twice. It first strips away from God divine qualities of infinite knowledge, perfect wisdom, and uncontested power that are God's alone and by which God robes himself in majestic glory and supreme majesty over all that he has made. In doing this, the open view likewise clothes us with garments stolen from the wardrobe of deity, that we might take to ourselves supposed and self-imposed significance, worth, importance, independence, heightened value, and, through all of this, human glory. As we put on coverings of *our* choosing, *our* deciding, *our* planning, *our* contributing, *our* participation, we seek that all who observe what is done in our partnership with God may boast, then, in God *and man*.

Divine demotion and human elevation work together in open theism. They are twins, born of the same womb, conceived in the same sin of human pride. Illicit human honor is bred with divine dishonor, so that the honor shown to man is achieved only at the expense of the honor owed to God alone. And what will God say of this view which so robs him of his rightful and exclusive claim to infinite glory (Isa. 42:8)? Our only right response is to repent, fall on our faces, and cry for mercy.

The impact of this view on our question of divine guidance then is enormous. Open theism does to the believer's confidence in God's leading what the incoming tide does to a beautifully crafted and elaborate sand castle. Little by little, room by room, wall by wall, the surety of our faith is swept away. We can hardly tell any longer what was there before. The God we once thought of as trustworthy sadly regrets even his own mistakes. The One in whom we placed our unquestioning confidence now changes his mind to improve a well-intended yet faulty plan. The hope we had for complete victory now is replaced with a question mark hanging over our lives like a black, billowy thundercloud over an out-door wedding.

When all is said and done, does it not seem clear that, while suppos-edly "gaining" God-as-friend-through-life, one has simultaneously lost God-as-Lord-over-life? When facing rough waters on the open sea, it is nice to know that you have a friend. But as the waters get ever rougher and the ship begins to veer, it is even nicer if your friend knows how to navigate the ship in order to get you safely and surely to your distant, unseen destination.

CONCLUSION

Over the centuries, innumerable Christians have been deeply comforted by the realization that, whatever difficulties they face, they can know that God has good and wise purposes, often including distant purposes, that he is fulfilling. Furthermore, they can be confident that those pur-poses, both near and far, are best accomplished only as God providen-tially takes them through the thorny paths they now walk. But now we are told to give this up. Do not expect God to know with certainty whether his will for you is good in the long run or, for that matter, quite honestly, in the short run. How could God *know* that? Settle for the real-ization instead that God, along with your capable assistance, is doing his best to guide you; be comforted by the fact that he will be your friend through all you face in life. Of course, just what it is you will face in life, no one knows, not even God. And of course, no one even knows whether you will live another day, much less what difficulties lay ahead—not even God. And of course, no one knows the long-range goals you should seek to fulfill—not even God. And of course, no one can plan what is best for you now in light of that future—not even God. And of course, when you discern God's will and decide to follow it, real-ize that even God might have gotten things a bit wrong. But, no matter what, put all your trust in God!

This ending satire is biting, I know. But there is much at stake. The openness proposal offers a vision of a warm, relational, loving God, and certainly it is right—even necessary—to seek the incorporation of these qualities into one's overall conception of God. But shall we not think of God also as infinitely perfect and gloriously supreme? May I suggest, by way of illustration, that many Christians have sung, "What a friend we have in Jesus" along with "Immortal, invisible, God only wise" with no conflict and, in fact, with mutual reinforcement. No loss of the friendship and nearness of God is necessary when affirming his absolute and sovereign rulership over creation, since the God of the Bible is both. May God grant us grace to behold afresh his supremacy, and may we trust him without reservation and in full confidence, knowing that we can be in no better place than in full, humble, and joyful dependence before his feet.

9

Despair amid Suffering and Pain

When tragedy and suffering occur, how should Christians respond? The reader will recall that in chapter 3 we summarized the openness approach toward suffering. Now in this chapter we propose to assess the adequacy of this approach, both in relation to Scripture and on the basis of practical Christian living. A few reminders of some of the key themes of the openness approach toward suffering will be helpful as we move into this assessment.

Clearly, one of the crucial commitments of openness proponents is their rejection of God's *knowledge* of the future free actions of moral creatures. And tied closely to this is God's inability to *control* such future free actions including, at times, some deeply tragic occurrences. So, while God feels the pain of our suffering, he often is unable to prevent it. In other cases, God offers us what he fully believes at the time is perfectly wise counsel, but even here he sometimes realizes that his well-intended leading proves not to have been the best. And for this or other reasons, he may even regret some of his own past choices and decisions. While God always stands ready to offer grace to direct and rebuild our lives, some suffering must be understood as fully gratuitous and point-less. But when such pointless evil occurs, we are not to blame God. He feels as badly about it as we do. In the midst of our pain we can know with assurance that he had nothing to do with our suffering and that his disposition toward us is one of uncompromising love.

This view has many attractive elements to it. I have no doubt that, upon hearing this approach, a number of Christians may conclude that it sounds and feels at least very promising. But is it right? The task before us is to assess this openness model as it relates to tragedy and suffering, and we will consider its adequacy both on the basis of scriptural teaching and in relation to practical Christian living. How do the central commitments of open theism's response to suffering stand up when examined in these two arenas?

THE BIBLICAL ADEQUACY OF OPEN THEISM'S RESPONSE TO SUFFERING

A number of important biblical passages speak directly to the themes and issues raised by the openness response to suffering. Since as Christians we want both our choices and our responses to reflect how God would want us to live, we must consider seriously the question of how the Scriptures lead us to think about suffering. Are we given guidance in how we should respond to suffering? And does open theism reflect the mindset and disposition of this biblical teaching? Consider a number of passages bearing on the question of the Christian's response to suffering.

Romans 8:28-32

We begin this brief biblical survey with a passage of Scripture that has brought great comfort and strength to Christians throughout the centuries. In Romans 8:28-32, Paul writes:

> And we know that God causes all things to work together for good to those who love God, to those who are called according to His purpose. For those whom He foreknew, He also predestined to become conformed to the image of His Son, so that He would be the firstborn among many brethren; and these whom He predestined, He also called; and these whom He called, He also justified; and these whom He justified, He also glorified. What then shall we say to these things? If God is for us, who is against us? He who did not spare His own Son, but delivered Him over for us all, how will He not also with Him freely give us all things?

The staggering promise of Romans 8:28, that *God causes all things to work together for good* to those who love him, has three aspects, each of which is crucial in assessing the openness proposal. First, *God works* all things for good. For the believer, there simply are no accidents or tragedies in which God is, as it were, a passive bystander. He never help-lessly watches while some tragedy occurs, wishing it were different. Rather, God is at work to bring about good. He is altogether active in all the events of our lives, never merely passively—and certainly not helplessly—watching.

Second, God works *all things* for good. This precludes the notion so prevalent in open theism that God may be involved in the good of life but not in its suffering and pain. Contrary to this view, Paul states that the scope of God's work is absolutely comprehensive. There is nothing he is not actively working in to bring about good for his own.

Third, God works all things *for the good* of those who love him. While the framework of this promise concerns God's disposition toward his own (and so does not include unbelievers), yet for all believers this promise from God assures them that there is no pointless suffering. God works *everything* for their good.[1] We will have to look at Scripture's teaching elsewhere to see whether gratuitous evil is allowed for (or sup-ported) more generally or in relation to those who stand outside of God's love in Christ; but clearly here, *there is, for believers, no such pointless suffering or evil.* To say that there is, is to deny the explicit promise of God in this wondrous text.

---

[1] Notice how fundamentally different this is from Boyd's understanding of Romans 8:28. Boyd (*God of the Possible: A Biblical Introduction to the Open View of God* [Grand Rapids, Mich.: Baker, 2000], 155-156) writes, "It [the open view] affirms that whatever happens, God will work with us to bring a redemptive purpose out of the event (Rom. 8:28)." Notice two things. First, for Boyd, God does not work "all things," as Romans 8:28 says, but he works *with us* in response to all things. This verse never says that God works with us (though, perhaps, he may); it says he causes *all things* to work for believers' *good*. Second, the surety of the promise is subtly missing in Boyd's version of the promise. Boyd's claim is merely that "God will work with us to bring a redemptive purpose out of the event," but then, there are no guarantees that this will happen. Since God must work with us, and since we may or may not cooperate with him, God simply cannot guarantee that he *will* bring good out of the events of our lives. Yet, Romans 8:28 offers a guarantee: God works all things for the good of those who love him. The simple fact is that open theism offers a model that is incompatible with the promise of this text.

John Sanders (*The God Who Risks: A Theology of Providence* [Downers Grove, Ill.: InterVarsity, 1998], 127-128) is wrong when he says that Romans 8:28 does not say that all things in fact work for good but that "God is working to accomplish good in all things," yet "the purposes of God meet with resistance, and even God does not always get what he wants." This interpretation defies the context following this verse, in which Paul buttresses the claim of 8:28 by declaring that *God gets just what he wants on behalf of his elect.* Whom God foreknows, he predestines, calls, justifies, and glorifies (8:29-30). Furthermore, no one can successfully stand against God's own, for God gives them "all things" as he has already given them his own Son (8:31-32). Finally, absolutely nothing can separate them from his love in Christ, including all the suffering and tragedy life may hold (8:33-39). Nothing in this context would suggest that Paul has reservations about whether God will be successful in working all things for the good of his own. Just the opposite, instead, is the case. The God who gave them his own Son will not fail to give them all good things (8:32).

Think again of the weightiness of this promise in light of open theism's response to suffering. Openness proponents suggest that, despite his love, God is not always able to prevent unwanted suffering; that he sometimes inadvertently contributes to our suffering; and that we must accept the reality of pointless suffering as part of human life. Contrary to each of these notions, Romans 8:28 states that in his love *God works all things* for good, and as such he never stands unable to prevent what he does not want, and he never contributes to our harm. Further, in all these things he ensures us that *good is accomplished,* thus relieving us of the worry of pointless suffering. For believers, what assurance, what confidence, what peace, and what hope are here given! Yet, if we followed the proposals of open theism, the certain promise of this rich text would be obliterated. At the most, the God of open theism commits himself to doing his best to trying within his significant limitations to work things out for the good of his own. No guarantees, however. After all, God does not know what choices might be made in the future that will frustrate his efforts to work things out for good. Remember "God's guidance" to Suzanne, according to Boyd:[2] God tried to work out her marriage to this college friend in a way that would be good for her, but in the end God failed. And even in the work God succeeded in accomplishing (getting the two of them together in college), God actually contributed to Suzanne's pain and hardship, not her good. To suggest that God is just as sorry about Suzanne's divorce and dashed hopes as she is acknowledges that the promise of Romans 8:28 is empty and hollow. But since Romans 8:28 is true, it follows that the model of God and suffering proposed in open theism simply is not plausible.

Consider also the promise of Romans 8:32: "He who did not spare His own Son, but delivered Him over for us all, how will He not also with Him freely give us all things?" Again we see a promise of almost unbelievable proportions. Paul uses a light/heavy line of argument to suggest that, if God has done the *heavy* thing (sent his own Son, whom he gave up for us all), how will he not also do the *light* thing (give us all things, by his grace). That is, in keeping with promises such as Psalm 34:10 ("The young lions do lack and suffer hunger; but they who seek the LORD shall not be in want of any good thing.") and Psalm 84:11

---

[2] See chapter 3.

("For the LORD God is a sun and shield; the LORD gives grace and glory; no good thing does he withhold from those who walk uprightly"), Paul revels in God's commitment to give *every good thing* to the elect. Now, it stands to reason that, among the good things God gives his own is the prevention of suffering that would not serve good purposes for them, and suffering that would be, in fact, altogether pointless and positively destructive. God, then, must stand in control of all that happens in believers' lives in order to ensure that they encounter only those circumstances and events that will advance the good he knows and plans for them. If God is in a position in which he must watch tragedies occur to his people, unable to prevent them; and if he at times gives them direction which later proves to bring them harm, not good; and if he sees that some of the suffering and pain they must endure is pointless; then the promise of Romans 8:32 (and related texts) is nullified. Again, it is clear that open theism's proposal stands in direct conflict with God's own stated promise to his people: He will not fail to bring to their lives all of the good—and only the good—that he plans for them.

Before leaving this passage, one more comment is needed. One must not think that these promises of Romans 8:28 and 32 indicate that God will exempt his people from suffering. In Romans 5:3 Paul has spoken about exulting in our tribulations, not because of those difficulties considered in and of themselves, but because of the good that God works into our lives *through* those tribulations (see 5:3-5). So, when Paul speaks of God working all things *for good,* or when he revels in God who will bring to his people *all* (*good*) *things,* one must see that this includes the tribulations of life that God designs for believers to endure *for the sake of the good* that those trials produce. So the promise of God stands: Whether through great trials and suffering, or through rapturous joys, God will bring all good things to his people and work all things in life for their good. The openness proposal simply cannot affirm these promises without invoking a thousand qualifications that empty and tarnish them beyond recognition.

2 Corinthians 12:7-10

In the same breath, Paul speaks of a particular time of suffering he had endured as having come both from God (to produce good in him) and from Satan (to torment him). How can it be both? And what can we learn from this episode in Paul's life?

> Because of the surpassing greatness of the revelations, for this reason, to keep me from exalting myself, there was given me a thorn in the flesh, a messenger of Satan to torment me—to keep me from exalting myself! Concerning this I implored the Lord three times that it might leave me. And He has said to me, "My grace is sufficient for you, for power is perfected in weakness." Most gladly, therefore, I will rather boast about my weaknesses, so that the power of Christ may dwell in me. Therefore I am well content with weaknesses, with insults, with distresses, with persecutions, with difficulties, for Christ's sake; for when I am weak, then I am strong.

Paul's perspective on this suffering could not be further from the openness point of view. First, notice that Paul sees his suffering, while brought to him by Satan, as being ultimately under God's sovereign control. After all, the main purpose of this "thorn in the flesh" was an altogether positive and good one. Paul had been given wondrous revelations from God (see 2 Cor. 12:1-6), and God wanted to keep him humble and dependent. Satan's torment was only a tool in God's hand to produce in Paul some good and constructive result. Paul's perspective is not that *Satan* decided to torment him and that God, in response to Satan's prior mischief, devised a way to use this for good. Rather, *God* chose to keep Paul humble, and *he* decided to use Satan to accomplish his own ends. Far from being out of God's control, this suffering is ordained by God and it stands fully within his good purposes for Paul.

Second, Paul's three-fold prayer to the Lord indicates that Paul knew that it was God, not Satan, who had the power both to *give* and to *relieve* this suffering. Paul simply did not have the attitude that, because this is suffering, it cannot be from God. Nor did Paul wonder whether God was watching this suffering occur at the hands of one of his free moral creatures (i.e., Satan), helpless and unable to do anything about what was happening. Nor would it have been any comfort for Paul in prayer to know that God "felt his pain" while being unable to intervene to bring it to an end.[3] Open theists may think this way, but the apostle did not. Rather, he knew that God stood behind this messenger from Satan, and that God had the power to relieve the suffering if he so chose.

Third, God's answer to Paul—that his grace is sufficient, for his power is manifest in weakness—shows that God designed this suffering for the good that it would produce. This is not pointless suffering, but pointed, intentional, divinely chosen, end-directed suffering, for the good purposes that would not be accomplished apart from it.

Fourth, notice how Paul generalizes in 2 Corinthians 12:10, joyfully accepting the whole range of weaknesses, insults, hardships, persecutions, and difficulties. Paul's suffering of 12:7-9 is not an isolated case, and Paul understands that in whatever difficulties and hardships he faces, God is working in and through them to bring about his good purposes. Is there pointless and gratuitous suffering for Paul? Absolutely not. Rather, he sees the whole sweep of suffering in life as coming from God, given by his gracious hand to produce good.

Joseph's Story

One of the clearest illustrations in all of Scripture of how God *intentionally* ordains and uses the *intentional* evil actions of people to bring about good is the story of Joseph's providentially guided slavery in Egypt and rise to prominence, all to bring about good both for Egypt and for his family. As one reads the account of Joseph's brothers' jealousy, leading to their selling him into Egypt as a slave (Gen. 37), one would not naturally think that God was involved in these actions. After all, apart from the dreams that God gave Joseph, there is no clear indication that God is unfolding his purposes through the hatred and spirit of revenge that is growing in Joseph's brothers' hearts. From Genesis 37 alone, if

---

[3] The sense in which the God of open theism is "unable to intervene" in such a case must be understood clearly. For openness proponents, surely God *could* intervene if he wished to violate creaturely freedom. And this is always the case. But the fact that God has chosen to create creaturely libertarian freedom and to respect its use leaves him in a position in which the integrity of that very freedom is jeopardized by his interference with it. The minute God starts to micromanage human affairs by canceling either the exercise or consequences of libertarian freedom in an ad hoc manner, the whole structure of his "creation project" is imperiled. For this reason, God puts himself in the position where he accepts massive amounts of immoral and despicable, even fully pointless and gratuitous, free creaturely choices (witness the Holocaust, for example) in which he is "unable to intervene" and still honor the freedom he has bestowed on his creation.

one were asked, "Who sent Joseph into Egypt?" the answer would clearly be, "His jealous brothers, and they alone, did this wicked deed!" Skip ahead several years. Joseph has been favored by God in every position he has been given. Even when Joseph is falsely accused by Potiphar's wife and thrown into prison, God blesses him. Because of the interpretations of dreams God gave Joseph in prison, he was eventually called to interpret Pharaoh's dreams, leading to his appointment to second in command in Egypt. So, during Joseph's years in Egypt, Scripture gives indicators that God is actively working to promote Joseph to this place where he will be able to bring good to his people; but such indicators seem absent earlier, when we read of the brothers' wicked scheming and plotting. Before, it would seem, God is passive and uninvolved; only after Joseph is in Egypt does it appear that God is actively involved in promoting Joseph.

How amazing, then, are the words we read in Genesis 45:4-8. Here, Joseph finally reveals his identity to his brothers, and in the process he interprets for us what *actually* happened in his being sold into Egypt:

> [4] Then Joseph said to his brothers, "Please come closer to me." And they came closer. And he said, "I am your brother Joseph, whom you sold into Egypt. [5] Now do not be grieved or angry with yourselves, because you sold me here, for God sent me before you to preserve life. [6] For the famine has been in the land these two years, and there are still five years in which there will be neither plowing nor harvesting. [7] God sent me before you to preserve for you a remnant in the earth, and to keep you alive by a great deliverance. [8] Now therefore, it was not you who sent me here, but God; and He has made me a father to Pharaoh and lord of all his household and ruler over all the land of Egypt."

No reader would complain a bit when, in verses 4 and 5a, Joseph says that his brothers sold him into Egypt. Everything in the preceding narrative would indicate this is exactly true. The surprise comes as Joseph continues. Beginning in 45:5b, Joseph now makes clear the real reason and ultimate cause behind his being sent to Egypt. Here he deliberately switches from saying that his brothers sent him to saying that *God* sent him into Egypt. Notice Joseph's language. He does not say, "You sent me here, and God responded by using this bad situation and turning it into good." No, rather, he shifts the ultimate causal force of his being sent to Egypt from his brothers to God. In 45:7-8, Joseph has come full circle. The brothers, whom he began by saying were the ones who sent him to Egypt, are now completely excluded. Joseph boldly declares, "God sent me before you to preserve for you a remnant in the earth, and to keep you alive by a great deliverance." The brothers are out; God is in. Even the dreams God gave Joseph back in Canaan testify that God *knew* and *planned* that precise moment when the brothers would fulfill their predictions and bow at Joseph's feet. It is as if Joseph and the narrative say, if you want to know the real cause of Joseph's being sent to Egypt, don't look at the wicked actions of the brothers. No, Joseph affirms, *God sent me here,* and my brothers were his tools to accomplish the work he intentionally purposed to accomplish. To confirm this line of thought, Joseph declares in 45:8, "Now, therefore, it was not you who sent me here, but God."

This is staggering! What it illustrates so well is that God is not passively uninvolved and inactive in the wicked actions of mankind. Rather, he ordains those actions for purposes that may not be apparent at all to the people at the time, and that in fact in this life they may never know. Joseph certainly had no clue, for many years, as to why all this happened in Egypt. Then, graciously, the good design of God was made crystal clear.

Open theism simply cannot adequately account for such a text. The openness insistence that God is *not* involved in evil, and its firm rejection of the notion that God ordains and then uses evil to accomplish his good purposes, are both flatly denied by the story of Joseph. Imagine Joseph's dismay had he thought about his situation while in prison the way open theism would encourage! *Gratuitous evil happens,* Joseph would reason, *and it has happened to me. I am a victim of this pointless evil and revengeful plotting of my brothers and now of the false accusations of Potiphar's wife. Even the dreams God gave me about my brothers, dreams he meant to be an encouragement to me, have actually contributed to their hatred of me and thus to my increased suffering. God didn't mean to do this, but the fact is that he has made my life immeasurably worse, and the dreams—ha! Imagine my brothers bowing down before me! How absurd—the dreams were wrong anyway! Furthermore, God did not even know this was going to happen to me, and he is totally unable to control these horrible events or to do anything about it. After all, free agents have done these things to me and God cannot know in advance what they will do, and he certainly cannot control their actions. And all I can do is accept the fact that this pointless suffering has been directed at me and that it has now ruined my life. Yes, I'm glad to know that God is with me in this prison. But how I got here, when if ever I might get out, and whether there is any purpose served from it, are all beyond God's control. Woe is me, Joseph would think. What hope is there in this? My life is over. All I can do is despair.*

That this was *not* Joseph's understanding is evidence that he saw the hand of God in the wicked deeds of his brothers and in every other event leading to his promotion in Egypt. God was not uninvolved; rather, he was orchestrating all that occurred! Joseph's own summary statement of this episode of his life says it all. The book of Genesis ends with the death of Jacob and the fear of Joseph's brothers that Joseph might now take revenge on them. In Genesis 50:20, Joseph responds, "As for you, you meant evil against me, but God meant it for good in order to bring about this present result, to preserve many people alive." To God be the glory, great things he has done! And his great and glorious work relates as much to God's ordaining and use of *evil* for the purposes he designs as it does to the clearly *good* gifts that he gives. God's people may be confident: God *does* work all things together for good for those who love him! Joseph's story tells us so.

Job's Story

The story of Job stands in the biblical canon as a monument to God's control over wicked and even satanically wrought suffering, all so that God might accomplish his good (though hidden) purposes. Job 1 and 2 set the stage for the book's discussion of the meaning of human culpability, human suffering, divine sovereignty, and divine justice. Job is presented in the strongest terms as a righteous man (Job 1:1, 8; 2:3) whom Satan accuses of serving God for personal gain. God then permits Satan to inflict suffering on Job to demonstrate Job's integrity. God controls the extent of the suffering, first allowing Satan to bring about enormous loss of family and possessions, while leaving Job's own life and body untouched (1:12). In the second instance, God again reigned in Satan's evil intentions, allowing him to torment Job's body but not to take his life (2:6). In answer to the question, "Who is responsible for inflicting this weighty suffering on Job?" it is clear that two answers are needed: *God* specifically permitted and gave approval to the precise suffering Job experienced; and *Satan* actively, willfully, and maliciously carried it out.

Amazingly, Job's initial response to the enormous loss of his family and possessions affirms that it is *God* who has both given and taken. Job says, "Naked I came from my mother's womb, and naked I shall return there. The LORD gave and the LORD has taken away. Blessed be the name of the LORD" (Job 1:21). As Job's "counselors" come and begin to charge that Job's great affliction has resulted from his great wrongdoing, Job does not say what open theists would encourage: Job never suggests that this suffering is not from God or is not controlled by God. Job does not say that Satan as a free agent has brought on this suffering and that God cannot prevent Satan from doing what he freely chooses to do. Job never suggests that this suffering is gratuitous. No, from beginning to end the understanding of Job and all concerned is that, in some ultimate sense, Job's suffering is *from God* and has some *meaning*. The precise nature of that meaning is the dispute within the book itself.

As the story continues, Job wearies of hearing his friends' accusations against him, and in his own defense he begins moving closer toward a position of charging God with unjustly inflicting this pain upon him. Again, for Job this is not Satan's doing but *God's!*

God's response to Job and Job's counter-response are very instructive. God confronts Job in chapter 38 and for the next four chapters humbles Job by pointing to Job's extensive limitations in contrast to God's infinite majesty, power, rulership, wisdom, and supremacy. At a pivotal point in God's case against Job, we read that the Lord answers Job out of the storm, saying, "Now gird up your loins like a man; I will ask you, and you instruct Me. Will you really annul My judgment? Will you condemn Me that you may be justified?" (Job 40:7-8). Since this is God speaking directly in regard to a situation of enormous and prolonged suffering, it is crucial that we see what God says and what he does not say. God does *not* say, "Job, why are you blaming *me* for this suffering? I am not the one behind it! I haven't brought this on you! In fact, I feel as badly about your suffering as you do, and I wish it could have been avoided. Unfortunately, Satan is a very powerful being whose free choices I cannot control, and he has brought on you this suffering. So, stop blaming me for something I have not done and realize that sometimes pointless evil is inflicted on others in a world of sinful creatures who possess moral freedom."

God says no such thing. Instead, he spends four chapters humbling Job by asserting that since God's wisdom, power, and glory are simply beyond the comprehension of a finite creature like Job, *it is simply presumptuous, arrogant, wrong, and out of place for Job to challenge the justice and wisdom of what God has done.* God never backs away from the book's uniform assertion that *God* (not Satan) is the ultimate cause behind Job's suffering. So, what Job is to learn is not that God is totally passive and uninvolved in his suffering, but that God is fully just and righteous in causing, ultimately, all the suffering Job has experienced.

The book ends with Job repenting in dust and ashes (42:6) after realizing how wrong he has been to challenge God's justice. He admits that God *as God* can do all things (including the inflicting of suffering) and that no purpose of God's can be thwarted (42:2). He admits that he has spoken out of turn and has erred gravely in what he has said (42:3). And he pledges now to listen and learn instead of attempting to instruct the Almighty (42:4-5). Chapter 42 concludes with God restoring to Job double for all his prior loss, and his siblings and friends come to bring him comfort. Some of the last words in the book announce again the theme that *God* has reigned over all of Job's suffering. Job 42:11 reads, "Then all his brothers and all his sisters and all who had known him before came to him, and they ate bread with him in his house; and they consoled him and comforted him for all the adversities *that the LORD* had brought on him" (emphasis added).

Open theism's theological framework stands in blatant and irreconcilable conflict with the theology of the book of Job. Where Job says that God ultimately controls human suffering, open theism renders God inactive and uninvolved in relation to the inflicting of suffering. Where Job says that God restrains Satan's evil choices and activities, open theism stresses God's inability to control the choices of his free creatures. Where Job says that extensive, weighty, debilitating suffering is meaningful because it is used by God for good, open theism flees to the concept of gratuitous evil, thereby robbing sufferers of all sense of true meaningfulness amid deep pain. Where Job says that no purpose of God's can be thwarted (42:2), open theism says that God's purposes are thwarted constantly, so that God must routinely accept defeat and frustration. Where Job says it is impertinent and insolent to challenge God's wisdom and justice in his use of suffering to fulfill his purposes, open theism brazenly declares that God would be both unjust and unloving were he to bring about affliction for the sake of accomplishing greater good purposes. All in all, we have here two mutually exclusive models of God and his relation to the world. The reader will have to decide which model to follow. One thing is clear: One cannot adopt the mindset, worldview, and theology of Job and at the same time follow the course of open theism. The contrasts are that great.

"Spectrum Texts"

While the above passages deal with suffering in relation to believers in particular, several other passages indicate that the whole sweep of life— both ends of the spectrum, so to speak, and everything in between—are in God's control. Open theists are simply wrong in their denial that God has nothing to do with pain, suffering, disease, hardship, and death. In fact, Scripture clearly teaches that God not only has something to do with all of these matters—even more, he ordains and governs them all. Such a view is deeply troubling for open theists. Greg Boyd, for example, ends his recent book on this theme by saying:

> The world is still scary. It is in a state of war, under siege by the enemy of our souls, and this is not a comforting thought (1 John 5:19). The open view grants this. Even God takes risks. But the world is less scary in this view than if we try to find consolation in the belief that *everything that occurs is controlled by God and thus reflects his dubious character.*[4]

Does Scripture in fact teach that God controls all things? If so, what can be said of Boyd's implicit charge that such a view results in a God of "dubious character"? First, consider a number of passages in which God

---

[4] Boyd, *God of the Possible,* 156 (emphasis added).

is referred to as having control of all facets of life, the bad as well as the good. These "spectrum" references obviously indicate that he controls both extremes and all that is in between. For example (emphasis added throughout):

The LORD said to him, "Who has made man's mouth? Or who makes him mute or deaf, or *seeing* or *blind?* Is it not I, the LORD?" (Ex. 4:11).

"See now that I, I am He,
And there is no god besides Me;
It is I who put to *death* and give *life.*
I have *wounded* and it is I who *heal,*
And there is no one who can deliver from My hand"
  (Deut. 32:39).

The LORD *kills* and *makes alive;*
He *brings down to Sheol* and *raises up.*
The LORD makes *poor* and *rich;*
He *brings low,* He also *exalts* (1 Sam. 2:6-7).

Consider the work of God,
For who is able to straighten what He has bent?
In the day of *prosperity* be happy,
But in the day of *adversity* consider—
God has made the one as well as the other
So that man will not discover anything
  that will be after him (Eccles. 7:13-14).

I am the LORD, and there is no other;
Besides Me there is no God.
I will gird you, though you have not known Me;
That men may know from the rising to the setting of the sun
That there is no one besides Me.
I am the LORD, and there is no other,
The One forming *light* and creating *darkness,*
Causing *well-being* and creating *calamity;*
I am the LORD who does all these (Isa. 45:5-7).

Who is there who speaks and it comes to pass,
Unless the Lord has commanded it?
Is it not from the mouth of the Most High
That both *good* and *ill* go forth? (Lam. 3:37-38).

If a trumpet is blown in a city will not the people tremble?
If a *calamity* occurs in a city has not the LORD done it?
   (Amos 3:6).

He made known to us the mystery of His will, according to His
kind intention which He purposed in Him with a view to an
administration suitable to the fullness of the times, that is, the
summing up of all things in Christ, things in the heavens and
things on the earth. In Him also we have obtained an inheritance,
having been predestined according to His purpose who works *all
things* after the counsel of His will (Eph. 1:9-11).

 While it is true that the statements made in every one of these passages relate to specific, historical situations to which they apply, it is also
true that the truths they announce within those situations are truths that
transcend just those times and places. These are truths about God and
his overarching providential governance of the world he has made. Open
theists try to dismiss the force of these texts by limiting them to the very
restricted applications within which they are spoken.[5] Indeed, they do
relate in those situations, but the truths they proclaim are bigger than
those situations themselves. Take just one passage above to illustrate this
point. Isaiah 45:5-7 is a bold declaration of the Godness of God. The
very deity of the true and living God is asserted by virtue of his control
over and performance of absolutely everything that occurs in life. What
relevance does this have in the situation in Isaiah's own day? To God's
rebellious people, God makes clear that the peace and rest they enjoy
(they currently are at relative rest, although living in outright rebellion)
and the calamity and disaster they are about to experience (as the
Assyrians come to destroy them) are *both* from God's mighty and
sovereign hand. Indeed, we would miss much of the importance of this

---

[5] See, e.g., Sanders, *God Who Risks,* 82: "Isaiah 45:7 refers to the specific experiences of Israel in exile and not to divine pancausality."

text if we failed to see the principle of light and darkness, prosperity and disaster, as being brought to Israel by God at this time in history. But, just as wrong would be an interpretation that limited these truths to *this single historical episode alone*. What is true here is true always: God, *as God,* maintains providential governance over every facet in the full spectrum of life, for to fail to do so would mean that God, in fact, is not God.

What of Boyd's claim that such a view results in a God of "dubious character"? More will be said below on this key issue, but suffice it here to say that God's character is not hereby impugned if it can be established that, in respect to *all* the evil he ultimately controls, he is accomplishing his good purposes *through,* and *only through,* such horrible wrongdoing.

While many examples could be given (of God's ordaining that good come about only through some evil), none is better than God's control of the greatest, most horrendous, most vile and wicked evil ever perpetrated in the whole of human history: the murderous crucifixion of the innocent Son of God, Jesus the Messiah. Remember the familiar words of Acts 4:27-28: "For truly in this city there were gathered together against Your holy servant Jesus, whom You anointed, both Herod and Pontius Pilate, along with the Gentiles and the peoples of Israel, to do whatever Your hand and Your purpose predestined to occur." Luke names four different "players" in the crucifixion of Christ: Herod, Pontius Pilate, the Gentiles, and the people of Israel. Concerning all four of these, Luke says that they did precisely what *God* had previously decided that they should do. And certainly we must hold this view if we mean it when we say that *God the Father* sent his Son to die on that cross (John 3:16); that it pleased *the Father* to crush his Son to save guilty sinners (Isa. 53:10); that Christ was delivered up by the *predetermined plan and foreknowledge of God* (Acts 2:23). In other words, God planned and brought to pass the crucifixion of his Son, and he did so through the activities of the wicked people who murdered him. Now, why are these wicked people preeminently *blameworthy* while God is preeminently *praiseworthy* for carrying out the same action (i.e., the action of putting Christ on the cross)? The answer clearly is that *they* did their evil *for the sake of the evil,* while *God* worked through their evil *for the sake of the greater and glorious good that would result.* The God who controls all that happens, the light and the darkness, well-being and calamity, life and death, is not, then, a God of dubious character. His ways are always and only good, and his purposes are perfectly upright and wise. As we shall see below, it is only because of these truths that we can have unassailable comfort and peace amid suffering. *God is in absolute control,* and *God is absolutely good.* On these twin truths we find rest, comfort, and hope.

PRACTICAL CHRISTIAN LIVING AND OPEN THEISM'S RESPONSE TO SUFFERING

How well does the openness response to human suffering work when placed in the framework of practical Christian living? Is it a coherent approach that can be applied consistently? How pastorally, spiritually, and existentially adequate is the counsel offered by openness proponents?

At the heart of the pastoral counsel offered to suffering people by open theists is this claim: God did not bring about your suffering, so don't blame God for it; instead, be encouraged because he feels as badly about the suffering you are enduring as you do. To many, this has an initial appeal. On the surface, it offers suffering people comfort. "God didn't do this to me," they say. "And furthermore, God cares about the pain I'm experiencing." To many, this sounds like good and wise counsel.

On analysis, however, this line of pastoral counsel presents a deeply flawed and troubling perspective. Regarding the claim that God didn't bring about your suffering and that he feels as badly about it as you do, it is either true or not true that God could have prevented your suffering. Granted, in either case (whether he could have prevented it or not), he did not bring about the suffering. But how shall we assess this counsel if it turns out that God *could have prevented* the suffering and did not? And what shall we say of this view if God *could not have prevented* the suffering though he wished very badly that he could have? First we will consider the possibility that he could have prevented the suffering, and then ponder what is involved if such prevention was not possible for him.

God's Uncaring Ability *to Prevent the Suffering He Allows to Occur*

If it is true that God does not bring suffering upon us but feels as badly about it as we do, this may imply that, though God did not inflict the suffering on us, he did consciously and deliberately permit it to occur when he could have prevented it. Is this view valid within open theism, and what shall we make of it?

At the most general level, one must say that the God of open theism (unlike the God of process theism) *could,* if he so wanted and chose, prevent *all suffering at all times.* But the cost to do so would be great. Essentially, were he to ensure that there was no suffering, God would have to abandon the kind of world he has created. For open theists (and for Arminians generally), since God has given human and angelic creatures significant freedom, these creatures cannot possess and use this freedom and at the same time be controlled in how they use it. To be free entails, by necessity, the possibility of using that freedom in wicked, mean, unjust, and abusive ways. So at one level we might say that, given the kind of world God has chosen to create, i.e., a world within which free creatures choose to do good or evil, God cannot prevent suffering from occurring. It should be recognized, however, that God's inability to prevent suffering is a consequential, not absolute, inability. God is unable to prevent suffering only as a consequence of his prior decision to create a world of free beings. God did not have to create such a world. So three things are clear: 1) God chose to create a world in which *he knew* there existed the distinct possibility that free creatures would use their freedom to produce suffering; 2) because he could not know their choices in advance, and because he cannot control their choices, *he knew* that there existed the distinct possibility that gratuitous suffering would be inflicted on others—suffering over which he would have no control and out of which he could not bring any good; and 3) knowing these two things, God deliberately and freely chose to create this world of free creatures.

The openness position here is by no means problem-free. On the one hand, one might think that, while God knew of the *possibility* that freedom would be abused to bring about gratuitous suffering, he did not know this *would* occur; and furthermore, *he did not think it likely* that this would happen. As discussed earlier, John Sanders suggests thinking in this direction when he claims that the first sin in the garden caught God by surprise![6] If this is the case, however, in God's decision to create this world, might we not charge him with folly, negligence, poor judgment, and

---

[6] Sanders (ibid., 46): "In Genesis 3 the totally unexpected happens."

perhaps even stupidity? God obviously was greatly mistaken, especially when one considers the massive misuse of freedom that has occurred throughout human history. Could not God figure out pretty quickly that things were not going to go well, and so put an end to his "project"?

On the other hand, one might think that God was fairly sure that freedom would be misused pretty much as it has been. That is, even though God did not *know* that massive, extensive, and even significant amounts of gratuitous suffering would occur from the misuse of human freedom, *he believed that it was highly probable* that this would be the case. But here, on openness grounds themselves, one would question the moral goodness of God in very much the same way that openness advocates question proponents of classical theism. The fact is, God did not have to create a world, either this one or any other. And on this understanding, when he did create, he knew full well that massive human suffering was the highly probable result of his decision to create. He could have prevented all of this by not creating at all, or by creating a different kind of world, but he chose to create *this* world. Can the God of open theism escape the moral charges leveled against classical theism's God? The fact is that God did not have to create, and in choosing to create he could have created a world with no evil or suffering. In considering this fact, it appears that open theism is on the horns of a dilemma. Either God created a world with significant freedom believing wrongly that the misuse of freedom to bring about suffering was unlikely, or he created such a world believing that this misuse of freedom was probable. In the first case, God is apparently a fool; in the second, and by openness standards themselves, he is seemingly malevolent. Open theism is not commended by either option.

Consider a different expression of this issue (Did God choose to allow suffering that he could have prevented?). As I write, my wife, Jodi, is laid up in bed with a heavy plaster cast on her right arm. While taking a meal to a family with a new baby, Jodi tripped at the top of a staircase and tumbled to the landing, breaking her arm. As accidents go, this one was relatively minor (easy for me to say, I know!). Even with the pain of the surgery, plate, and screws that were required, prospects are very good for full recovery, and the main problem now is the inconvenience of the whole ordeal.

Now, I raise the question: Could the God of open theism have prevented this accident from occurring? I find it hard to see why not. This was not a case where my wife *willed* to take some action that would inflict suffering. Therefore, to prevent this suffering, God would not have had to override her freedom and so spoil, as it were, the integrity of the created moral order. No, in fact, since he is God, all he would have to do is cause my wife's foot not to trip at the top of the stairs; or he could have made sure that her foot recovered quickly enough to reach the step and avoid the fall; or even with a fall, he could have ensured that the bone withstood the impact and remained unbroken. In any of these cases (and how many more might God be able to think of!), Jodi would have simply walked away from this situation totally unaware that God had even intervened. No harm would have been done to the integrity of human freedom, no disruption to the regular course of natural law, no apparent drawback or harm to any divine purpose in God's relationship with his human creatures.

Yet, if the true God is the God of open theism, he did not prevent this accident. And if it is true that he could have prevented it, it follows that he deliberately allowed it to occur. Why? Two possible answers come to mind, the first seeing God as "hands off" and the second as "hands on." According to the first of these possible answers, God might have allowed what he could have prevented because he simply will not, on principle, intervene in such a way as to disrupt the natural course of life, the regular sequence of cause-effect relations that make up the tapestry of everyday existence. That is, God chooses to be hands off as it pertains to human decision-making and the flow of natural cause-effect relations. But if this is the case, is this God (this version of the God of open theism) really the intimately personal God he is touted so to be? As will also be seen below, this picture of God more resembles deism than the personal, deeply involved God of the Bible.

Concerning the second, "hands on" option, God might have allowed what he could have prevented because he envisioned some good purpose coming from the suffering. Of course, the God of open theism is often unable to *know* what will come of what. Perhaps, though, we could say that God is hopeful, or views it as probable, that good will come. But if this is the case, can we really tell people that God was not involved in the suffering that they experienced? If God has deliberately allowed it and is quite "hands on" in relation to the suffering, can we rightly comfort people by reassuring them that God had nothing to do with the tragedy that occurred? No, in fact, if it is possible that God purposely allows suffering to occur because of perceived benefits coming from it, then for what specific instance of suffering could we so dogmatically tell someone that God is not—surely *not*—involved in it? Do we know the mind of God? Can we say with such confidence that, while example A of suffering was allowed by God for some perceived good that would come from it, example B of suffering is clearly and certainly gratuitous and God had nothing at all to do with it? How immensely knowledgeable and wise the openness counselor must be to be able to discern instances of suffering with such precision! Satire aside, how presumptuous it is for the open theist to reject out of hand the possibility that, for some horrid instance of suffering, God was intentionally involved in it and he was so involved for some greater good. How much one must know to be able to say with such confidence that this cannot be the case! So, whether God is "hands off" or "hands on" in relation to instances of human suffering, it appears that, if the God of open theism allows what he could prevent, the pastoral counsel open theists offer in the face of suffering falters.

God's Caring Inability to Prevent Suffering He Wishes Did Not Occur

If it is true that God does not bring suffering upon us but feels as badly about it as we do, this may imply that God really stands just as helpless to have prevented the suffering as was the one who is now forced to endure it. Consider with great sobriety the honest yet weighty admission of Greg Boyd about this implication of the openness view. Boyd writes,

> It is true that according to the open view things can happen in our lives that God didn't plan or even foreknow with certainty (though he always foreknew they were possible). This means that in the open view things can happen to us that have no overarching divine purpose. In this view, *"trusting in God" provides no assurance that everything that happens to us will reflect his divine purposes,* for there are other agents who also have power to affect us, just as we have power to affect others.[7]

---

[7] Boyd, *God of the Possible*, 153 (emphasis added).

What does this say of God? For all the talk in open theism about a God of intimate personal relationship, here we have a view in which God is no more involved in some of life's most pressing and agonizing experiences than would be the god of deism. The God of open theism waits, watches, and learns what unfolds, *but he is passive, not active, in the moment of tragic suffering.* To take seriously the notion that God could not have prevented the suffering is to render God uninvolved, although clearly not uninterested or uncaring. But what do we typically think of someone who cares deeply about the unfolding of some tragedy but who can do nothing to stop it or change it? We would pity such a person, and we would hardly think this quality (caring but helpless passivity) to be characteristic of deity.

Openness proponents surely would counter that at least in their view God is not *inflicting* evil upon suffering people, as must be the case if God is the ultimate determining cause of all that occurs. At least, they would say, the problem of evil is due to *our* doing, not God's. Three responses are needed. First, in arguing that God is not the ultimate determining cause of all things, open theism flatly rejects Scripture's clear testimony to the contrary. The "spectrum texts" cited earlier make clear that darkness as well as light, death as well as life, calamity as well as prosperity, sickness as well as healing, are all under the sovereign and providential regulative control of God. Like it or not (Rom. 9:14, 19), this is the God of the Bible, who will have mercy on whom he desires and will harden whom he desires (Rom. 9:18).

Second, as illustrated earlier through our brief consideration of Acts 4:27-28, God works through evil people, and he uses evil decisions and actions, but *God never, never, never himself does evil.* God, who through the wicked actions of evil people put his Son on the cross, is fully glorious, righteous, and praiseworthy in his action, while the evil people God used to crucify his Son are fully despicable, deserving of judgment, and blameworthy. God ordains evil, uses evil, and accomplishes infinitely good purposes through evil, but he never *does* evil.

Third (and most important on the issue at hand), if it is true that God could not have prevented some horribly painful situation, and if it is true therefore that God is not in control of such tragic experiences, then who or what *is* in control of what happens? However we answer this question, the answer clearly is *not* "God." Perhaps Satan is in control, or his demons are in control, or wicked and vile people are in control, or forces of nature are in control, but clearly God is not in control. This raises the question, How much of life is in this category? That is, how much of life stands outside of God's control? Do I know whether at the next moment some tragedy might occur while God stands watching it develop, unable to prevent it? Do I know whether my children are being subjected to the assaults of satanic attack while God merely watches Satan have his way? Do I know whether natural disasters or traffic accidents or debilitating physical ailments await me or my family, and whether when I inquire, "Where is God?" I might hear only, "He's watching the events unfold, and if (because he also doesn't know what will occur) they are bad, be assured that he will feel your pain with you"?

Compare this with the long-standing Christian answer to human suffering: God has ordained this suffering and is working through it to accomplish purposes that are good, right, beautiful, and glorious. While we may or may not be able to see what those purposes are, *we know God;* we know that his character is good and righteous, and we know that he is in control of all things (Eph. 1:11), and so we rest in the assurance that God is doing what is best. As the songwriter puts it,

> God is too wise to be mistaken; God is too good to be unkind.
> So when you don't understand, when you can't see his plan;
> When you can't trace his hand, trust his heart.[8]

What it comes down to is this: Would you rather see your life as being at the mercy of the God of all knowledge, wisdom, righteousness, goodness, and love, who is in control of all that occurs? Or would you rather see your life as being at the mercy of Satan, demons, wicked people, and natural forces who have control over much of your life, bringing disaster and suffering upon you, some of which is entirely pointless in the great scheme of things, while God watches, unable to intervene? In the first case, you don't have to know or understand why God has ordained that you experience the suffering. *All you have to know is God!* All you need is the confidence that this "accident" or tragedy is not outside of his control (God forbid!) but rather is designed by him for purposes in keeping with his

---

[8] Words taken from "Trust His Heart," written by Eddie Carswell and Babbie Mason, © 1989, May Sun Music, Causing Change Music, Word Music and Dayspring Music.

own character. But in the second conception, when God is taken by surprise by the unfolding of future events, or when he cannot stop the freewill agency of some wicked person or demon, we realize that our lives are not in God's hands after all. Pointless evil happens! And all the comfort offered in the face of deep and tragic suffering is that God feels just as badly about this as you do. Such a view will lead Christian people to despair, not hope. They will question whether God is worthy of worship or trust or allegiance. Such a God is a pathetic being, a poor, marred, shallow, and empty substitute for the God of the Bible.

Here is your choice: *Do you want the God who risks?* Then you must take *with* him the uncertainty, the lack of confidence, and the despair that goes with this risk. Talk all you want about the personal relationship offered with such a God, but what you have in fact is great disappointment, fear of what may lie ahead, and shallow, faltering faith. Or, on the other hand, *do you want the God who controls all that is?* "But this brings with it the problem of evil," you say. Well, open theism has its own problem of evil (see above); and this problem, for classical theism, has a viable solution. Besides, what you really get (with classical theism) is the God in whom you have complete and full confidence. His character is impeccable, his wisdom flawless, his will and ways righteous, his heart holy and good; and he is the One who "does according to His will in the host of heaven and among the inhabitants of the earth; and no one can ward off His hand or say to Him, 'What have you done?'" (Dan. 4:35). What could possibly be better than to know that this God, the true and living God of the Bible, who rules over heaven and earth, governs every facet of your life!

Consider again the two deaths spoken of by John Sanders (see chapter 3). In both cases the question asked was, "Why did God kill" (my brother, or my child)? And, of course, the counsel offered by Sanders in the face of such tragic loss is to suggest that these are pointless deaths. God had nothing to do with killing his brother or this little child. But are these really words of comfort? Is it comforting to know that some other power, apart from both God's power and our own, controlled the taking of these lives? Is it comforting to know that, even though God would have liked it to be different, he couldn't prevent some drunk driver or some fatal disease from taking these lives? Is it comforting to know that our lives are subject to massive layers of control by human and demonic freewill agents in regard to which God cannot exert his control? Is it comforting to know that in every "next moment" of my life there awaits the possibility of some horrid gratuitous evil event occurring that God can only bemoan but not prevent? When the reality of this counsel settles in, the emotions produced in people will not be calmness and comfort but fear, anxiety, betrayal, dread, discouragement, dismay, disappointment, and despair. Such is life with the God who risks.

But shall we say to these grieving individuals that in fact *God did take these lives?* The answer is that with gentleness, with compassion, with deep sympathy for the unavoidable and natural sense of loss, we will say, "Yes, the God of all wisdom, goodness, and power has ordained to take these lives." Remember Deuteronomy 32:39 and 1 Samuel 2:6-7? The Lord gives life and he takes life. He is God, and this is his prerogative. But his ways are always righteous. So, his taking of these lives must be seen as fulfilling good purposes of which we may not now (nor perhaps throughout all of our life) be aware. But do we trust God's character? Do we know God for who he is? Can we say, with Job, "the LORD gave and the LORD has taken away. Blessed be the name of the LORD" (Job 1:21)?

CONCLUSION

One of open theism's strongest appeals is its claim to account for tragic human suffering in such a way that God is both blameless and caring. On the surface, this appeal appears strong. Upon examination, however, it is clear that open theism's counsel is unbiblical, incoherent, and shallow.

It is *unbiblical* insofar as it fails to account for the prevailing biblical vision of the God who reigns over human affairs and who ensures that his purposes are accomplished even through human wickedness and evil.

It is *incoherent* because it faces the horns of an untenable dilemma: Either God allows suffering he could prevent, which raises moral questions concerning God's blamelessness (though openness advocates would deny this); or, God stands idly by, unable to prevent great and agonizing human suffering, in which case one is led to despair at the realization that life is under the control of massive amounts of free choice over which God has no control and much of which is desperately evil.

And, the counsel of open theism is *shallow.* Many thoughtful

Christians will begin to wonder what hope there is if much of suffering is pointless and if God is unable either to prevent it or to bring good from it. Despair and lack of confidence in God will be the legacy of open theism, should it extend its influence in the church.

The simple truth is this: The God of the Bible is not the limited, passive, hand-wringing God open theism portrays. He is king, lord, sovereign, wise, good, and perfect in all his ways. The message of the Bible is that suffering has meaning, God is in control over it and over all else, and so life can be lived by faith in the infinitely wise and powerful God.

Conclusion

10

God's Greater Glory and
Our Everlasting Good

What kind of glory does the God of the Bible possess? And in what is our everlasting good found? These are the two questions with which we close our examination of open theism. One might wonder why these two particular questions should come together and why at the end of this treatment. First, they come together because it is the Bible's own view that, as the glory of God goes, so goes our temporal and everlasting good. For example, in the opening section of Ephesians 1, in which Paul extols the many blessings we enjoy in Christ, his regular refrain is, "to the praise of his glory." In this text, it is clear that God's glory is both the *source* from which our goodness comes and the *end* toward which our goodness aims. Our blessings come from the glorious, risen, and exalted Christ; and such goodness redounds to the glory of God in Christ. In brief, our goodness depends on God being glorified.

Second, the reason we have reserved discussion of this pair of questions until the end is that they bring together, perhaps better than any other relevant conceptions, the fundamental differences of theological vision between open theism and a more traditional model of divine providence. So, while some of what we discuss here will summarize ideas and materials from throughout the book, this also will afford us a study in contrasts: What is the nature of the glory that is God's alone; and in what is our good to be found? We will consider first the openness perspective on these issues, and then we will explore the contrast between the openness vision and a more traditional vision of God's greater glory and our greater good.

GOD'S GLORY AND OUR GOOD IN OPEN THEISM

Openness proponents tell us in many contexts and in many ways that the vision of God they commend is one in which his glory is greater and more fully manifest than in the classical model. Furthermore, they say, the well-being of God's human creation, in particular, is enhanced in the open view, for now real significance attaches to our choices and actions. Throughout Boyd's *God of the Possible*, for example, he commends the openness model as portraying God as being more glorious and human experience more satisfying. Consider a few sample statements:

> Open theists . . . maintain that God can and does predetermine and foreknow *whatever he wants to* about the future. Indeed, God is so confident in his sovereignty, we hold, he does not need to micromanage everything. He could if he wanted to, but this would demean his sovereignty. So he chooses to leave some of the future open to possibilities, allowing them to be resolved by the decisions of free agents. It takes a greater God to steer a world populated with free agents than it does to steer a world of preprogrammed automatons.[1]

> God is *so* wise, resourceful, and sovereign over history that he doesn't need or want to have everything in the future settled ahead of time. He is *so* confident in his power and wisdom that he is willing to grant an appropriate degree of freedom to humans (and angels) to determine their own futures.
>
> In my view, every other understanding of divine providence to some extent diminishes the sovereignty and glory of God. It brings God's wisdom and power down to the level of finite human thinking. *We* would need to control or possess a blueprint of all that is to occur ahead of time to steer world history effectively. But the true God is far wiser, far more powerful, and far more secure than we could ever imagine.[2]

---

[1] Gregory A. Boyd, *God of the Possible: A Biblical Introduction to the Open View of God* (Grand Rapids, Mich.: Baker, 2000), 31 (emphasis in original).

[2] Ibid., 68 (emphasis in original).

It takes a truly self-confident, sovereign God to make himself vulnerable. It takes a God who is truly in authority to give away some of his control, knowing that doing so might cause him incredible pain. By contrast, to simply control others so that you always get your way is the surest sign of insecurity and weakness. To do so simply because you *can* demonstrates nothing praiseworthy about one's character—unless you're inclined to worship sheer power and control. . . .

How different [than in Calvinism], and how much more glorious, is the portrait of a God who chooses to create a cosmos populated with free agents. Out of love, God empowers others to be personal beings. Out of love, he respects their God-given ability to make decisions even when doing so causes him pain. . . . Despite the various claims made by some today that we must protect "the sovereignty of God" by emphasizing his absolute control over creation and thus by denouncing the open view, I submit that we ought to denounce the view that God exercises total control over everything for this very same reason: *It demeans the sovereignty of God.*[3]

These quotations will suffice to lay out the main openness perspective. God is more glorious, in this view, precisely because he has limited his power and knowledge from what he might have done had he chosen to create a different kind of world. He *could* control all and know all that would take place in the future, but to do so would have precluded the introduction of other free agents. God's choice to share power and limit his knowledge *through allowing freedom in others*, according to this view, manifests his *greater self-confidence and praiseworthiness*. And we are benefited enormously. Had God not given us freedom, we would be, in Boyd's words, "preprogrammed automatons." Had God designed an exhaustive blueprint or written a divine script for all of life, we would be forced to play out our determined roles. What joy, fulfillment, or satisfaction would there be for us? But because God has given us freedom, we establish our own lives by our own choices and *life becomes truly meaningful*. In short, for open the-

---

[3] Ibid., 149-150 (emphasis in original).

ism both God's glory and our good centers around *the God-given capacity for and expression of moral freedom.*

Assessing the Openness Model: God's Lesser Glory and Our Lesser Good

In assessing the openness vision of God's glory and our good, several of the themes we have considered in earlier chapters will resurface. This will give us opportunity in this final chapter to pull together some of the main considerations throughout the book.

God's Glory and God's Success

First, the openness vision of God's glory and our good appears particularly attractive when one is assured that, because God is resourceful, he is able to guide creation toward his desired ends. By the use of his matchless wisdom and creativity, God is more greatly glorified as he successfully accomplishes for creation what he intends. Now, if this works very well, then we would naturally ascribe glory to God for his success; and because he has succeeded, we obviously have entered into greater fulfillment and experience of the goodness God intended for us. So long as God succeeds and so long as free creatures do not use their freedom in substantial and significant rebellion against him, his glory and our good are, to that degree, secured.

What happens, however, if God's success rate turns out to be low? What comes of both his glory and our good should a significant portion of his moral creation not follow in his ways? The answer, it appears to me, is that God, in the openness model, is *worthy of glory to the degree to which he succeeds,* and *unworthy of glory to the degree to which he fails.* For if it is the case that God is glorified precisely through the display of his resourcefulness to direct free creatures to freely choose his way, then it stands to reason that he deserves credit (glory) when his persuasion succeeds but not so when his persuasion fails (remember, it is the *resourcefulness to make it work* that is commended). So, not only is God's glory and our good tied to the exercise of moral freedom; the *degree of glory* and *degree of good* are likewise inextricably connected to the kinds of choices freedom produces.

But if this is true, then a very troubling aspect of the openness model cannot be avoided. Throughout their literature, open view proponents make clear that freedom makes it possible that horrible and pointless evil can occur. While God may try to avoid such horrendous suffering, they say, there simply are many times when he cannot do so. Furthermore, open theists believe that a number of people will likely reject God's salvation invitation and by this be separated from him forevermore. And, Satan and his demonic forces are at work in the world to bring many kinds of suffering and pain to bear. Make no mistake, freedom has its dark side. But to the degree to which evil prevails, the glory of God is necessarily diminished. If it is true, as Boyd stated, that "it takes a *greater* God to steer a world populated with free agents than it does to steer a world of preprogrammed automatons,"[4] then to the extent that God's steering goes awry, to that extent his greatness is minimized. God's glory, it seems, correlates with God's success rate.

So how do we evaluate the extent of God's glory at present? Essentially we have two factors to consider: how well God has thus far steered the world forward; and how well he might do in the future. Concerning God's *past* success rate, I think it fair to say that on openness standards (and on Arminian standards, generally) of what the world should be, God gets pretty mixed reviews. How well has he steered the masses of the peoples of the world to embrace his will and ways, given worldwide rates of theft, murder, rape, adultery, warfare, and so forth? Now, if one accounts for all these horrible features by appeal to the role of Satan (a free agent) and the exercise of our own free wills, one must realize that *to this extent God has failed altogether to steer the world forward in the ways he intended.* It is impossible to commend God as fully glorious since his glory is attached to how resourceful he is in leading the world forward, and since that resourcefulness seems in so many, many ways to have failed. If the world is in such obvious moral, spiritual, and physical disarray, the glory of God is similarly tattered.

What of God's *future* success rate? As we have seen earlier, it is simply not at all clear, on openness grounds, that God will in fact win (significantly and widely) in the end. Projecting from how well he has done

---

[4] Ibid., 31 (emphasis in original).

so far, one may be led to become quite discouraged at the prospects of God's ultimate decisive victory. Yes, there is the victory of the cross and empty tomb, but until free creatures embrace this crucified and risen Savior, they stand in their rebellion against God and, to this degree, God's purposes again fail.[5] And the sobering truth here is that, by the openness view, neither we nor God know now whether in fact God will so win in the end. If God is at war, and if God has taken significant risks, then we must wait to see if God will win, and so wait to see if God is in fact glorious.

From this first observation, then, I conclude that, from an openness perspective, *we simply cannot ascribe to God unqualified glory*. Maybe God will get lucky; maybe he won't. Maybe his free creatures will cooperate better in the future than they have in the past; but maybe things will get immeasurably worse! Can open theists assure us that this cannot happen? As developed earlier, given the implausibility of the first sin in a perfect environment, we have no basis for confidence that now, as sinners, God's creatures will do any better. If anything, the reverse is more likely. God's glory, then, according to open theism, is a relative matter, and at present all bets are off as to whether God will prove glorious in the end. Certainly, judging by how things are at present, one can make a strong case that God's losses have greatly outnumbered his wins. And since God's glory and our good are inextricably tied together, it is also true that our good[6] suffers greatly. Since our good is linked along with God's glory to the extent to which we use our freedom to follow in his wise and wondrous ways, it also appears that the level of our goodness is desperately low. So, given that God's glory and our good are tied to God's resourcefulness to direct the world forward in the ways he intends, and given that the divine directing perhaps is going quite badly, one can give at best a very qualified, diminished, marginal, and penultimate ascription of glory to God.

Let us linger a moment further and consider the effects of this line of

---

[5] As noted earlier in the book, when considering this problem, it is apparent why the doctrines of salvific inclusivism and annihilationism (perhaps also post-mortem evangelism) are so appealing to openness thinkers. In all of these misguided doctrines (none of which has legitimate biblical basis), the great benefit to the openness proposal is that perhaps things will be better in the end than what otherwise might be the case.

[6] I am referring here to real material or existential good and not the mere formal good of possessing libertarian freedom in itself.

thinking on worship. What will believers feel toward God when the mask of open theism's positive portrayal is removed and we see increasingly the mistakes, misjudgments, misdirections, miscalculations, and widespread failures of God? One can only wonder how many cases like Suzanne's, discussed in chapters 3 and 9, there are in the world. How often is it the case that God actually contributes to human hardship and suffering through his well-intended but misguided direction? What will happen when people realize that God's glory is unavoidably marred by these innumerable divine failures? Perhaps appeals to his love will prevail for some. But many will find this vision of God deeply distressing, and many more will see correctly that this sort of God is unworthy of unqualified and unreserved worship. This god is man writ large, they will see, full of so many of our weaknesses, but worse because he is not one of us but is touted to be God. His glory will be tarnished so fully that his appearance will evoke pity and mistrust, not devotion, awe, wonder, amazement, fear, respect, and honor. God's glory and our good, tied as they necessarily are in open theism to an unknowable and unpredictable future and to the use of our freedom over which God has no control, cannot survive when the dark side of our freedom prevails.

God's Glory and Our Glory

A second way in which God's glory is affected by its connection to creaturely freedom is this: To the extent that God allows us to share with him the ability to choose freely, to make decisions that to some degree shape how things will be, to assist in moving things in a positive direction when we could have resisted, to "partner" with him in charting the course for the unfolding of the future—to the extent that all this is true, the simple fact is that *we, not God,* should get credit for these contributions. At the heart of the open view is the value attached to human (and angelic) freedom. This freedom is so important to open theists that they reinterpret the Scriptures and overturn the tradition of the church in a concerted effort to deny that God exhaustively knows the future. When all is said and done, it is this value—the value of our human free will—that weighs heaviest on the scales of importance for open theism. Ultimately, all the moves made and the interpretations offered are to secure this one most cherished reality.

But one can ascribe to moral creatures the significance, value, and shaping importance of their freedom only at the expense of God's glory. Many will balk at this, I know. But balk or not, it is true nonetheless, and here is why: It is impossible for the actions of human freedom to be *outside of God's control* and for God, nonetheless, to *get the credit* for what good effects were produced by those free actions. If the problem of evil is solved (in Arminian and openness theologies) by appeal to human freedom, such that God is not responsible for the evil done by free creatures over whose actions he had no control, then one may regard this as the "problem of goodness." That is to say, if God should not take the *blame* for the evil done by human freedom, then correspondingly he should not get the *credit* for the good done equally freely and fully outside of his control.

The conclusion that God's glory is diminished by libertarian human freedom is impossible to avoid. If you say, "But the only reason this person used her freedom to do the good deed was that *God gave her the freedom* to do so," this argument becomes a two-edged sword. If God is to receive *glory* for the good we have done with our freedom *because he gave the freedom in the first place,* then does it not follow for exactly the same reason that he should also receive the *blame* for the evil done with our freedom? "Giving libertarian freedom" is a value that either connects with *all* of the morally significant uses of that freedom or connects with none of them. If it does connect, God is as blameworthy as he is praiseworthy for the various uses of freedom. If not, then God can no more take the credit for the good done with the freedom he gave than he can be blamed for the evil.

The effect of this is to say that, when we use our freedom for good, *we get the credit and God does not.* And of course, if we get the credit, we have a basis for boasting, for we did what we did not have to do (that is the point of libertarian freedom), and having done it, *we* are the ones, not anyone else, responsible for having done it. *We acted* in freedom, *we chose* the good, *we get the credit,* and *we have a basis for boasting.*

Tragically, this conception cuts directly across the teaching of the Bible. First Corinthians 1:26-31 forbids us in very strong terms to boast in anything except the Lord. And Ephesians 2:8-9 makes clear that our salvation by grace precludes any basis for human boasting. One of the themes repeatedly emphasized in our earlier examination of passages from Isaiah 40–48 is God's demand that he alone receive glory. God alone is fully rich and splendor-filled. He alone is eternally self-existent and self-sufficient (see Ps. 50; Isa. 40:12-18; 66:1-2; Acts 17:24-25; Rom. 11:33-36). Every quality in infinite measure is possessed intrinsically within the glorious nature of the triune God. The thought of belittling and diminishing God's infinite and eternal glory, especially by taking to ourselves (supposedly!) glory that is due to God alone, ought to strike fear and deep contrition within our hearts. We are to mean it when we sing, "To God Be the Glory"; yet in the openness view, in regular and significant measure, we cannot but think, *to us—yes! to US— be a significant portion of the glory.*

Perhaps someone will respond that the major purpose of freedom is for the good of us creatures. So, is God's glory diminished (by open theism) only to elevate our good? Ironically, this is not the case. While it is true that God's glory is diminished by open theism in a way that elevates our boasting, this is not at all the same thing as elevating our good. Wherein lies our good? The Scriptures make so very clear that our good is found not in our independent ability, our autonomy, or our self-reliance; rather, our good is found in humble, poor-of-spirit, dependence on God. The parable of the vine and branches in John 15 expresses it beautifully. As Jesus says, "he who abides in Me and I in him, he bears much fruit, for apart from Me you can do nothing" (John 15:5).

The exaltation of human freedom in open theism, then, ironically harms those whom it seeks to serve. It wishes to help Christian people and others by commending to them the importance of their choices, their actions, their contributions, their planning, their prayers. Yet, the best way Christian people are helped is by *disowning* all self-effort, by *renouncing* all self-ability, by humbly recognizing that nothing we can think or say or do can be done to the glory of God or for the real benefit of ourselves or others that is not done entirely by God's work within us and through us. Now, be sure: God's work within us never replaces our active involvement; this is not a call for passivity or quietism. Quite to the contrary, this is a call to embrace with joy and vigor the work God has given us to do *because he works in us both to will and to work for his good pleasure* (Phil. 2:12-13; cf. 1 Cor. 15:10; Eph. 2:10; Col. 1:29). God's work is manifest precisely as it engages us in the very work God accomplishes in and through us. But because *God* accomplishes the work, *he* receives the glory. The elevation of libertarian freedom in open theism cannot but diminish the glory of God as we take to ourselves in misguided presumption what belongs only to God.

The truth, then, is that the attachment of God's glory to human freedom robs God of the glory that is rightfully his while it also steals from us the good he intends us to have. God is the only one who can bring about his will on earth as it is in heaven. He alone is glorious for all his accomplishments both throughout the universe and in and through our lives. And, our good is found in humble submission, joyful obedience, wholehearted surrender—and in no place else. We find our greatest joy when we realize our wholesale need to depend on God. And these two ideas of God's glory and our good are designed to go together in a way strikingly different from what is commended in open theism. We are meant to see that we are weak, but he is strong; we are ignorant, he is knowledgeable; we are foolish, he is wise; we are poor, he is rich; we are needy, he is giving; we are sinful, he is Savior. Only as we see God and ourselves in this way, with God as the bountiful, lavish Giver and ourselves as the needy, helpless recipients, will we resign our claims of self-ability and self-accomplishment and flee to our gracious God who alone provides for us all that we need. When this happens, we realize that our true source of satisfaction is in dependence on his character and in the honor of his name. As John Piper has stated so well, God is most glorified in us as we are most satisfied in him.[7]

God's Glory and God's Sovereignty

Third, as is apparent particularly from chapter 6, God attaches his glory, honor, majesty, and very deity to his *rulership over all*. There are so many passages that speak to this. Recall, for example, Deuteronomy 32, Isaiah 45, Daniel 4, and Ephesians 1. God goes on record as the one and only true God, unique and unlike any impostor. He will not share his glory with another (Isa. 42:8; 48:11). And what establishes his rightful claim on such glory and majesty? In significant part, it is his uncontested rulership over all (e.g., "He does according to His will in the host of heaven and among the inhabitants of earth; and no one can ward off His hand

---

[7] This is the theme of John Piper, *Desiring God: Meditations of a Christian Hedonist* (Sisters, Ore.: Multnomah, 1996).

or say to Him, 'What have You done?'" [Dan. 4:35]). God's glory is the manifestation of his sovereignty, and his sovereignty reigns over all.

Recall that in the first point above, we saw that God's glory suffers in open theism because it is tied to his success rate which arguably is flawed. It appears, however, that the instinct that tied God's glory to his success rate is correct and fully biblical! The only difference between the view of Daniel 4, for example, and that of open theism is that in Daniel, *God is fully successful!* His glory is undiminished because he accomplishes all his will.

Unlike the open view of God, the God of the Bible ordains and accomplishes everything as he alone knows is best. He is not thwarted by creaturely freedom, and he successfully "does whatever he pleases" (Ps. 115:3). As we considered earlier, Ephesians 1:11 places the certainty of believers' reception of their future inheritance in Christ precisely in the context of the purpose of God "who works all things after the counsel of His will." The God of the Bible has no failures, and yes, his glory is tied to his successes. But since he is entirely successful, in working through all the evil done by his creatures as well as in working in them all the good that they do, God succeeds fully. Yes, God *is* glorious, in part, because of his works; and here he is *fully glorious,* because his works *always succeed.*[8]

CONCLUSION: GOD'S GREATER GLORY AND OUR EVERLASTING GOOD

In closing, I urge readers to weigh carefully the diminished view of God and the distorted view of our good proposed in open theism. What is here lost in so many places and in so many ways is the infinite supremacy of God, and this loss is unimaginably great. Nothing less than the uncontested deity of God, his absolute lordship over all space and time, his universal, unrivaled, and inviolable sovereignty, his flawlessly wise and meticulous providence, his undiminished and infinite perfection, and his majestic and incomparable glory—all this and more has been compro-

---

[8] I am fully aware that this vividly raises the problem of evil faced in any overall determinist model, such as the one I believe Scripture clearly teaches. While many very fine discussions are available (works by D. A. Carson, John S. Feinberg, and Paul Helm are among the finest), in a forthcoming book on divine providence from a moderately Calvinist perspective, I intend to offer my own treatment of this issue along with an overall defense of this model as most fully biblical and satisfying.

mised by open theism. We have here, then, a fundamentally different god, not merely a different version of God. For the sake of the glory that is God's alone we have no choice but to reject the openness model. And with joy and gladness we affirm afresh that the true and living God reigns supreme as King over all, knowing the end from the beginning, and regulating the affairs of all creation to accomplish his infallibly wise and perfect will. As such, he is infinitely worthy of our worship and trust. His word and promise are absolutely reliable. He is for us our sure and constant source of all that we need, so that as supreme Giver of every good and perfect gift he alone may receive all the glory due his name. The true and living God, the God of the Bible, is incomparably wise and great, and in him we are immeasurably blessed. In his infinite glory we find our everlasting good. He truly is for all who believe in him alone their "Maker, Defender, Redeemer, and Friend."[9] *Soli Deo gloria*, indeed.

---

[9] Taken from the last line of the fourth verse of Robert Grant's hymn, "O Worship the King."

General Index

Scripture Index

3:7	54, 132, 170		**Luke**	
3:19-20	54, 55, 132		22:31-32	129
7:31	77-78		22:34	129
18	133-135		22:42	185
18:1-4	134-135			
18:4	134		**John**	
18:5	133-135		1:14, 18	145
18:5-10	133-136		3:16	206
18:11-12	134		6:64	70-71, 127
19:5	77, 78		8	184, 185
26:3	80		8:26	184
31:31-34	84		8:28	184, 193, 194
32:35	54, 77-78, 170		8:29	33, 184, 193
			8:31-32	185, 193
Lamentations			12:37-41	127
3:37-38	150, 205		13:19	38, 127
			14:29	127
Ezekiel			15:5	227
12:3	80		16:4	127
36:26-36	84		17:3	185
			17:5	145
Daniel			18:19-27	127
2, 4, 5, 7, 8, 9, 10, 11	126		21:18-19	127
4	149, 151, 228-229		**Acts**	
4:29-30	149		2:23	137, 206
4:34-35	149, 151		4:27-28	137, 206, 212
4:35	175, 214, 229		17:24-25	227
4:37	150			
11	126		**Romans**	
			4	70, 71, 72
Hosea			4:18-22	70
8:5	82		5:3-5	195
11:8-9	87-90		6:15-23	186
11:9b	89		8:28	21, 192-195
			8:28 and 32	195
Amos			8:28-32	192
3:6	205		8:29-30	193
			8:31	125
Jonah			8:31-32	185, 193
3:4	94		8:32	193-195
3:5-10	91		8:33-39	193
4:2	94		9:11	152
			9:14, 19	212
Matthew			9:18	152, 212
6:10	170		9:19	152
26:21-25	127		9:22-23	152
			11:33-36	227